A Practical Guide to University and College Management

Written for managers and administrators in higher education, *A Practical Guide to University and College Management* is a highly accessible text that offers practical guidance on how to manage the day-to-day life of universities. The authors take a proactive approach and offer a range of good practice examples and solutions designed to resolve the dilemmas that arise in today's rapidly changing higher education environment.

Drawing on a wealth of management experience, this edited collection pulls together advice and practical guidance from expert managers working in the field of higher education. Each chapter is underpinned by theoretical perspectives to support invaluable pragmatic hints, mini-case studies, practical examples and sample guidelines. The book covers four main areas:

- *Selecting and inducting students*: This part of the book outlines the essential process for targeting, attracting, recruiting and inducting students.
- *Managing throughout the university year*: Advice on the student experience, from the admissions process right up to graduation.
- *Assuring the quality of the student learning experience*: How to manage course administration, student learning through assessment, student complaints and issues of quality assurance.
- *Maximising staff and student engagement*: This part looks at how to maximise commitment and involvement by both staff and students, and includes approaches and examples of engagement implementation at other universities.

A Practical Guide to University and College Management will be of interest to higher education managers, administrators and anyone looking for a pragmatic 'how to' navigational guide that informs the working life of a university, from attracting students through to graduation. It offers managers and administrators essential training and support required to promote highly successful and efficient higher education institutions (HEIs). *A Practical Guide to University and College Management* is designed to help manage HEIs effectively, efficiently and to the highest standard. It is essential reading for anyone who works in university administration or aspires to do so.

Steve Denton is Pro-Vice-Chancellor and Registrar and Secretary at Leeds Metropolitan University, bringing together university-wide student administrative and support services, including governance and legal matters, the academic registry, planning, student services, communication and marketing, and widening access and participation.

Sally Brown is Pro-Vice-Chancellor for Assessment, Learning and Teaching at Leeds Metropolitan University. She has published widely on innovations in teaching, learning and, particularly, assessment.

A Practical Guide to University and College Management

Beyond Bureaucracy

Edited by
Steve Denton and Sally Brown

Routledge
Taylor & Francis Group

NEW YORK AND LONDON

First published 2010
by Routledge
270 Madison Ave, New York, NY 10016

Simultaneously published in the UK
by Routledge
2 Park Square, Milton Park, Abingdon, Oxon OX14 4RN

Routledge is an imprint of the Taylor & Francis Group, an informa business

© 2010 Taylor and Francis

Typeset in Minion by
Keystroke, Tettenhall, Wolverhampton
Printed and bound in the United Kingdom on acid-free paper by
CPI Antony Rowe, Chippenham, Wiltshire

Library of Congress Cataloging-in-Publication Data
A practical guide to university and college management : beyond
bureaucracy / by Steve Denton and Sally Brown, editors.
p. cm.
Includes bibliographical references and index.
1. Universities and colleges—Great Britain–Administration. I. Denton, Steve.
II. Brown, Sally A.
LB2341.8.G7P72 2009
378.1'010943--dc22
2009005211

ISBN 10: 0–415–99717–8 (hbk)
ISBN 10: 0–415–99718–6 (pbk)
ISBN 10: 0–203–87455–2 (ebk)

ISBN 13: 978–0–415–99717–1 (hbk)
ISBN 13: 978–0–415–99718–8 (pbk)
ISBN 13: 978–0–203–87455–4 (ebk)

Contents

Illustrations

CHAPTER 1

Beyond Bureaucracy

Managing the University Year

STEVE DENTON with **SALLY BROWN**

Leeds Metropolitan University

Introduction

For almost as long as there have been universities, there have been those who taught, and those who supported those who taught and were being taught. However, university administrators have historically been associated with some of the more negative aspects of managerialism, in what Ramsden characterises as 'The Bureaucracy':

> Its focus is on regulation, consistency and rules. Its managerial style is formal-rational. A cohort of senior administrators wields considerable power. Standards are related to regulatory bodies and external references: evaluation is based on the audit of procedures. Decision making is rule-based and students are statistics.
>
> (Ramsden, 1998: 349)

This book aims to rehabilitate the work of the university administrator, reframing it in terms of the positive contribution our work can make to universities becoming successful, high-achieving and efficient organisations where academic practices are at the heart of all we do but where high standards are the *sine qua non* of our existence. As Baldwin (2009) suggests, 'Universities need great academic staff to deliver the research and teaching that are core to their mission. But if their talent is to thrive, it needs to be underpinned and supported by an effective organisational structure'.

Administration, the art of successfully managing the university year, has a long and proud heritage. Many would acknowledge that Cambridge is one of the world's oldest universities. Much can be learned from the lessons of the history of the administration of the University of Cambridge. Cambridge was established as a university in 1209, and there is evidence of early forms of 'administration' being established to support academia from around 1226. Many of the executive office holders still recognised today were established. Shortly after formation, the university had a chancellor and vice-chancellor. Other administrative office holders drew on universities' early connections with the church: bedells, who preside over ceremonies, chaplains and deans (University of Cambridge, 2008).

Administrative systems were established to identify and authenticate persons to whom degrees had been granted through enrolment with a licensed master, to moderate and supervise examinations, and to mark progress by admission (graduation) to different grades, or degrees of membership of the university. Authorities were also established to keep accounts (the first finance directors!). In 1506, Robert Hobys became the first registrary of Cambridge. He was responsible for matriculation and enrolment, admission to degrees, recording decisions of Regent Masters (the teachers) and adoption of statutes (University of Cambridge, 2008).

Five hundred years on, the current registrary in 2009, Jonathan Nicholls, still performs these vital functions of ensuring that students are properly admitted, that records are kept of the terms of their admittance, that their examinations and assessments are properly conducted and recorded, and that the university has a common system of rules and regulations. As a profession, administration and management have a sustained value and importance, and are a necessary condition for the success of institutions.

Definitions

The terms 'administrator' and 'manager' are often used interchangeably (even in chapters of this book), with an increasing preference to use the term 'manager' in the United Kingdom to designate senior staff (vice-chancellors and pro-vice-chancellors of British universities are sometimes surprised to find themselves described as administrators when they visit US universities!). While, as this book demonstrates, management of the university year is increasingly complex, with a growth of specific professional functions, this is happening alongside a growing crisis of identity and also a potential lack of confidence in the profession of administration.

We use the term 'administration' in its broadest sense, to include a range of administrative and professional functions, including:

- *Registry*: which traditionally includes the admission and registration of students, the administration of examinations and the authentification and conferment of awards. It also now commonly includes strategic and operational planning, data management and the formulation of statutory returns, student systems support and management, timetabling, fee management and quality assurance, enhancement and audit.
- *Human resources*: which includes attracting, recruiting and supporting staff, supporting appraisal and performance management, staff development, and the management of discipline and grievances.
- *Finance*: including keeping track of various sources of income (fees, grants, contracts, endowments) and expenditure (staff, buildings, facilities and infrastructure, pensions) and ensuring that they comply with internal and external audit and accounting standards.
- *Marketing*: including publicity and promotion, reputation and crisis management, but also intelligence-gathering on the higher education market, and may also include fund-raising, particularly seeking income from benefactors.
- *Estates, facilities and infrastructure*: including buildings, plant, maintenance, furniture and equipment, and the information technology necessary to support activity across the university.
- *Student services and pastoral support services to students*: health and welfare, counselling, disability support, careers.
- *Alumni*: including maintaining relationships and affinities with graduates for a variety of purposes, including alumni events, fund-raising and sponsorship.
- *Faculty, school and corporate services*: many administrative functions, such as course administration, are carried out in academic units close to teaching and research activity, for instance in subject groups, schools and faculties. Others are undertaken as pan-university functions, often described as the 'centre' (sometimes with derogatory overtones). What is undertaken in academic-related organisational units and what will be undertaken in pan-university organisational units will vary from institution to institution, dependent on the particular university's history, culture, size and leadership preference.

The *Oxford English Dictionary* (OED) defines 'administration' as 'the organisation and running of a business or system' and the verb 'to manage' as 'to be in charge of', 'to supervise' or 'to administer and regulate'. Interestingly, it also has among the definitions 'to succeed despite difficulties', which will resonate with many university administrators.

The term 'professional' as an adjective is defined by the OED as being 'engaged in activity as a professional occupation rather than as an amateur' or 'competent' and as a noun as 'a person having competence in a particular activity'. We therefore describe ourselves as professional administrators and managers since:

- We have particular abilities and skills, increasingly the subject of various accredited awards and subject to the oversight of professional bodies; therefore we have acknowledged competence.
- We are involved in and integral to the organisation and running of a business or system.
- We administer and regulate.
- Many of us are in charge of or supervise staff.

The term 'professional administration' should therefore, we argue, be applied to those who:

- attract and recruit students, support them in their learning and research, and in their experience as a student;
- support staff in the delivery of teaching, learning and research;
- provide assurance to governors and external stakeholders on the organisation and running of universities.

Why is Focus on Competence Important?

We argue that competence is important so that we have confident individuals who can work across disciplines, at all levels, within and between institutions. What is required is a professional administrators' cadre who have what Baldwin (2009) calls the 'Warwick way' of doing things: 'It is most visible in the short lines of communication between administrative and academic staff, the high degree of mutual respect, and the can-do spirit that is shared by administrators, academics and students'.

Elsewhere in this book are descriptions of some particular approaches to staff development (see Chapter 14). These can include development of both generic and skills-specific knowledge, the acquisition of diverse experience and values through both internal and external development opportunities, and personal growth through coaching, mentoring and professional training.

In the United Kingdom there has been much progress in recent years in the provision of external development opportunities, through the Association of University Administrators (AUA) and other organisations such as the Leadership Foundation and the Higher Education Academy and their antecedents, including the Universities' and Colleges' Staff Development Agency (UCoSDA) and the Committee of Vice-Chancellors and Principals (CVCP), as well as voluntary bodies including the Staff and Educational Development Association (SEDA) in the United Kingdom and the Higher Education Research and Development Society of Australasia (HERDSA). While these have been welcome developments, such organisations largely offer, by their very nature, broad-brush approaches, and can often be relatively expensive, particularly in many universities, where administrative staff have traditionally been given a low priority in the allocation of departmental training budgets. Such organisations can offer fairly well-established ways of developing competence through programmes of training and courses, but we suggest that we could learn much from other sectors about making better use of development opportunities such as internal and external sabbaticals and secondments, to enable professional administrative staff to experience work in higher education and/or other organisations.

There can, however, be barriers to such development: continuing professional development (CPD) is, regrettably, not always seen as a high priority for professional administrative staff. Secondments and sabbaticals for university administrative staff have in the past been rare by comparison with those offered to academics, usually because of the differences between administrative organisational structures in diverse universities previously described, but also because of perceived competition between institutions, and sometimes actual competition within institutions, for resources and staff. Those who see such competition in negative terms are regrettably short-sighted. Baldwin (2009), using a football transfer analogy, would argue that for staff to move on from universities where they have experienced outstanding professional development and support is a manifestation of organisational maturity and renewal that is to be welcomed rather than regretted.

> Warwick's ambition was laid down in the 1960s. High expectations were established, leadership was strong and learning was rapid. That baton has been handed to the generation that followed. But there has been constant and continual refreshment of the university's culture and its way of working and behaving that appears normal to all concerned.
>
> (Baldwin, 2009: 28)

Internal Staff Development

The Civil Service and local government have for many years used secondments and attachments widely and to great effect in developing individual competencies and to achieve organisational goals. The Graduate Trainee scheme at Leeds Metropolitan University (Leeds Met) is a welcome step in promoting higher education administration as a valuable and worthwhile career.

The Leeds Met Graduate Trainee Scheme

Leeds Met, like many other universities, is keen to ensure that students who have had really good experiences of studying with us consider us as potential employers. We are keen to 'grow our own' high-quality employees in both teaching and administration. Following the success of our appointment of 100 PhD students in our centenary year, some of whom are likely to seek employment with us as academics when they complete their studies, we decided to establish a graduate trainee scheme to open up opportunities for some of our graduates to seek employment in other kinds of roles across the university. In the first year of the scheme, only four graduate trainees were employed. This was followed in the second year with ten and in the third with 14.

Graduate trainees are appointed through a competitive process, and over the three years of the scheme to date, competition for the posts has become fierce as graduates recognise the value of the opportunities such roles can offer. Typically, over a two-year period a graduate trainee can be expected to have six placements of four months each in different sections of the university, including finance, governance, sport, the office of the Pro-Vice-Chancellor for Assessment, Learning and Teaching, within faculties and elsewhere. In addition to supporting pan-university projects and festivals including Freshers' Week, graduation ceremonies and the Staff Development Festival (see Chapter 14), graduate trainees undertake a range of projects that are designed to be both useful to the university and developmental for the individual. Managers of graduate trainees are expected to provide weekly mentoring sessions and a working context in an open-plan office to encourage cross-institutional learning, and graduate trainees also benefit from weekly coaching sessions from the director of the Graduate Trainee scheme and from the vice-chancellor, who takes a close interest in their progress. On the completion of their two-year internship, graduate trainees are well placed to seek university administrator or project officer roles within Leeds Met or other universities.

Sally Brown

Confidence in the value of higher education administration as a career is all-important in engendering a positive attitude to the profession, which comes, we argue, through:

- self-belief, which stems from confidence that one has the right tools, skills and experience (competence) to undertake the relevant role;
- the belief of others, including managers, academics, stakeholders, family and friends, that this is a profession worth pursuing;
- the way we portray ourselves and our achievements, individually and collectively.

As a profession and as institutions, we already demonstrate self-belief through developing competence, but we need to do more to inspire belief by others in what we do, particularly by the way we portray ourselves, and in this domain the work of the UK AUA has been particularly valuable.

The term 'non-academic' has historically been used as a descriptor for professional administrators, often with negative overtones, but this is a view that must be challenged. The experiences described in this book provide examples of how senior management in institutions can address such misconceptions through:

- ascribing a high value to the administration functions;
- raising the profile of the importance of administration within the institution and beyond;
- establishing administration as a worthy and rewarding career;
- fostering confidence in administrative staff.

We have a duty, however, to inspire confidence in others through what we do, how we do it and how we conduct ourselves. In respect of the latter, we need to move towards a model where administrative staff are equal partners with academic colleagues rather than subservient, in a model that is described by Shattock (2002) as 'shared governance'. He subsequently described how this might work best:

A centre which only comprises administrative, that is non-teaching, officers will certainly be regarded as monolithic by those outside it, even if it is effective (which is unlikely); a centre comprising only part-time members, that is, academics, will find it hard to be effective and may become factionalised over particular issues. For this reason, the centre should include a mixture of academics, elected or appointed, to serve as members of particular committees working in close consort with a vice-chancellor and full-time professionals in the field.

(Shattock, 2003: 82–3)

The Founder of the Profession of University Administrator

As the founding registrar of the University of Warwick, Michael Shattock established, through thorough training, support and development, a system of professional administration. Many staff who worked for him are now in senior management posts in universities and other organisations. His book *Managing Successful Universities* is one of the most widely read and quoted texts among the university professional administrative community. It extols the virtue and value of administration not only in the day-to-day management and running of universities, but also in the collaborative development of policy and strategy.

> Institutions need close working relationships and trust between the academic and administrative communities so that administrators have the self-confidence to work with the academic community as equal partners and can challenge it on policy issues without appearing to seek to become a dominant partner.
>
> (Shattock, 2003: 156)

He urges administrators to be systematic, but creative and responsive, arguing that innovation and creativity in administration and management make creative opportunities for institutions. He eschews the views of those who argue that there is no place for administration and management in a community of self-governing scholars, arguing that management makes a difference, and drawing attention to the contribution of administration.

His experiences of recruitment, training and development of administrative staff were clearly ahead of their time, and indeed ahead of current practice in some institutions today. He argues, 'In a labour intensive industry it can be argued that university strengths lie chiefly in the quality of staff they employ' (Shattock, 2003: 17). He contends that universities will be able to attract and retain the best administrators only if those administrators are offered support and encouraged to develop a rounded set of skills and experiences in a creative environment, with varied rather than monotonous work.

Effective university administration is crucial, he suggests, if universities are to become successful entrepreneurs, with academics and administrators working as partners together in cohesive, functional project units, including interdisciplinary research centres, consultancy offices, technology and science parks, and incubators (Shattock, 2009: 192). He also argues that administrators should have intellectual confidence, and describes how in his early days as a registrar he encouraged administrative staff to work for higher or research degrees in order to be able to engage with academic colleagues, arguing that it is incumbent on administrators to promote tolerance and understanding between academics and administrators. His books are required reading for new and ambitious administrators, who can learn much from them about the importance of administration.

The registrar of the University of Warwick today, Jon Baldwin, provides a useful summary of what he regards as the attributes of first-rate administrators, reproduced below.

What Does it Take to be an Effective Administrator Today?

Good administrators are committed and have an affinity with their institution. They are team players, talented individuals, a jack of all trades working in a diverse and complex environment. They need to demonstrate tact and diplomacy, show honesty and integrity, and have a keen sense of empathy. Possessing razor-sharp intellect is as essential as it always has been – possibly even more important than formerly. A good administrator needs to be able to hold their own with bright academics, and to know all the answers (or at least where to look for them). Ambition is important – to have the desire to win, not to settle for second best. And particularly in today's economic climate, administrators should be financially literate, possibly financially puritanical, and certainly entrepreneurial. They should be flexible, navigating their way with a compass rather than a roadmap, so that they can deviate along the way to make the most of new opportunities and avoid potential pitfalls. Networking should be second nature, as should an inquiring mind, with the ability to generate good ideas and to speak up about them. They should be dynamic – hungry for new challenges, for change and for winning – and not afraid to question and try new things out.

Good administrators also need to love and respect their profession, and that of their academic colleagues. To succeed, an administration needs to promote a unity of purpose across the institution, and have clarity about shared goals. We should not forget what we are 'administering' for – the advancement of learning and knowledge by teaching and research and the provision of a university education

---

continued

(Baldwin and Greatrix, 2006). Administrators are here because of the university – without academics and students, research and teaching, we would be unnecessary. Our sector is unique. Despite the challenges, the strengths, importance and resilience of universities should not be forgotten, and we should not stop contributing to that.

Source: Baldwin (2008: 12–13)

Going Beyond Bureaucracy: The Approach of This Book

Building upon the foundations of good practice established by Michael Shattock, we aim in this volume to provide useful perspectives from a range of administrative colleagues on each key phase of the cycle of student engagement with universities. Our contributors provide perspectives from a range of very diverse institutions in the United Kingdom and internationally, and they describe practices and viewpoints that vary according to local, regional and national contexts.

This volume is divided into four parts that broadly mirror the life cycle of students in a university. In Part I, 'Selecting and Inducting Students', our contributing authors discuss effective marketing (Stamp, Kelly and Maruma); how to manage the admissions process effectively (Grier, Cross and Oshun); how we can best welcome and develop students through inductions and freshers' events (Morgan and Brown); and how to go about offering scholarship programmes (Forshaw). Part II, 'Managing Throughout the University Year', offers a student perspective on how students' unions can provide support throughout the year (Grayling and Stephens); discusses the managing of course administration (Child, King, Lander and Ryan); and provides guidance and examples on how to manage graduation ceremonies (Fearnley, Frost, Brook and Arthur). In Part III, entitled 'Assuring the Quality of the Student Learning Experience', we discuss the management of assessment systems and processes (Mienczakowski, Kelly, Bexton and Hamley); dealing with complaints and appeals (Buckton, Child and Flowers); scrutinising quality (Akerman and Cardew); establishing and launching a new university (Funnell and Rich); and working with external agencies on quality audit (Dishman). The final part of the book, 'Maximising Student and Staff Engagement', includes chapters on getting the most from our staff (Harper, Gray, North and Brown with Ashton); engaging students with the wider community (Farrar and Taylor); practical examples of student engagement (Brown, Ward, Bailey, Rodgers, Conkar, Gray, McClure, Hunjan and Adam); and fostering employability (Barrie, Andrews, Dean and Heimanis). The final chapter (Brown and Denton) offers some conclusions to the volume as a whole by particular reference to the role of the most senior administrators in universities, vice-chancellors.

Common themes emerge across the chapters, however, including the necessity to:

- celebrate and promote our individual heritages, and promote individual approaches of universities with diverse missions;
- demonstrate confidence about such diversity, with clearly articulated systems that are fit for purpose for the organisations for which they are designed;
- vigorously pursue a wide range of continuous professional development approaches that are tailored to the administrative function and that encourage both inter- and intra-institutional working;
- encourage bright graduates to consider university administration as a career of first choice, and foster their capabilities through graduate training schemes;
- offer high-quality administrative services that refute the stereotypical reputation of administrators as 'bean counters' and bureaucrats who are obsessed with regulations and red tape, to which Ramsden (1998) alludes, promoting instead a culture that sees administrators as problem-solvers and gate-openers (rather than gate-keepers);
- develop an appreciation of the academic culture, of the traditions and values of the organisations and institutions through which it is sustained, and of the roles of colleagues in all branches of higher education;
- be sensitive to the multiplicity of clients served by the higher education administrator and the need to balance conflicting demands;
- act with integrity, honesty, fairness, professional impartiality and diligence, and without discrimination;
- observe due care, objectivity and respect for confidentiality;
- be explicit and straightforward in our dealings with colleagues and clients;
- ensure that personal interest does not override the needs of clients and stakeholders, including students, colleagues, employers, governors and others;
- accept responsibility for our actions and the implications they have for the work of others;
- challenge existing practices and ideas when necessary, without rejecting out of hand those approaches that have served previous generations well;
- be committed to our own personal and professional development by seeking new knowledge, skills and opportunities to enhance

professional performance, including, for example, contributing to conferences and publications;

- foster the development of others by sharing expertise and good practice and by encouraging employers to support professional development.

Many of the above points draw extensively on the Association of University Administrators' *Code of Professional Standards* (AUA, 2000), which can act as a useful guide to administrative colleagues about how we conduct ourselves in all aspects of our working lives.

University administration has a long history and, we would argue, a healthy future. A mature profession that is able to be sufficiently confident in its approaches to scrutinise rigorously its own practices and to reform them fearlessly where they are inappropriate, unviable or outdated is one that has much to offer the organisation it serves. This volume aims to contribute to enhancing the reputation of university administration and ensure its rightful place as the bedrock on which university processes and practices have their sound foundations.

References

Association of University Administrators (2000) *Code of Professional Standards*. Online, available at: www.aua.ac.uk/about/code/ (accessed December 2008).

Baldwin, J. F. (2008) 'The future shape and structure of higher education: challenges for administrators and managers', *The Bulletin*, December, pp. 12–13.

Baldwin, J. F. (2009) 'A culture of excellence', *Times Higher Education*, 1 January, p. 28.

Ramsden, P. (1998) 'Managing the effective university', *Higher Education Research and Development*, 17 (3): 347–70.

Shattock, M. L. (2002) 'Rebalancing modern concepts of university governance', *Higher Education Quarterly*, 56 (3): 235–45.

Shattock, M. L. (2003) *Managing Successful Universities*, Buckingham: Society for Research into Higher Education/Open University Press.

Shattock, M. L. (2009) *Entrepreneurialism in Universities and the Knowledge Economy: Diversification and Organizational Change in European Higher Education*, Maidenhead: Society for Research into Higher Education/Open University Press.

University of Cambridge (2008) *A Brief History: The Medieval University*. Online, available at: www.cam.ac.uk/univ/history/medieval.html (accessed December 2008).

PART **I**

Selecting and Inducting Students

CHAPTER 2

Effective Marketing in Higher Education

ROSEMARY STAMP

Stamp Consulting

DENNIS KELLY

University of Teesside

and **ANNE MARUMA**

University of Kent

The Context for Marketing in Higher Education

Marketing in higher education (HE) has been the focus of a series of major changes within recent years. It first began to make a significant appearance on the corporate agenda within the United Kingdom in the early 1990s (it had occupied centre stage for some forward-thinking US institutions for many years). However, for UK universities it was still at that time primarily driven by the need to recruit and admit students and communicate the portfolio offer. Since then, for many UK higher education institutions marketing has increased in remit and influence, and has begun to be recognised as a specialist professional function, fundamental to managing how an organisation communicates with key stakeholders and manages its profile. In this chapter, the authors – who work in a private consultancy, a UK post-1992 university (former polytechnic) and a UK pre-1992 university respectively – aim to review the context and propose some guidelines on how best to market universities effectively.

The greatest changes, however, have occurred within the past five years. For some institutions, marketing has moved on from the status of specialist function to being acknowledged, rightly, as an integral strategic function critical to the successful development of business planning, corporate strategy, branding, portfolio development and reputation management, and as a driving force behind the achievement of long-term corporate strategic objectives for higher education institutions.

The scale of marketing development has been dependent upon the need of institutions. Marketing innovation has often been driven most aggressively by an awareness of acute market need, shifting stakeholder demands and expectations, together with the threats and risks presented by an increasingly competitive marketplace. Those organisations most conscious of their market environment and competitive positioning have been those most likely to recognise the value of investment in marketing as a strategic function.

The 2006 survey *Marketing as a Catalyst in Higher Education* (Stamp, 2006) highlighted a major concern: almost half of the survey respondents from UK higher education institutions felt that their institutions were still extremely unrealistic about the competitive environment in which they were operating. This had led to a lack of investment (in terms of resources or corporate belief) in the marketing function and, inevitably, had subsequently led to vulnerability (among some institutions) to competitive challenges and market change.

The need for effective marketing and the opportunities for engaging with it have never been greater in British higher education than now. This is a worldwide trend, as the market for higher education has become global, particularly considering recent economic conditions. Factors that extend the remit of the institutional marketing function in universities include:

- the year-on-year rise of the expectations of stakeholders such as students, advisers, parents and employers (especially within an increasingly fees-driven, 'investment-aware' international student cohort);
- the ease of 'best in class' comparisons of service within but also beyond the HE sector (first considered by Hamel and Prahalad, 1994);
- the substantial surge in user-led comparative information sources such as blogs and social networking websites providing non-official or first-hand feedback on institutions;
- the imperative to recruit and retain not only students, but key staff in an aggressively competitive skills market;
- the need to manage education-to-business marketing and commercially focused ('third arm') activity;
- the need for strategic market intelligence to drive and inform activity plus an increasingly global context for many organisations.

Marketing is now beginning to take its place as core to the process of strategic corporate planning and is being increasingly recognised as a function that is not simply responsive to or pulled along by corporate objectives, but rather is one that should drive and inform the strategic planning process in higher education.

The Cyclical Marketing Process

First and foremost, marketing is a cyclical process: it demands a continuous cycle of market and consumer analysis, development of strategies and linked tactical implementation plans, the testing of the reception of marketing activity and service delivery, and the subsequent refinement of marketing operations. Practical marketing activity can be seen as the tip of the iceberg: before any outputs, activity or delivery of services to stakeholders can take place, market intelligence must be gathered to provide a realistic context for the development of plans and activities. Ill-informed marketing may deliver relatively little return on investment for the time, resource and effort made.

Understanding Markets and Consumers

Marketing is centred on the concept of understanding the market and the needs of target stakeholders: market intelligence must be at the heart of all that marketing does. The marketing team needs to be in charge of market intelligence-gathering, managing (or sourcing) a service that can facilitate research analysis and map the issues that will shape the structure and targeting of marketing effort. For example, it can assist the institution through the provision of information regarding:

- stakeholder motivations and perceptions;
- stakeholder profiling and segmentation;
- decision and choice drivers;
- market trends;
- opportunities for new market entry;
- portfolio management and new product development;
- the competitiveness of the institutional proposition;
- the extent to which the institution delivers on its brand promise;
- the factors that deliver the perceived relative strength of the institution's brand and reputation.

Analysis of the factors that drive decision-making and choice among existing students and the perceptions of potential applicants, for example, is a basic need for all institutions and provides insight into how well an organisation performs, and how perceptions of its services, style and culture affect choice (whether positively or negatively). This is also integral to the decision-making of other institutional stakeholders, for example business partners through 'third arm' activity.

Successful marketing to potential students is built upon a resource of key information. It demands both a detailed understanding of recruitment and decision-making processes and the ability to develop distinctive propositions that are appealing and have relevance to prospective students.

Case Study 1:
Aberystwyth University: Brand Insight and Influence

In 2007, Aberystwyth University planned to analyse the accuracy of stakeholders' perceptions of its proposition in order to inform its future marketing and positioning strategies. Steve Lawrence, its Director of Development and External Affairs at that time, recognised the powerful and positive influence that an accurate understanding of the organisational brand can have on a wide range of audiences. He commented, 'The real challenge for Aberystwyth was grasping the major opportunity presented by the analysis to outline to new and existing audiences the key values that underpinned the university brand'.

A process of consultation enabled the university to reconsider just how important and influential were the messages about Aberystwyth that it communicated to both its internal and external groups. The brand analysis consultation process consisted of four core phases:

1 stakeholder perceptions research;
2 mapping Aberystwyth's brand equity: key factors that comprise the differentiated brand;
3 tracking brand synergy and brand dissonance: where, when and how did the university succeed in delivering on its brand promise?
4 recommendations for strategic brand enhancement and the effective deployment of the differentiated brand proposition.

The stakeholder perceptions process provided the foundation for the brand analysis consultation. It enabled anecdotal or received information about the university to be rigorously tested against robust and accurate research analysis, which subsequently informed evidence-based recommendations. The university gained an accurate picture of the perceptions held by its stakeholders about a wide range of issues, including the university's culture, style, student experience, location brand factors and the portfolio offer.

Aberystwyth gained in-depth insight into the core components of its brand equity. It was able to reassess, for example, how it could leverage its competitive success in areas such as sustainability – a brand facet currently emerging within the UK higher education sector – and the uniqueness of its student experience. Tracking brand synergy and brand dissonance enabled the university to identify specific areas of success upon which to build, and opportunities to enhance infra-structure and services in ways that would deliver tangible and positive advantages for all its stakeholders.

Possibly more than anything else, the consultation demonstrated how brand strategy can drive pragmatic outputs and inform the marketing process to the institution's benefit. The analyses of specific Aberystwyth 'push' and 'pull' factors that drive motivations for student choice were invaluable. They highlighted many positives about Aberystwyth that had been taken for granted but which, in reality, proved to be critical influencers in driving student choice. This enabled the university to refine and refocus its marketing activity to maximise the effective use of these factors through targeted marketing activity.

Rosemary Stamp
Director, Stamp Consulting

Identifying Points of Differentiation

There can be a lack of clear differentiation between institutions in the minds of potential students. In the United Kingdom, for example, there are more than 160 higher education institutions, many of which would regard them-selves as completely distinctive from one another, and similar considerations are true for other nations that offer higher education to an international audience. However, the real challenge all organisations face is to make any potential distinctiveness credible and apparent to students in a way that is helpful to them – that is, enabling them to better understand the organisa-tional proposition and thereby assisting them in making informed choices: credible differentiation gives prospective students reasons to choose one university over another.

From the cyclical marketing perspective, the core need is, therefore, for HE institutions to understand the recruitment marketplace for diverse student prospects, but they also need to gain insight into the motivations that drive their stakeholders. Once motivations are understood, they can be mapped against the organisational proposition, since a key element of student satisfaction is realistic expectations of what the university they choose will provide and confidence that changes will be made following student complaints (the UK National Student Survey increasingly plays a role in stakeholder awareness of how well an institution delivers on the various promises that it makes). The organisation can then identify prospective students to whom their proposition will most appeal and have most pragmatic relevance. To do so, it will need to field a competitive positioning – that is, a level of demonstrable difference between its offer and that of other organisations. In planning and developing the portfolio of the future, institutions need to monitor the market and stakeholder needs, and to develop services and the portfolio offer accordingly.

Case Study 2:
Evaluation as Part of Service Development and Delivery

The role of evaluation and feedback to enable the consistent refinement of services is critical to the Information Services team at the University of Kent. Surveys and feedback help identify the changing needs of customers and establish a map for change. Year-on-year, this helps us establish a baseline for benchmarking progress.

Surveys and customer feedback help to identify the gap between what users want and what they expect. All feedback is, of course, incredibly valuable for any organisation, but it is critical to ensure that the feedback and its evaluation are integrated with service roll-out or delivery at the planning stage. Evaluation needs to be part of the equation, rather than an after-thought.

Management of customer feedback helps to pinpoint which services are meeting expectations and which are not, and enables organisations to identify the specific services that are delivering well or failing to deliver from the stakeholder perspective. In addressing what matters most to the consumer and focusing resources on meeting their expectations, an organisation can hope to make the most effective contribution to delivering upon stakeholders' needs and expectations.

Recent survey and feedback outcomes for Information Services at the University of Kent have included the following:

- The 2007 annual student satisfaction survey suggested that computer availability was a top priority for students. The perception was that there were an insufficient number of computers to meet demand during peak times. Data suggested that overall computer availability was being judged on the number of machines free in the library rather than the number of computers free on campus. Large display screens have now been introduced throughout the library and are programmed to indicate not only the number of computers available but their location in both the library and the colleges around the Canterbury campus.

- The annual study bedroom network survey in 2008 saw increasing numbers of students satisfied, following a significant drop in computer virus infections. This was due partly to the introduction two years previously of a network access control mechanism that scans the student's laptop or PC when it is connected to the network to ensure that the machine has up-to-date anti-virus software and critical updates installed. If the computer fails the scan, it cannot connect.

- Customer feedback from students requesting specialised software revealed that students using the software had only limited access. Representation by Information Services to the specific department on behalf of the students was made and as a result the department agreed to run a trial the following month, allowing late-night, seven-days-a-week (subsequently extended to 24/7) access following the introduction of high-definition CCTV and controlled access to the building.

Evaluation outputs, in this way, can act as direct 'modifiers' of services, communications and delivery to the stakeholder end-user. Evaluation is an integral process in service planning and delivery, and an organisation's responsiveness to stakeholder needs is fundamental to the market analysis, development and delivery cycle.

Anne Maruma
University of Kent

Differentiating factors for higher education institutions are many and complex, but can include the following:

- Credibility of the university's reputation: some students, for example, may only be interested in studying at leading organisations, and this may serve to determine (or limit) the range of disciplines they wish to study.

- The assessment, learning and teaching approach: for example, whether problem-based learning or technology-enhanced learning are used extensively, or whether a traditional tutorial-based pedagogy can be expected.
- Factors driving the holistic student experience: for example, the extent to which sporting or cultural opportunities are on offer.
- The corporate culture: for example, is the university consultative and responsive to the needs of its stakeholders?
- Portfolio expertise: for example, does the university have national or world-class expertise in a specific academic discipline?
- Location issues and opportunities: the attraction of the capital city, for example. Universities in Leeds and Manchester, for example, also benefit from their host city's national and international reputation as a great place to study.
- A further wide range of added value factors, often driven by an institution's current profile or an association with emerging popular trends.

A major challenge facing all higher education institutions is the increase in new 'hygiene' factors in brand equity. For example, in the 1990s a focus on sustainability might have been considered to be offering added value to an institution's proposition; today it has become a must-have brand facet. Similarly, internationalisation of the student cohort and the curriculum is now increasingly a required component for many institutions' offer.

Reputation and Experience of the Institutional Brand

It is not enough simply to own these facets: institutions must also be able to bring them to life and communicate the organisation's relative positioning and proposition to target stakeholders such as prospective students, their parents and employers through the effective deployment of a wide range of activities and media channels. The unique blend of tangible and intangible assets that comprises the institutional proposition is the foundation of its brand equity. Its reputation, however, will be centred on the narrowness of the gaps between what the organisation says about itself and how the organisation is experienced by stakeholders – that is, does the organisation deliver on the promises that it makes?

As Ind (2004) has shown, the growing imperative to 'live the brand' is a major challenge for all organisations. For complex institutions with devolved decision-making structures, such as universities and colleges, however, the challenge can be even greater. It is the relative success of this experience of the institutional brand that fuels positive or negative perceptions of the organisation within its target markets and among its target stakeholders (and so informs an understanding of the organisation's reputation, compared to that of other institutions).

The student decision-making process regarding higher education is complex and highly individual. Of the many determinants that can be identified, the relative reputation of an institution can be of paramount importance to specific prospective student cohorts and their influencers: for example, international and postgraduate student cohorts. While in the past it may have been a temptation for higher education organisations to believe that their institutional reputation would develop through a focus on academic endeavour, a wide range of additional factors now drive the development of reputation and, for forward-thinking institutions, reputation cannot be left to organic growth but needs to be managed actively and regarded as a prime organisational asset.

Institutional reputation is multifaceted and the components can include, for example:

- relative rates of graduate employment;
- potential return on investment (RoI) for stakeholders;
- strength of the academic portfolio and a department's academic 'stars', including well-known professors or faculty staff;
- profile of corporate social responsibility on issues such as sustainability;
- visibility of strategic alliances, for example with other internationally known universities, sporting, cultural and business partners;
- quality of facilities and infrastructure, including teaching accommodation, IT infrastructure, social, sporting and leisure facilities, and so on;
- realities of student experience as evidenced through informal information sources such as social networking sites;
- peer-group endorsement: recommendations by friends and siblings, which is increasingly a strong factor in student choice;
- regional, national or global profile and positioning.

Planned marketing activity provides the key to promoting a climate of favourability, through which prospective students (plus staff and other internal stakeholders) are well disposed towards the institution and happy and willing to communicate this to others.

To develop favourable impressions of the organisation, media management will encompass a wide range of communications channels, including television, radio, national and local newspapers as well as digital and online communications such as podcasts, SMS messaging and the use of social networking sites. From the perspective of the potential student, active media management will help to build reputation with decision-influencers, such as family, parents, teachers and careers advisers, and thereby generate positive word-of-mouth communications plus the comfort of peer endorsement for choices made. This is especially important now that league tables play such a major role in student decision-making, and particularly so for international students.

Case Study 3:
Leeds Metropolitan University and Sporting Partnerships

Leeds Metropolitan University (Leeds Met) goes beyond the boundaries of traditional forms of marketing by using its partnerships with professional sport to raise awareness of the university and to support directly the recruitment of new students. Leeds Met's first sporting partnership was with Leeds Rhinos, rugby league's world champions. This partnership gives unique opportunities for students and staff to become involved in professional sport and for professional sportsmen to become involved with the university as students and coaches – 'rubbing shoulders with champions', as it is described at Leeds Met. This partnership enables the university to raise awareness of itself as a potential destination for some of the many young people, particularly from disadvantaged backgrounds, who watch rugby league live or on television and who might never otherwise have thought of studying at university. The enthusiasm associated with supporting a rugby league team then becomes associated with enthusiasm for a higher education institution, a connection that is made better than any television advertising could. A unique collaboration to co-use newly built faculties at the rugby ground for corporate events on match days and teaching on other days reinforces the link and provides highly cost-effective usage of otherwise potentially underused faculties.

This pioneering partnership was extended in January 2007 when Leeds Met became the official education partner of the Rugby Football League. This unique link included the branding of the world-famous Challenge Cup, which was transformed into the Carnegie Challenge Cup, a brand that makes the university much better known in all areas of the world where rugby league is played. The partnership also saw the advent of the Carnegie Champion Schools Tournament, which opened access to the university to participating pupils. This is particularly rewarding as it involves schoolchildren in localities that traditionally have had little engagement with higher education. The Carnegie Challenge Cup final is played at the world-famous Wembley Stadium. This is the first time that a UK university has promoted its brand to a worldwide TV audience with supporting print and electronic media exposure. The university also displays the Carnegie Challenge Cup at UCAS (Universities and Colleges Admissions Service) fairs and at university open days, to the fascination of enthusiastic pupils.

In July 2007, Leeds Tykes rugby union club was renamed 'Leeds Carnegie' after winning the National Division One Championship, enabling the benefits of association with rugby league to be extended to rugby union. This was a ground-breaking arrangement in British sport at that time, with an educational institution taking over ownership of a professional sporting organisation. Students and staff have access to world-class venues and facilities, training, support and advice, in addition to the recruitment and brand awareness benefits.

A further pioneering partnership with the Irish Football Association (IFA) reflects Leeds Met's commitment to recruiting students from Northern Ireland. The partnership between Leeds Met and the IFA comprises support for the Carnegie Schools Soccer Cup and the Carnegie Women's League in addition to the Carnegie Premier League. Strong relationships have been formed with hundreds of schools and colleges through this partnership. The number of applications to Leeds Met from Northern Irish students has doubled year-on-year since the initiation of the partnership.

As an example of good marketing practice, Leeds Met's use of sporting partnerships is demonstrably effective. Positive feedback from prospective students has been endorsed by a rise in applications for undergraduate programmes that is significantly higher than the national average.

See also Chapter 15 on diverse examples of university partnerships at Leeds Met.

Dennis Kelly
formerly at Leeds Metropolitan University

Communications Channels and Disintermediation

However digitally based future communications may become, it will continue to be critical to guard against 'disintermediation' – that is, when stakeholders become so remote from the organisation that positive and mutually beneficial relationship-building is compromised. It is well known that despite the growth of multi-channel communications, stakeholders still crave the reassurance of person-to-person interaction with an organisation. In this way, face-to-face communications are becoming more, and not less, critical in the marketing of the organisation to its prospective students. They provide opportunities to build institutional reputation and so help influence choice of study destination. An institution has opportunities to meet and influence students through international recruitment missions, careers fairs, open days, partnerships, community involvement and applicant days, for example. For potential international students, virtual versions of these interactions are on the increase, with organisations around the world offering online virtual student guides, podcasts of lectures and virtual open days, to maximise opportunities to substitute virtual for live interaction and experience with institutions, however physically remote they may be.

Practical Marketing Operations

For prospective students as well as other institutional consumer targets, marketing materials and outreach activity, in whatever form, need to inform choice and provide accurate information about an institution's proposition, including its values, vision and programme offer, to a diverse range of stakeholders whose needs will be very varied. To achieve this, it is critical that marketing tailors outputs, communications and activity to specific target audiences, and the means and channels for this will, of course, be informed by the market intelligence-gathering process.

For prospective students, the prospectus is, inevitably, a core information source, but the format in which it is presented is changing radically. Increasingly, innovative communications channels are employed to deliver information about the institutional portfolio via the web, video streaming, DVDs, CDs and memory sticks as well as traditional print formats. In the next five years it is likely that major shifts in the production of core marketing material such as prospectuses, course brochures and so on will centre on the transition in production methodology to the provision of online and digital channels first and hard copy second, reversing the traditional production cycle.

Linking Marketing with Consumer Decision-Making

Marketing materials and activity focused on student recruitment must be designed with the student decision-maker in mind, and the most effective outputs will be those that not only present the information in an appealing and accessible way, but are also tailored to specific audience segments' needs and wants. There will, inevitably, be a significant difference in the information needs of post-school entrants, mature applicants and international students. One form or source of information will not necessarily suit all applicants.

A simple but fundamental imperative for all marketing is to plan activity proactively to link, integrate with and inform the key stages of consumer decision-making. In this way, those making choices are likely to receive the most appropriate information at the most useful time and via the most effective communications channels. This approach demands that organisations rigorously map decision-making across the full range of stakeholder groups and plan for the long term, cross-referencing stakeholder wants and needs against tailored marketing outputs, services and activity.

Loyalty and Customer Relationship Management

Marketing is most effective when it acts as a catalyst to stimulate a response from the customer and initiates a relationship between customer and organisation. Customer relationship management (CRM) is now critical to managing long-term cyclical marketing activity in higher education. Data management technology offers a mechanism by which to tailor both the management of prospect information and the opportunities for both parties to stay in touch. Contact details of enquirers can be captured and the initial response can be followed with personalised information together with useful material that incrementally informs the prospective students' understanding of the organisation and adds to their awareness of the institution and its differential offer, enabling them to make informed choices.

In this way, long-term institution-driven CRM has the potential to track and support prospective students through each stage of their engagement with the organisation: from pre-enquiry awareness-raising through to application; enrolled students through to postgraduates and alumni. Doyle (2000) mapped the rise of mutual benefits for the organisation and stakeholder as a driver of corporate success, and this is now increasingly apparent in higher education. The customer relationship management of the future is centred on the value of maintaining long-term, mutually beneficial contacts with target stakeholders to ensure that the institution can be of relevance and value to them as prospects, students and lifelong alumni.

Raising Awareness for Non-Traditional Entrants to Higher Education

Increasingly, institutions recognise the need to engage with prospective students early on, and certainly before they might usually begin to think about higher education study choices, for example through community involvement, Aimhigher initiatives or mentoring and strategic alliances with linked feeder organisations. (Aimhigher, as outlined in Chapter 5, is a UK-wide initiative to familiarise children with higher education and the opportunities it can bring.)

Case Study 4:
Widening Participation at Leeds Met

At Leeds Met the Get Ahead team works with young people from school years 5 to 11 on a series of activities designed to raise aspirations. A programme of events takes place both on and off campus, tailored to the age group of participants. The activities are directed particularly at pupils who traditionally would not have considered progression into higher education. All activities allow students to see what university life is like and to learn in an enjoyable and interactive way. They range from one-day taster sessions to campus trails. Many young people from disadvantaged backgrounds have concerns about higher education. Some have no idea about what or where they want to study or whether they want to move away or stay at home. Others know exactly what they want to do and where they want to go but may be concerned about where they will live or the size of the campus, and many students have concerns over the ever-increasing cost of studying for a degree.

The Get Ahead team has developed workshops that focus on finance, accommodation, course choices, interview skills, completing the university admissions (UCAS) form and writing the personal statements required by the UCAS form. Leeds Met also runs, in conjunction with other universities in Yorkshire, Easter and summer schools to promote awareness of higher education to people who are under-represented in higher education, including pupils with disabilities, Afro-Caribbean boys, Asian girls, and bright young people from local schools where traditionally very few enter higher education, to help them achieve higher GCSE (General Certificate of Secondary Education) grades ('Reaching for A*').

In addition to the workshops, Leeds Met has developed a formal programme of study called the Progression Module, which guides the young people through the decision-making process and provides an opportunity for them to make an informed choice about their future.

Each year the Get Ahead team works with over 15,000 young people on Aimhigher activities.

Inder Hunjan,
Leeds Metropolitan University

Marketing Organisation

The structure of a higher education institution's marketing function will be conditioned by the culture of the organisation and the relative importance attributed to key marketing responsibilities. These will range from student recruitment, corporate profile and reputation management, branding and competitor scoping through to strategic alliances, partnerships and education-to-business activity (that is, knowledge transfer, consultancy and research provision for industry, for example).

Specialist staff within the communications and marketing team should lead the development of the core marketing strategy, which will then support the development and maintenance of an institutional reputation, in line with organisational aspirations. This overarching marketing strategy should be underpinned with tactical plans that aim to deliver the right information to target consumers (such as prospective students) engaged in the decision-making cycle, together with their influencers, at the right time and via the most appropriate and effective channels. Ideally, all marketing sub-strategies across the organisation – for example, education-to-business, international profile, strategic alliances, alumni relations strategies, and so on – will need to cross-reference each other and be developed within the context of the organisation's long-term objectives.

Marketing Influence

The level of success or influence the higher education marketing function achieves can be dependent upon its relationship with the senior management team. For many organisations that have newly developed marketing director roles, access or reporting lines to senior managers can make or break the effectiveness of marketing activities, as these channels determine whether an individual will have the influence and decision-making powers to drive through real change and strategic innovation. Inevitably, if marketing is not represented effectively within the decision-making arena of an organisation, it can have little power to drive corporate strategy proactively, but instead is destined to manage a response to a strategic direction that is decided by others and is beyond its reach. To be effective, marketing needs to be integral to corporate strategy and, as a function, to be able to drive and influence the direction of long-term corporate planning processes. One of the greatest difficulties facing organisations attempting to restructure marketing operations along more integrated and strategic lines is the problem of shaking off traditional reporting lines and a task-driven approach to marketing operations.

Inevitably, marketing is often called upon to focus on the year-on-year tasks of student recruitment, but the survey outlined by Stamp (2006) suggested that this may be at the expense of the bigger-picture challenges of reputation management, positioning and threatening competitive market issues. The survey indicated that endorsement from senior managers and principal officers is the most significant factor in the effectiveness of delivering support to (and for) marketing effort within organisations. It also illustrated that marketing is most valued within institutions when they are realistic about their competitive challenges.

Marketing Culture

How positively marketing is received and perceived within organisations is directly related to its performance and interaction with internal stakeholders. When marketing is well understood and is perceived to bring direct benefits, it is welcomed, and levels of awareness of a marketing-orientated culture rise. Where there is a gap in internal stakeholders' understanding of marketing, it can be regarded as less beneficial or purposeful. Such gaps do exist: two key stakeholder groups, namely academic staff and the student cohort, are known, potentially, to have difficulty in perceiving the benefit of organisational marketing. This is a major concern, especially when both groups are central to marketing an organisation's proposition as corporate advocates and have the opportunity to benefit from successful strategic marketing activity. To work effectively, therefore, marketing as a function needs, itself, to be marketed to internal stakeholders to increase levels of positive awareness and understanding. To succeed, it needs to be demonstrably relevant to stakeholders: marketing cannot be done *to* stakeholders but needs to be achieved *with* them.

Conclusions: The Future Challenge

The main challenge for marketing in the future is to be recognised as core to the institution's business processes. For an institution to be successful, sustainable and competitive, marketing must be fully integrated with the organisation's strategic planning processes. Marketing has a critical role to play in the development of the institutional strategic plan, scoping future market opportunities and competitor action, exploring new portfolio areas and mapping stakeholder needs to inform the development of new products and services. The existence of a marketing-orientated culture will enable an institution to plan effectively for its future within the context of a realistic awareness of its market opportunities and competitive threats.

We conclude with some pointers derived from our collective experiences that others might find useful.

Ten Guidelines for Marketing Success

1 Promise only what you can realistically deliver, but be sure your institution delivers what it promises.
2 Understand your stakeholders: constantly monitor their needs, wants and expectations.
3 Remember that market intelligence is critical: monitor the market and stakeholders constantly and evaluate the performance of your marketing activity to inform and develop marketing operations and stakeholder services.
4 Monitor the competitive context, but remember: competition may not be about 'other institutions'; it could be centred on competing for stakeholders' attention, motivation and their understanding of your offer.
5 Note that for brand or proposition differentiation to be effective, staff, students and managers must perceive the difference in the institution and believe it is of relevance and value to them.
6 In all communications with stakeholders, speak their language: do not ask them to learn yours.
7 Utilise the power of credible advocacy: for example, your best marketing ambassadors are likely to be current students, staff, business partners and alumni.
8 Remember the 'features versus benefits' equation: spell out the benefits of what you do for stakeholders; don't simply tell them about the features of your offer.
9 Link marketing activity to the consumer decision-making cycle.
10 Remember that marketing should be integral to corporate planning: it needs to drive and inform corporate strategy rather than be pulled along by it.

References

Aimhigher: information available www.direct.gov.uk/en/EducationAndLearning/UniversityAnd HigherEducation/DG_073697 (accessed 8 August 2008).

Doyle, P. (2000) *Value-Based Marketing*, Chichester: Wiley.

Hamel, G. and Prahalad, C. K. (1994) *Competing for the Future*, Boston, MA: Harvard Business School Press.

Ind, N. (2004) *Living the Brand: How to Transform Every Member of Your Organization into a Brand Champion*, London: Kogan Page.

Stamp, R. (2006) *Marketing as a Catalyst in Higher Education: The Survey of Decision Makers*, 2nd edn, Kenilworth: Stamp Consulting Ltd. Available at: www.stampconsulting.co.uk (accessed 8 August 2008).

CHAPTER 3

Making Students Welcome

The Admissions Process

JEAN GRIER
University of Edinburgh

ROSEANNA CROSS
University of Bristol

and **OLUWATOYIN GLADSTONE OSHUN**
Lagos State University

The Admissions Framework

First impressions matter a great deal, and the way a university welcomes students who choose to enrol with it can be hugely important in determining how they subsequently regard the organisation. National systems for admissions vary substantially, and this chapter sets out to describe admissions processes in different countries and to draw from them some transferable guiding principles.

Admissions Processes in the United Kingdom and Nigeria

The application process for undergraduate students in the United Kingdom is managed through UCAS (the Universities and Colleges Admissions Service). UCAS is a well-established organisation that provides a centralised processing system for applications to the vast majority of undergraduate degree programmes.

The postgraduate application process is a different story, with most applications currently going direct to the institution concerned, with the exception of a small number of professional Master's programmes such as those in social work, which are handled through UCAS. However, UCAS has recently developed UKPASS (UK Postgraduate Application and Statistical Service, www.ukpass.ac.uk), an online postgraduate application service. Very few institutions have signed up to this at the time of writing, but it is likely that more will join in the future, and that the postgraduate applications system may in time come to resemble more closely the undergraduate system.

Nigeria's university system started in 1948 with the establishment of University College, Ibadan, as a college of the University of London. There are now 93 universities in Nigeria. Two bodies, the West African Examinations Council (WAEC) and the National Examinations Council (NECO), are responsible for conducting Ordinary level (O level) examinations in Nigeria; university applicants are expected to have at least five passes at O level, including English language and (for science-based subjects) mathematics. Some universities run specific sub-degree programmes that qualify successful participants for admission into undergraduate programmes at the same university; (Higher) National Diplomas obtained from Nigerian polytechnics are considered from applicants for engineering. Creation of places at each university is a function of the individual university in conjunction with the National Universities Commission, which oversees the capacity of each university for its respective first degree programmes.

From the Applicant's Viewpoint: The UK Experience

Applicants to UK universities, many of whom will be in their final year at secondary school, complete an online application form. They choose from programmes on offer at institutions across the United Kingdom. The UCAS website (www.ucas.ac.uk) provides brief details of all programmes and their 'asking rates' (the results required by the various programmes in the public A level and similar exams) in a standardised format. Most universities will also post entry profiles for each of their programmes on the UCAS Course Search part of their website, giving details about programmes, the university, and other information about entry qualifications, selection criteria and admissions policy. Most applicants will also consult the relevant university's website and its prospectus, either online or in hard copy, for more information on the institution itself, on life as a student there, on the programme and its teaching methods, and so on. Mature applicants who are not applying straight from school may wish to consult the university before making an application, to check that they meet the entry requirements (as they may be offering non-standard qualifications), and gain further detail on the structure of the course (for instance in order to fit it around work and family commitments).

UCAS procedures are reviewed from time to time. At the time of writing, applicants may apply for up to five programmes, and are not required to specify a priority order for those applications. In recent history, applicants applied for up to six programmes; some years earlier the number was eight, with applications prioritised. An applicant can currently apply for more than one programme at an institution (for example, for medicine and also for biological sciences at the same institution), or can apply for five programmes at five different institutions. Time limits and deadlines are clearly laid down by UCAS, with applicants for medicine, dentistry and veterinary science and all Oxford and Cambridge programmes submitting in October for admission the following academic year (September/October); applicants for all other institutions and programmes must submit by a deadline in January of the year in which they hope to begin their programme, although most universities will accept late applications, especially from international applicants.

The applicant's school or college usually provides a reference for the applicant, and confirms the 'predicted grades' for the applicant's forthcoming public exams. Applicants not applying straight from school will already have achieved grades, and will supply a reference from someone who can comment on their academic suitability for the programme. A major part of the application to be considered by the admissions tutor is the 'personal statement', a statement by the applicant on why they wish to study the subject in question, and on what they think they can offer to a university. Applicants typically wax lyrical about their extra-curricular activities, including sporting prowess, musical achievements, work experience, and so on, and do what they can to persuade the institution that they are worthy of an offer. Each applicant has an 'account' with UCAS that they can access at any time to check on the progress of their application.

UCAS receives confirmation of most UK and some international public examination grades directly from the examining bodies, and admissions offices can therefore be confident that the information they are working from is accurate: applicants who have taken these exams do not need to send certificates or other confirmation to UCAS themselves. Applicants with exam passes from some time ago will usually be asked to send their certificates to the university to be verified. Admissions offices within institutions consider the applications they have received and make offers via UCAS.

Institutions vary in how they process applications. Some will assess all applications as they are received, but wait until the UCAS deadline in January before making any offers. Others will try to make offers as soon as the applications are received, but will have procedures in place to ensure that they treat all applicants who apply by the deadline fairly and equally. There can be advantages in making offers swiftly, particularly where an institution or subject needs to 'recruit' rather than 'select' (where 'recruit' means that there are generally fewer applicants than there are places available on a programme, and 'select' means that the number of applications for a popular programme far exceeds the number of places available): applicants receiving a speedy offer may look more favourably on an institution that appears to have 'chosen' them early in the process.

Case Study 1:
The Winning Approach

Joanna applied to five universities. She found the choice of the initial four relatively easy, but had difficulty identifying a fifth place. She opted for a university in a city she had never been to, and felt quite unsure about it, but her school told her she really ought to have five choices. Within 48 hours of submitting her online application, she received a letter from her fifth-choice university. The admissions office addressed her by her first name, said how interested they had been to read her application, confirmed that they would like to offer her a place and invited her to attend a visit day, for which they would meet her travel costs and provide her with overnight accommodation, given that she was travelling from a distance. If the date they had suggested did not suit her, they asked her to ring to sort out an alternative date. Excited by this, she arranged to visit the university, loved the city, was impressed by the tour and eventually took up the offer. This is an example of how a university with a very welcoming approach can ensure that it is more attractive to potential applicants than the competition.

Applicants in the United Kingdom learn via their UCAS account of offers made; a proactive admissions office is also likely to write direct to the applicant with information on open days, etc. Some subjects in some institutions require an interview before an offer is made, and applicants will be contacted about this direct by the institution.

Urban myths abound at what is inevitably a stressful time for applicants: 'University X won't make you an offer if they know you've applied to University Y', 'University Z doesn't offer places to applicants from independent [in the UK, private] schools', and so on. While many of these are just that – myths – it is important for institutions to be open and honest about their admissions policies, and to work with schools, colleges and independent applicants to ensure that prospective students know their current policies. At the same time, it is worth looking at the difference between 'recruitment' and 'selection' (as mentioned earlier); typically in the United Kingdom at present, there is an over-supply of applicants to arts programmes and a shortage of well-qualified applicants to some science programmes. Regardless of whether one is recruiting or selecting, the importance of treating candidates fairly and courteously cannot be over-emphasised, as is demonstrated in the following case study.

Case Study 2:
An Off-Putting Offer

Michael is a keen musician but is aiming to go to university to do science. He applied to five universities and received offers from four of them. The fifth, a very prestigious university and the one he really wanted to go to, took a long time to contact him. When it did so, it called him for interview at less than a week's notice. The interview date clashed with a major concert he'd been preparing for at school, in which he was due to play a violin solo. He was devastated, and asked the school's advice. The careers teacher told him he couldn't possibly ask that university to reschedule the interview, and he therefore missed the concert. The interview went reasonably well, but he was left sitting in a waiting room for a couple of hours at one point with no information. The tour of the university was conducted by a student who was unable to tell Michael anything about the musical life of the university (other than – erroneously – that she thought the orchestra was only open to people studying music for a degree course), or indeed anything beyond the science department he'd applied to. When eventually told that he was free to go, Michael was unclear what the next stage in the admissions process would be. In fact, three weeks later he was made an offer, but by that point had already decided he didn't want to go to that institution.

Once UK applicants have heard from all the institutions to which they applied, they need to make decisions on which offers (assuming they have more than one) they wish to keep in play; applicants are given a deadline by UCAS for replying to their offers. By this deadline, applicants need to reduce the offers they are holding to two: ideally, their first choice of institution and programme, plus an 'insurance' offer. The first choice may be asking for high grades in the public exams, for example grades AA and B at A level, while the insurance offer may be for an institution or programme that is less attractive to the applicant but with a lower asking rate, perhaps BB and B.

Holding such an insurance offer means that if the applicant fails to meet the grades predicted for them of (in this case) AAB, they can still take up the offer at the second choice of institution provided that the lower offer (in this case, BBB) is met. From 2009, all this will change, as applicants will be able to seek an alternative place if they exceed the offer of their firm choice and want to apply to what they regard as a better university. The implications of this decision are that it will be difficult for universities to plan intake numbers, as they will not know how many applicants may choose to adjust to another university; it may also impact on retention rates, as students who make a hasty decision to change university may later regret their decision. Universities will also need to consider how to manage the expectations of applicants; they may not have the places available to admit adjustment applicants, unless they plan to keep back a number of places for this purpose. Universities will also need to decide whether they will exclude applicants who have previously been rejected by them during that cycle.

From the Applicant's Viewpoint: The Nigerian Experience

In Nigeria, a brochure produced annually by the Joint Admissions and Matriculation Board (JAMB) fulfils a similar function to the UCAS website in providing a compendium of all first degree programmes on offer and their specific entry requirements. Since 1989, JAMB has covered admissions to polytechnics and colleges of education as well as all universities in Nigeria, providing a co-ordinated admissions process across the country. For more information on JAMB, see www.jambng.com/history.php.

In line with government aims towards technological development in Nigeria, there is a 60:40 bias towards science-based programmes. Applicants indicate their preferred two universities and programmes, with candidates in 'educationally less developed areas' knowing that some local universities offer remedial programmes for applicants who do not meet the normal entrance requirements for university. Students on remedial programmes sit the Universities Matriculation Examination (UME), which is conducted nationally by JAMB, and must obtain an acceptable level of performance in subjects relevant to the proposed programme of study. The UME subjects that are mandatory for different programmes are set out in the JAMB brochure. Use of English is mandatory for all programmes. A Pre-Degree Science (PDS) Programme ran until 2006–7, enabling a significant increase in entrant numbers to science-based undergraduate programmes. Until recently, candidates who did not secure admission in one year repeatedly sat the UME in subsequent years. This has led to a new arrangement of post-UME screening tests and interviews, allowing universities to look more closely at candidates before final selections are made.

Finance is a key factor in an applicant's decision to accept (or not) the offer of admission and, in due course, to complete on schedule. This has been a concern for some time to the federal government, the respective state governments and the universities themselves. As happens in the United Kingdom, many students are supported by their parents or guardians. Scholarships are also offered by corporate organisations, such as oil companies operating in Nigeria; state and federal bursaries also exist, as do scholarships based on academic performance. Some of the older universities offer university scholarships.

Employability on completion of the degree is an important consideration in Nigeria, as in the United Kingdom, and many universities are currently restructuring and repackaging their programmes to make them more relevant and skills orientated, allowing graduates to compete successfully in a world market for jobs.

From the University's Viewpoint

Undergraduate applications in the United Kingdom are frequently received and processed by a central admissions office, and then assessed by departmental admissions tutors (usually academics), although this pattern is changing, as what have traditionally been academic roles are passed to administrators in many universities. The central admissions office or registrar's department will also usually be responsible for ensuring the provision of a fair and efficient admissions service, the management of applicant communication, developing admissions policy, ensuring that intake targets and legal obligations are met, and staying up-to-date with best practice and national imperatives.

Within each university in Nigeria, the Examinations Division, Registry and Admissions Offices liaise with WAEC and other examination bodies to verify O level and A level results submitted by applicants. Candidates are selected by each university on merit, with each university having a first-choice list of applicants; this is submitted to JAMB for endorsement and JAMB then issues the provisional offer of admission to the applicant. Supplementary selection of candidates from the remainder of applicants (otherwise referred to as 'the University Discretion List') augments the merit list and ensures that places on respective programmes are filled.

The main concern of any admissions process should be to admit students who have the ability, motivation and potential to benefit from the programme. UK universities favour the method of holistic assessment, which generally involves varying degrees of emphasis on three factors: the academic record, the personal statement and the reference. In addition, many institutions also use other forms of assessment, such as an interview, a request for a piece of written work, or a separate test (e.g. LNAT, the National Admissions Test for Law, www.lnat.ac.uk). Universities sometimes find it appropriate to use other methods to distinguish between applicants of similar merit, such as consideration of an applicant's unit grades as well as aggregated grades, or even consideration of actual marks obtained (UMS marks). Some courses or programmes in the United Kingdom and in Scandinavia use a lottery system to select from equally qualified candidates in an approach to fair selection. Recent national qualification changes in the United Kingdom, such as the introduction of an A* grade (a grade higher than an A grade) to A levels, can also be useful for this purpose. In the future, contextual information, such as relative school performance against benchmarks, may become a bigger factor in the attempt to ensure fair access for disadvantaged students, and there is currently a national debate on the merits or otherwise of routinely providing this information with the UCAS form.

The Schwartz Review of HE Admissions of 2004 (www.admissions-review. org.uk) established as one of the principles of a fair admissions system the need for transparency (other principles included selection on achievements and potential, the use of reliable and valid assessment methods, the need to minimise any barriers for applicants, and the need to have a professional, high-quality and efficient admissions system). In response to the review, universities have tended to be much more transparent about their admissions criteria and how the admissions process will be conducted, and it is wise to ensure that this is the case in any institution. It has become increasingly common for universities to provide publicly available admissions policy statements and detailed application advice on their websites, at university level or even at programme level. As we have mentioned, many universities have also published entry profiles on the UCAS website for each of their programmes, which are documents that clearly explain the relevant programme content, the skills and qualities necessary to succeed on the programme, and the application process. The aim of all this work is not only to reduce the apparent mystery of applying to university, but also to provide a better fit between programme and applicant, so that wasted choices are avoided.

Some universities in Nigeria have taken the move towards transparency in the admissions process much further, posting information on their websites at various stages in the admissions process, including lists of candidates admitted, and emphasising that admission has been on merit (www.lasunigeria.org). By emphasising academic merit as the hallmark of the admissions exercise, such universities are able to win the confidence of applicants, staff, other stakeholders and the global community. Students are proud to belong to a system that so clearly and publicly recognises their academic worth – a marked contrast, perhaps, with the United

Kingdom, where the Data Protection Act would clearly prevent such public disclosure.

Unsurprisingly, owing to increased media and governmental interest in admissions in the United Kingdom, there has also been a growing emphasis on the need for national good-practice guidelines to be developed. One of the recommendations of the Schwartz Review was the creation of a central source of expertise and advice on admissions issues, and the 'Supporting Professionalism in Admissions' (SPA) programme was set up in 2006 for this purpose (www.spa.ac.uk). Its website is a good source of practical guidance for aspiring and current admissions professionals.

Another driver for this move to openness has been the increased number of applications made to universities (for example, UCAS reported an increase of over nine per cent in the total number of applicants in the 2007–8 admissions cycle). An unfortunate side effect of this popularity is that there will be more students who are not successful in obtaining a place at their preferred institution. A university can therefore expect to receive letters of complaint from applicants who have been rejected, often asking the university to explain the exact reasons for rejection, and even challenging its decisions. Any university will need to have procedures in place that will enable justification and production of evidence for all decisions, in the likely event of external scrutiny. For example, in the United Kingdom the Office for Fair Access (OFFA) (www.offa.org.uk) requires all universities that charge tuition fees above the standard level to submit an access agreement that sets out how they will safeguard and promote fair access through financial support and outreach work. Another source of independent scrutiny on admissions policy is the Office of the Independent Adjudicator for Higher Education (www. oiahe.org.uk), which handles individual complaints against HE institutions (e.g. from unsuccessful applicants).

International Applicants

International students pay full tuition fees in the United Kingdom, rather than being subsidised by the Funding Councils, so there is usually less competition for places, since universities are free to admit as many international students as they can comfortably accommodate, rather than having their numbers capped, as is the case with UK students. However, the concern should still be whether the applicant has the potential to succeed on the programme, so the same admissions criteria should be used. From an administrative point of view, specific priorities for international admissions are to help assessors to understand the equivalence of qualifications, to make decisions on fee status (using government guidelines), to ensure that any English language requisites are met, and to ensure that appropriate qualification checks are made, owing to increased opportunity for fraud. For this reason, admissions tutors need to check the identity of applicants and ascertain that their qualifications are genuine. It is also good practice to ensure that applicants are sent helpful information about visa applications, accommodation and any other information to help them settle in. An emerging issue is pressure from international students to receive more support from the institution once they arrive than was traditionally the case, and this is expected to increase in future years.

There can be a surprising lack of cultural awareness in some institutions. Many universities now offer an 'alternative prospectus' produced by students, and all universities rely on current students to lead tours for prospective students. But while some school leavers may be attracted to an institution by a tour guide who proudly points out the landmarks of 'pub, pub, nightclub, pub, club' from the steps of the hall of residence, others will not be so keen on this aspect – and some may be actively put off. Consider the case of Shalima.

Case Study 3:
Cultural Insensitivity

Shalima had a government scholarship from her home country. She had already had to work hard to convince her family that it is acceptable these days for a woman to go to university, and indeed to go to university abroad. Freshers' Week, however, came as a bit of a shock. Shalima learned little about study facilities and met only one member of the academic staff. She was horrified that everything seemed to revolve around the consumption of alcohol. She was surprised to be in a hall of residence with male students on the same corridor, and she wouldn't dare tell her family about this. And when she was woken in the early hours of the morning for the fourth day in a row by fellow students returning drunk from a club, she was very upset and decided to go home.

Universities need to have mechanisms in place to spot and support students like Shalima, who on some programmes may be in the majority. International students are likely to need help with many practical aspects of life in the United Kingdom – for example, sorting out a bank account and a mobile phone contract, registering with the health centre, learning how and where to shop economically – as well as potentially needing help with the cultural issues. At postgraduate level in particular, many applicants are likely to be expecting to bring a spouse and children, and the welfare of the whole family may therefore be an issue. If they are serious in wishing to attract more international students, institutions need to ensure that their structures for support of such students are properly in place.

Changes and Developments in the United Kingdom and Nigeria

Overview

The UK admissions system in the early years of the millennium is in a state of flux owing to government reviews of higher education admissions policies, and this is likely to continue if there is a change of government. A number of recent changes have been made with a view towards introducing a post-qualification application system by 2012 – that is, admitting students on the basis of achieved rather than expected examination results (further information is available at www.universitiesuk.ac.uk/ABOUTUS/ASSOCIATEDORGANISATIONS/PARTNERSHIPS/Pages/AdmissionsDeliveryPartnership.aspx). For example, as was discussed on p. 35, applicants who have exceeded the terms of their original conditional offer will, from 2009, be allowed to seek an alternative place following the publication of their results. Other changes have included the recommendation to have UCAS Entry Profiles for every single programme (to provide more detailed advice to applicants before they apply), and the provision of feedback to unsuccessful applicants (the SPA statement on feedback was approved in January 2008; www.spa.ac.uk/good-practice/applicant-feedback.html). Both issues will require the commitment of additional resources, and the second requirement will also have legal implications. Many institutions are therefore in the position of having to revisit their earlier policies of refusing to provide any reasons for a rejection of an application, and consider how best to respond to this new obligation.

In Nigeria too, there are concerns that candidates who have performed well at UME in April or May and been offered provisional admission will not be able to register until the results of their Senior School Certificate Examination (WASSCE), sat in June/July, are issued. Some potential candidates therefore sit Cambridge O level examinations instead, though WAEC has been successful in ensuring the release of results on schedule in recent years. Post-UME screening tests and interviews are increasingly being used to look closely at potential students.

Post-Award Application: The Pros and Cons

There has been much discussion over whether the current system in the United Kingdom should be revised. At present, applicants apply before knowing the outcome of the public exams they will take in their final year at school. This means that the application process is an uncertain one, depending heavily on teachers' predictions of grades, which are notoriously unreliable. An applicant who eventually performs much better (or much worse) than was predicted might have made different choices of institution or programme had they known what their exam results would be in a nation where there are perceived hierarchies of universities, rather than a system where students apply to their nearest university, as is the case in some countries. The process is also an uncertain one for universities, requiring them to guess, to some extent, how each applicant will perform in school exams and therefore how many offers might actually be taken up. On the other hand, any system of 'post-award application' would require a very tight turnaround on the part of applicants and institutions; with A level results currently being issued mid-August and the university year starting in September/October, there would be little time for processing of applications, conducting of interviews, and so on unless the date of entry were moved from the autumn to the new year. Applicants would also have less time to arrange accommodation or travel, and would need to do much of the visiting and trips to open days in advance of applying, at a time when their efforts should be concentrated on preparation for their exams. Such a move would also be likely to have a very adverse impact on some of the less favoured universities, which might, on average, find themselves with weaker students applying to them.

Diversity of Qualifications

The 14–19 qualifications changes in England and Wales (www.dcsf.gov. uk/14–19/) have served to increase the range of qualifications that students can offer. This has created some uncertainty for both applicants and universities: the latter may be unsure about the content and grading of a new qualification, and so it will be difficult to formulate offer require-ments. It may also mean that the first year of degree programmes may need to be adapted to meet the needs of students offering the new quali-fication. Equally, students will need to know that opting to study a new qualification will not disqualify them from applying for certain programmes. A future trend will probably see students offering a mixture of different qualifications, for example Cambridge Pre-U (a new post-16 qualification specifically designed to prepare students for the skills needed at university: www.cie.org.uk/qualifications/academic/uppersec/preu/index_ html) and one or two A levels. This trend will be made even more complex by the increasing numbers of continental European (European Union, EU) and international students who will study in the United Kingdom. From an admissions point of view, it will be increasingly difficult to make standard offers, and entry requirements will have to become more flexible. A university will probably need to develop detailed equivalence tables, or use the UCAS tariff (currently under review) to help assessors make informed decisions. Another issue likely to arise is the increased difficulty academics are likely to experience in planning their first-year programmes when the prior experiences of their students will have been so different.

Students in Nigeria present with a range of qualifications, too, from the nationally recognised WAEC-controlled O level examinations to Cambridge O levels, private examinations, remedial programmes and National Diplomas, and first-year tutors will similarly need to take account of these complexities.

The Changing Demographic

A projected drop from 2010 onwards in the number of 18- to 20-year-olds, the traditional market in the United Kingdom, will mean that UK higher education institutions will have to recruit more heavily in continental Europe and in non-traditional UK markets (particularly from the pool of mature students and those from disadvantaged backgrounds) in order to fill their places. Again, any increases in the success of EU recruitment are likely to lead to an increased diversity of qualifications being presented for admission. In addition, if the cap on fees is lifted and/or if the UK government reduces or withdraws funding for UK students, there will be direct competition between home and international students for places.

The Application System

The current UK system is principally paper based, although applicants apply online, but it is likely that the system will become totally electronic in future. In turn, this may mean that applicants will be able to make applications more tailored to their own particular circumstances, for example by being able to submit a separate personal statement for each programme, and adding other information about their achievements to date, such as an e-portfolio. The way that applicants apply in future may also be affected by the recent adoption of similarity detection software by UCAS, which is used to notify an institution if an applicant is suspected of plagiarising his or her personal statement.

An issue that will probably continue to surface periodically in the media is the idea of assigning university places to applicants by a lottery system as discussed earlier. However, such a system might not be politically acceptable since it does not tend to satisfy the wishes of schools or parents, who usually prefer a holistic system that takes account of the ability and potential of each individual applicant.

In Nigeria, a major problem arising from the existence of remedial programmes is that applicants who failed to secure a university place in one year repeatedly sat the UME in subsequent years. Some universities have therefore started to favour applicants who obtain good results in one sitting of WAEC exams, and the examining bodies are being encouraged to release results within two months of completion of the examinations to enable universities to consider applicants swiftly. As we have already mentioned, post-UME screening tests and interviews have also been introduced. As happens in the United Kingdom at postgraduate level, it is currently possible for a candidate in Nigeria to accept more than one offer of admission, leaving institutions with little idea as to their likely intake numbers until the start of the session. A recent development is that candidates are now allowed to select only two universities to which to apply, which addresses this issue to some extent. ·

Applicant Communication

Many UK universities have already started exploring the potential of making their communication with applicants more sophisticated by the use of new technologies, for example with tailored, automatically generated email responses to encourage applicants throughout the application process. With the advent of higher fees, applicants are now expecting a high-quality consumer experience, and this can only intensify in future years. Nigerian universities are also exploiting the benefits of new technology, with students registering online, paying fees online and also having access to online complaints and suggestions mechanisms.

Conclusion

An element of bureaucracy is inevitable in any large system, especially one in which so much is at stake for applicants and institutions. Applicants are becoming increasingly aware of their rights and inclined to challenge any perceived breach of those rights. Institutions therefore need to be increasingly 'customer-focused'; long gone in the United Kingdom are the days of government grant-funded students largely accepting what is done to them. Undertaking a degree is a major financial as well as intellectual commitment, and applicants and students (and, increasingly, their parents too, for whom this is likely to be a financial strain) are quite rightly expecting value for money, fair and courteous treatment, and transparently equitable processes. At the same time, improved technology facilitates communication at all stages of the application process, and institutions should ensure that they have appropriate mechanisms in place at all levels to ensure that the application process works as smoothly as possible.

CHAPTER 4

Commencement of the Academic Year

Welcoming, Inducting and Developing Students

MICHELLE MORGAN
Kingston University

and **SALLY BROWN**
Leeds Metropolitan University

Introduction

When students first start at university, there is a relatively short period in which a favourable impression can be made. If we get things right, we can set the tone for a productive and positive higher education experience as well as laying the foundation for nurturing lifelong learning behaviour and a relationship with education. However, all too often in the first couple of weeks of university life, students are faced with confusion, queuing and excessive bureaucracy. Sometimes this experience can continue throughout the life cycle of the student. In this chapter we will outline how in our respective universities we have tackled the challenge of improving the student experience from welcoming, orientation and induction to graduation, for both undergraduates and postgraduates starting courses of all kinds.

As is described elsewhere in this volume, recent trends, including the massification of higher education (HE), an increase in the diversity among the student body due to widening participation approaches, and greater numbers of international students studying in countries other than their own, have added to the complexity of the issues faced. Governments around the world, including that of the United Kingdom, are committed to increasing the take-up of HE to fuel the knowledge-driven economy (Department of Trade and Industry, 1998), in which universities have an important role to play (Department for Education and Skills, 2003).

Around the world, nations are being faced with demographic changes leading to near-saturation of the HE market for qualified 18-year-olds. Universities are increasingly recognising that in the past they have not been successful in providing a quality student experience, and many are rethinking their approaches to supporting and retaining an increasingly diverse student body. By 2011, the pool of 18-year-olds from which universities can recruit will be smaller than the population over 60 years of age (Directgov, 2008), so retaining students is going to be an even more critical activity for HE institutions than before. In recent years, HE has benefited from and relied on the international student market to boost its income and its student numbers. For example, postgraduate student numbers have remained relatively stable because the increase in the international market has counteracted the UK decline (Bekhradnia, 2005). However, the downturn in the economy near the end of the first decade of the century, visa requirements and the new points system for international students mean that universities can no longer rely on this market.

National and international research has increased understanding of student needs, and so we are better placed to ensure that students starting university life have every possible advantage. The student experience is complex, and the challenge for the HE sector in recent years has been trying to understand the elements that make up that experience. As HE has changed in terms of student diversity, the complexity has increased. HE institutions in many countries have responded in improving the student experience by, for example, improving orientation, induction and student support services; enhancing student welfare, teaching and learning support within institutions; and providing better opportunities to enable the student voice to be heard, through course representative schemes and close working relations with student unions. All of these factors are important in enabling the students of today to succeed, whether they are undertaking a traditional degree, are distance or work-based learners, or are new or returning students. However, proactivity in this area has not just been a matter of philanthropy. Increasingly, universities are judged by funding bodies and others on their success in recruiting, supporting and retaining students, thus making the need for effective induction paramount. Latterly, the National Student Survey, whose main purpose is to 'help inform the choices of prospective higher education students about where and what to study', has been a key driver in focusing institutions' attention on improving the student experience (Ipsos MORI, 2008).

In the United Kingdom there have been a number of initiatives to improve students' experience of welcoming, orientation and induction within institutions and through the UK Higher Education Academy Subject Centres. Future developments include improving the transitions from level to level as well as 'outduction' – that is, helping students move smoothly from university to the next stages of their life, including employment.

The Challenges

There are three broad challenges for universities wishing to improve the student experience, especially in the area of welcoming, orientation and induction. The first is identifying what support the 'student of today' in a diverse student population needs in order to succeed: the 'one size fits all' approach needs to be avoided. The needs of the individual are important even though they may seem small and insignificant to an institution that has to look after the needs of thousands of students. The second challenge is to demonstrate to colleagues that practices adopted and utilised 20 years ago are not necessarily suitable for students today, who have a very different skill base as compared to those of 10 or 20 years ago. The final challenge is to develop a student experience comprising quality learning and teaching, targeted administrative, support and welfare services, and effective social networks which all seamlessly link together from the point of first contact until graduation. The case studies in this chapter show how these broad challenges have been met.

Making a Difference

Staff across a university can make a real difference to the student experience. Increasingly, institutions are recruiting senior managers who are student experience champions or proactive practitioners. Targeted initiatives and good practice to improve the student experience need to be part of the ethos and culture of every unit and department within an institution. Top-down initiatives, no matter how logical and beneficial, will fail if they are not understood, accepted and adopted by all those working with applicants and students on the ground. And often, as perceptions of 'student need' by academic and support staff differ, there can be tensions and challenges regarding how to support students effectively. Providing a quality student experience is complex, and a huge undertaking that requires the agreement and input of all stakeholders.

Where to Start?

Students go to university to learn and get a degree, but what is the role of the university in that process and the relationship it has with that student? Defining the role the university plays can be very helpful in starting to unpick what it needs to do to start improving the student experience.

Universities educate several thousands of new students every year, provide academic and welfare advice and guidance, and help develop new relationships (students with students, students and academics). They teach new skills, inculcate the rules of the educational community (which can be subtle), promote independence in a range of areas (teaching and learning, how to be a student) and prepare the students for life afterwards, whether that be employment or further study ('outduction').

Importantly, the institution's rules may have to adapt and evolve to changing environments (economic climate and the knowledge-driven economy) and the changing nature of the student body. Today, maybe more than ever before, staff need to play a more explicit and constructive role in the life of students if those students are to succeed. The journey for both the student and the university starts with 'first contact' and continues until the students are alumni.

For many years, universities only engaged with the student experience (and often poorly at that) once the student had arrived at university, and the experience ended on graduation. It is a long journey for the student and a critical one, with all sorts of implications if the relationship breaks down somewhere along the way. If expectations are not managed from first contact onwards, the student can feel let down. Disappointed expectations can be a dangerous thing because students are more likely to withdraw. Yorke and Longden (2008) found in their research looking into the reasons for non-continuation among first-year students that disappointed expectations were a major issue in withdrawal.

> It was totally different from what I expecting, both academically and socially, and [it] totally let me down. Academically, I had no idea what was going on as we were never explicitly told about what was expected of us.
>
> (Yorke and Longden, 2008)

The Importance of Efficient Bureaucracy

Delivering a quality student experience from first contact to beyond graduation requires bureaucracy to be efficient. Bureaucracy need not be inefficient and negative. Efficient bureaucracy requires a symbiosis between effective collaboration and processes, good communication, and understanding the importance of responsibilities and the management of all stakeholders' expectations.

All stakeholders within an institution, whether they be academic or support staff working in faculties or schools, student support units, or infrastructure services, need to collaborate to achieve their institution's vision. They cannot work in isolation. For example, students will not benefit from quality learning and teaching practices if the lecture and tutorial rooms are not fit for purpose or if an institution recruits too many applicants with special learning needs but the support services cannot adequately provide support owing to lack of resources.

To work efficiently together requires having effective communication processes, whether between university staff or between the university and the applicant or student. Poor communication processes and a lack of 'joined-up thinking' are all too commonly found within the HE sector. The old adage that the one key thread tying a range of functions or activities together is 'communication, communication, communication' is true when it comes to providing a quality student experience. For example, if the promises made by a central recruitment and marketing department about the student experience are not reflected in the faculty's or school's information, nor delivered by them, then this not only causes confusion for the applicant or student and parent or guardian, but undermines the credibility of the institution as a whole. It takes time to build up a reputation but it can be lost quickly. All marketing and recruitment information across an institution needs to be clear, concise and consistent regardless of the mode of delivery.

All stakeholders within an educational system from university staff to potential students (including their parents or guardians in the case of younger students) need to understand their responsibilities in ensuring that quality student experience is achieved. Student charters became quite popular in the 1990s but they tended to be one-sided, with students being asked to take full responsibility for their experience. The delivery of a quality student experience is a two-way street, with the university responsible for delivering a range of services and students responsible for participating fully in the learning and teaching process and the rules of the educational community.

Managing the expectations and experiences of an applicant starts with first contact. Applicants and students are often described as 'customers', but such a description is fraught with problems. They are certainly consumers of education. The gym membership analogy is quite a good one when describing the relationship between the student and their institution. The fact that someone may have a gym membership does not in itself mean that they will get fit. They have to work at it. It is the same with education. However, it is important that the equipment in the gym is not broken, preventing fitness from being achieved.

The expectations and experiences of an applicant are established in a variety of ways. Importantly, their own pre-university educational experiences are very influential in shaping their opinions on university. For example, research tells us that low levels of preparedness for entering HE can increase transition difficulties (Richardson, 2003). Pre-registration information could also be obtained via a sibling, a friend, a member of staff at an open or admissions day or from an institution's website or prospectus. In recent years, we have increasingly seen expectations set by the 'helicopter parent', a term coined by Cline and Fay (1990) to describe a parent who pays extremely close attention to his or her child's experiences and problems. With the increase in tuition fees, more students living at home while studying, the economic downturn and more students returning to live at home post-study, it is hardly surprising that parental and guardian input has increased. However, sometimes expectations by the applicant or student and the parent or guardian are neither realistic nor correct, so it is important from the moment of first contact to be clear about what is expected of an applicant when they become a student and what their experience will be. The challenge for an institution is how to communicate with parents or guardians without compromising its relationship with the applicant during the admissions process and respecting the confidentiality of the student thereafter. Institutions are increasingly running parent/guardian admissions and open-day programmes alongside those for applicants. Advice and guidance for parents and guardians can be found on many university websites.

First Contact to Pre-Arrival

The period from first contact to pre-arrival is critical for all stakeholders as it is when opinions and first impressions are created. Information needs to be clear, fair, transparent, immediate, non-bureaucratic and accurate. It needs to be delivered via a variety of sources and integrated, whether via the web, face-to-face activities or by phone. Oblinger (2002) calls these sources 'touch points' and suggests that integrating them not only helps with bringing students into the institution but can help with 'at-risk learners' once they are enrolled.

It is during the pre-arrival period that any extra support for students, whether it be a conditional or an unconditional requirement of their application, needs to be given. Extra support could be in the form of a language pre-sessional for international students, an introductory day to ease mature students back into study and university life, or a maths summer school for engineering and science students. These activities need to link seamlessly into the arrival, orientation and induction process, which we talk about next.

Arrival, Orientation, Induction of New Students and Supporting Transition

In the past, universities may have been too quick to assume that students need very little support to help them adapt to university life, but adapting is particularly hard for international students at both undergraduate and postgraduate level. Guidance for students on what support and advice is available has tended to be compressed into a brief period at the beginning of the first year of study. And as imperatives to maximise student retention in the United Kingdom, as in many other countries, have taken hold, there has been a growing realisation that many well-intentioned induction activities, such as the traditional cheese and wine evening giving students a chance to get to know their tutors informally, are not enough to lay the foundations of a good student experience, nor are they necessarily culturally appropriate for students for whom alcohol is unacceptable. And on occasions, students start programmes late through no fault of their own, and they can feel disadvantaged if they have missed out on the induction experience.

Orientation, welcome and induction is the time when the promises we make during the recruitment and admissions process and the pre-arrival period need to be delivered. Students need to see that the product they have chosen and are getting is what was 'on the tin'. It is also important to remember that not all students will have visited their chosen institution before they arrive. The induction period is about managing expectations.

The term 'induction' implies a one-off introductory experience, but many working in the area consider the word deficient, as it suggests too brief a process. Similarly, the term 'orientation' gives the impression that once students can find their way around, literally and metaphorically, the job can be considered to have been done.

Induction has often been viewed as an activity that starts in Freshers' Week and lasts for one or two weeks. The types of activities traditionally undertaken by students during induction include settling into accommodation, finding their way around campus and their new town, enrolling, completing administrative tasks, getting their timetables and course information, attending Freshers' Fair and joining clubs and societies, and being introduced to a range of services such as welfare, ICT and library support. However, most of these activities are 'orientation' activities, meaning activities that help settle students into their new living and studying environment. These activities do have a short lifespan, with many tending to be administrative based. Very often, academic activity does not take place until the week following induction. Of course students are at university to have fun, but they are primarily there to get a degree. In recent years, research has demonstrated that as well as friendships being important in helping students settle into university life (Stuart, 2006; Wilcox *et al.*, 2005), getting new students embedded into their academic studies as soon as possible is critical in aiding retention and enabling them to succeed in their course (Kantanis, 2002; Morgan and Lister, 2004; Stuart, 2005). As a result, many institutions are adapting their induction programmes to make them more academic based. Academic and administrative collaboration is critical in developing a successful induction programme.

Research by Yorke and Longden (2004) tells us that the first six weeks of study are crucial to student achievement and retention; in the United Kingdom, students are more likely to drop out in the first year than at any other time, and the first peak for attrition is at around the six weeks point. If students feel that they do not belong, that they are out of their depth or that they are simply a number in an anonymous context, they are more likely to be discouraged than if they start to feel part of the programme.

There is a balance to be drawn between overloading students with too much information given out on arrival and leaving them underinformed. Students in the first couple of weeks may be overwhelmed and bemused by the sheer size and diversity of the organisation compared to where they were studying before and may feel exhausted by all the new information. It can be particularly hard to find their feet for students who have had a long gap between completing their qualifying examinations and taking up a university place.

All key players in an institution who are involved in the orientation, welcoming and induction of new students need to take responsibility for supporting students in transition as a means of demonstrating their commitment to students. It is all too easy to delegate information to staff involved in the induction of new students without sufficient follow-through and support of those staff. Induction provides an opportunity to give students a toolkit to support their experiences, enabling them to build the foundations for their next stages of study and university life. It is when they should be taught that they are expected to become independent learners. For this reason, a number of universities are exploring suspending normal teaching for the first six weeks of the first semester to focus on group activities that help to engender cohort cohesion and to foster independent learning approaches.

Induction should start in (or before) Freshers' Week but continue over a much longer period of time than that of orientation. So, maybe the first week, known as Freshers' Week, should also be referred to as initial induction, which includes academic activities such as getting course information and timetables, meeting academic staff and starting some form of study. Introducing new students to other academic, fun-based activities in Freshers' Week, such as attending an enjoyable, non-threatening lecture in a large lecture theatre, which can be an intimidating experience, can be a good ice-breaking activity. Involving existing students in the initial induction of new students via roles such as student induction helpers and peer-assisted learning schemes can be highly beneficial in helping new students relax and settle in. The University of Westminster's e-mentoring scheme, which is now into its sixth year, has a successful track record of students supporting students, especially during induction period.

Initial induction should roll into a longer induction programme and be designed to introduce and reinforce academic rules, standards, skills, behaviour and regulations in the following few weeks to prevent information overload and new students feeling confused, overwhelmed and possibly panicky.

Recruitment, pre-arrival, orientation and all induction activities should seamlessly fit together without causing information overload for students. The above applies to all new students starting at university, whether they are undergraduates, postgraduates, direct entry students or late arrivals. A good-quality orientation and initial induction programme is very important for direct entry students who go straight into year 2 or 3 of a degree programme. This is especially critical for direct entry international students, who have to learn to adapt to not only a different living environment, but also an academic one. They are expected to understand the academic conventions of a course and university overnight without having the adjustment period that students who started the course in year 0 or 1 will have had. This can create enormous pressure on the student as well as barriers to success. Some institutions continue recruiting students after the start of the new academic year. It is important that these students, who have been unable to participate in the main arrival, orientation, welcome and induction process, are not disadvantaged.

The case studies that follow demonstrate success as a result of academic and administrative collaboration, communication between the key players and a lot of will and determination. Case Studies 1 and 2 show how two institutions deal with the arrival, orientation, welcome and induction of their students. Case Study 1 shows how the University of Sussex, through internal and external research, designed a new induction programme encompassing the above elements for both new undergraduate and postgraduate students. A critical element in the construction of the programme was listening to the needs of students rather than just the institution and what staff wanted or thought would be useful. Case Study 2 illustrates how Leeds Metropolitan University addressed the needs of arrival, orientation, welcome and induction of its diverse student body through its Freshers' Festival. Case Study 3 shows how the Faculty of Engineering at Kingston University has designed an initial induction programme for all direct entry students, with a specific focus on international students, who make up a significant proportion of the direct entry cohort.

Case Study 1:
The Eight-Strand Approach to Induction at the University
of Sussex: Initial Induction Developed by Michelle Morgan,
Student Experience Manager

Recognising that students of today, who are now educational consumers, face very different pressures and educational experiences compared to those of a decade ago, the University of Sussex decided to look at its orientation and welcome programmes, which varied across the schools and had little university co-ordination. Research indicated that both played an important role in the student experience and retention.

We undertook a major review and extensive research with students and staff via questionnaires and focus groups. The research showed that there were a number of basic activities that all students needed to undertake, regardless of whether they were undergraduate or postgraduate students, full-time or part-time learners. Students were specific about what support, advice and help they needed, and staff recognised through the review that there were real weaknesses in our existing strategy.

We wanted to produce a common, cross-school induction programme that addressed the needs of a diverse student body. It needed to be friendly, not bureaucratic, appropriately pitched and with fully structured academic and social ice-breaking activities. Overall coherency and continuity of activities through the week and the weekend were critical. The challenges included engaging faculty and all staff. External and internal evidence was used to demonstrate the need for change. The new induction process needed to 'involve all stakeholders (academic, non-academic staff and internal organisations such as the Students Union)' (Four Counties, 2002).

We wanted a balance between academic and social events as well as a move away from the traditional administrative-led induction at Sussex, which fitted around the needs of the university rather than those of our increasingly diverse body of students. For example, Freshers' Week was purposely started mid-week so that university facilities such as accommodation and hospitality services did not have to open at the weekend. This meant that initial induction took place at the end of Freshers' Week and at the start of week 1, resulting in teaching not starting until mid-week of week 1, causing a number of problems for students, including their ability to settle in quickly.

Freshers' Week did not include academic input, which internal and external research showed was important for enabling students to embed themselves into academic life and forge relationships with the academics responsible for their first-year learning experience. 'It is pertinent that students' initial experience of university, especially experiences associated with teaching staff, teaching methods and assessment, be recognised as a significant factor in determining students' course persistence' (Kantanis, 2002).

The Plan

A number of new interlinked initiatives were developed, but the centrepiece of the new 'initial' induction programme was the Eight-Strand Approach, encompassing good external practice. It could be moulded to suit any type of student, whether undergraduate or postgraduate, reflected that what students said was important, and could be undertaken over a week or collapsed into two days or less. The strands were compulsory and provided a balance of social and academic introductions to the university, the new student's home department and our teaching processes, thus ensuring that all students received a similar basic induction experience. Activities unique to the schools were fitted into slots in the timetable purposely left empty for these activities. The strands were distributed equally throughout the week in the order students had requested. The programme required a major shift in thinking by academic, administrative and support staff across the university. Recognising that students identified with the department and not the school, departmental activities were prioritised. Having too many welcome sessions was avoided.

Departmental Welcome Academic Orientation – Monday Morning

In this session, students were given the university student handbook and the school or departmental handbook. They were told how to use them, how to choose course options and shown how to use the teaching timetable. Students met faculty in their 'home' subject, heard about the department's approach to the subject, were given a sketch of the coming first year, and given a chance to ask questions of faculty and second- and third-year students.

Departmental Social Event – Monday Afternoon

Departments were asked to avoid the 'wine and nibbles' approach and think of more imaginative formats such as quizzes, which acted as an

continued

effective ice-breaker for both new students and staff. Faculty representatives were required to attend at their departmental welcome and social event. This event was designed to finish a hectic day on an informal and fun note.

University Registration and Enrolment – Schools Allocated Time During the Week

For most students, registration and enrolment was completed online before arrival. This session was for those who were unable to register online. Students who had already completed the activity would be able to use the allotted time to sort out any queries or issues.

Library Tour – Tuesday

New students all had a compulsory library talk and were given the opportunity to attend a library tour. Trail activity leaflets were given to all students to help them orientate themselves with library services.

University, School Welcome and Introduction to University Services – Wednesday

The Wednesday saw a university- and school-level welcome by the vice-chancellor and the dean of the school. University services such as the Computing Service and Students' Union would all present a five-minute introduction to the services they could provide. At this session, students were given a one-page 'Who's who' guide to all support services and key players within their school, which was designed to be pinned on a noticeboard.

ICT Introductory Sessions – Wednesday

All new students were required to undertake a session introducing them to the ICT systems at the university. Free and useful software as well as information on extra support services were given at this session.

Study Skills and/or Mentoring Opportunities – Thursday

On Thursday a workshop-type session took place to help students with the distinctive features of university-level study. Study skills training was undertaken by faculty or student mentors. Mentoring opportunities were also offered by current second- and third-year students.

Personal Tutor Meetings – Thursday

A personal tutoring meeting (possibly group-based – just to make friendly contact) was held.

Timetables for all school, department and university-based events were drafted centrally in collaboration with the key players in order to avoid clashes. Once the departmental slots and activities unique to them were added, these were passed on to the Students' Union and other central services so they could build their programme around them.

How it was implemented

Successful implementation of the Eight-Strand Approach across the university was achieved by engaging, convincing, influencing and negotiating with key players, rather than by imposing and compelling. All staff received an induction handbook detailing the programme and providing advice and guidance on supporting new students.

Effectiveness of the Project

All schools voluntarily adopted the Eight-Strand Approach. The induction review of 2003 demonstrated that staff and students were very happy about the induction process. Faculty stated that the best part of the Eight-Strand Approach was that students were more confident entering the first week of teaching. The solid and comprehensive programme took continuous hard work, through talking and disseminating information and good practice, to keep staff engaged. The induction programme is adaptable, flexible, comprehensive, targets streamlined information and meets the needs of a diverse student body.

Case Study 2:
Leeds Metropolitan's Freshers' Festival

In many UK universities, Freshers' Weeks tend to centre on pub crawls and binge drinking. Leeds Met is a very diverse university, with students from at least 105 nations studying with us. We have a high proportion of students from ethnic minorities whose cultural practices preclude drinking alcohol and participating in uninhibited social behaviour. At the highest level there was strong support from 2004 to offer a different kind of student welcome that would be inclusive and engaging for all students, not just those who enjoy high-octane

continued

partying. As a university of festivals and partnerships, and working together with our Students' Union, we decided to create a university-wide fortnight-long Freshers' Festival located in our Festivals village (marquees erected at our Headingley campus for our graduation ceremonies and used for our Staff Development Festival prior to the freshers' event). The festival starts with a family welcome weekend, where parents and carers dropping off students can get a feel for our university life and young children can be entertained while the students are settling in.

As well as local induction activities in the faculties and schools, each faculty uses the marquees for half a day each within the fortnight for generic induction for all students in that faculty. These sessions are wrapped around with a highly diverse range of activities to suit our diverse students, including dancing displays, sporting and cultural activities, concerts, and welcome parties. The Students' Union mounts a substantial Students' Fair in the marquee, where all student societies have an opportunity to recruit new members, and there are displays and exhibitions from the police, the Health, Disability, Counselling and Learning Support Services, and our cultural and sporting partners, including Northern Ballet, Opera North, West Yorkshire Playhouse, Leeds Rhinos (Rugby League), Leeds Carnegie (Rugby Union), Yorkshire County Cricket Club and many others.

In earlier years we held a separate induction for international students prior to the Freshers' Festival, but this proved to have the unintended consequence of making them feel separate and different from home students, since they had already started to make fixed friendship groups prior to the arrival of the other students, and some-times felt they had already been involved in orientation and did not need to do it again. Consequently, we have now moved to adding special welcome events for international students after the universal freshers' events, to encourage a homogeneous approach.

Case Study 3:
Initial Induction for Direct Entry Students (UK, EU and elsewhere Internationally) in the Faculty of Engineering at Kingston University

The research undertaken within the Faculty of Engineering highlighted that direct entry students coming into year 2 and the final year of a degree were not getting the same induction experience as new students. That in turn was affecting their ability to settle into university life and their studies. International students who arrived the week before tended to migrate together instead of mixing with the main cohort. The aim of the initial induction programme for direct entry students is to embed them quickly into their studies, integrate them into their year cohort and enable them to make friends. Their orientation and initial induction programme starts before the official arrival period.

June – Pre-enrolment Information

In June, students expected in the following September receive a handbook providing advice on the transition process, what to expect when they arrive and how to study at a UK institution. This information links to the arrival activities in the week before Freshers' Week.

Pre-Freshers' Week – Arrival and Orientation of Students

International direct entry students are asked to arrive mid-week, the week before Freshers' Week starts. They are picked up from the airport and student helpers assist them with the settling-in process. They undertake a specific orientation programme designed to settle them as quickly as possible into their new living environment. They get the opportunity to meet other international and UK students as part of the programme. UK students in university accommodation are expected to arrive by the Sunday morning before the start of Freshers' Week.

Freshers' Week

The Freshers' Week programme for direct entry students in the Faculty of Engineering starts on the Sunday afternoon. The initial induction programme consists of core activities that all direct entry students need to undertake to help settle them into their studies as well as providing them with free time to sort out any issues or problems relating to their studies or university life. All students are provided with a comprehensive welcome and orientation handbook, which contains practical orientation advice, a jargon buster so students can make sense of the acronyms and jargon we use, study advice and a 'who's who' guide and useful contact details for specific services they may need while settling in.

continued

Sunday

Enrolment is undertaken partly online but the process must be completed in person by all new students. For the faculty, enrolment takes place on Sunday afternoon. Students, parents, guardians and spouses have access to a welfare fair and afternoon tea. It is not uncommon for some parents of international students to accompany their son or daughter on their journey to the United Kingdom. This event is well attended and appreciated.

Although the initial induction timetable has a significant number of sessions that students must attend, the information is focused and designed not to overload the students. Direct entry students should be experienced students in terms of knowing how to study. However, the week is designed to provide them with the information they need to study in a different institution and to make friends. International students are required to undertake specific sessions during the week such as the International Student Welcome and Language Diagnostics.

Monday
- International specific student welcome and information session.
- Faculty welcome and introduction to what's on in Freshers' Week for all direct entry students.
- Academic Information Session.
- Working lunch.
- Departmental welcome and fun activity designed to get all direct entry students talking to one another.

Tuesday

All students undertake a range of refresher study skill lectures and workshops on time management, report writing, referencing, and tackling assignments.

Wednesday

Students undertake sessions on health and safety, library and ICT, welfare and support, and specific technical ICT sessions required for years 2 and 3.

Thursday

The Thursday offers some free time for UK students, plus the Freshers' Fair. International students are required to attend a language diagnostic and support session in the morning. They then have the opportunity to attend the Freshers' Fair in the afternoon.

Friday
The Stomp Rocket Challenge is a fun activity day for all direct entry and returning students, although not compulsory. The aim is for direct entry students to mix with existing students and make new friends before the start of teaching by undertaking a fun engineering activity.

Supporting the Transition of Returning Students

It is important to remember that each academic year brings a different set of student expectations that need managing, and a fresh need to understand what is required by students and what new skills they need to learn in the coming year. It also brings a different set of pressures for the student. The transition period for all students can be a vulnerable time. The RaPSS Study (2007), which was the first in-depth UK study to look at student suicide, found that students were more likely to commit suicide at the start or near the end of the academic year.

Raising students' awareness of what to expect throughout the life cycle, whether they are undergraduates or postgraduates, is critical in helping them succeed. Institutions are increasingly recognising the importance of this activity and are introducing re-induction sessions for returning students.

As well as recognising the need to induct returning students, institutions are realising that institutions need to participate more in preparing students for life after university. As Adnett and Slack (2008) state, having a degree still offers graduates an advantage in the marketplace. However,

> a concern is that the recent rapid expansion of HE in the UK has increased the inflow of graduates into the labour market at a faster rate than the creation of new graduate-level jobs, thereby lowering the earnings premiums of new graduates (the 'over-education' phenomenon).

Not all degree programmes are designed to equip students with employability and career advancing skills. In an increasingly saturated graduate market, equipping graduates with transferable skills that are useful in the employment arena is becoming important. The Quality Assurance Agency (QAA) requirement for institutions to provide students with the opportunity to engage in personal development planning aims to facilitate this activity. Personal development planning (PDP) is defined as 'a structured and supported process undertaken by an individual to reflect upon their own learning, performance and/or achievement and to plan for their personal, educational and career development' (Higher Education Academy, 2005).

Also, it is important to understand that the drivers for students undertaking a degree may be changing. UNITE found in its 2001 Student Living Survey that 52 per cent of those in its sample were undertaking a degree to improve their employment chances (MORI, 2001). In 2007 this figure had risen to 65 per cent, and of the sample, 44 per cent saw a degree as a way of improving their earning potential. Only 19 per cent said it was for the chance to be creative (MORI, 2007). The 2008 NUS Student Experience Report has reported similar findings (NUS, 2008).

Some institutions are already addressing these issues by designing degrees with enhanced employability skills in preparation for a student's life after university and to meet the needs of the knowledge-driven economy. An example of this is the increase in work-based learning degrees. Also, just as we induct students, many argue that we should be 'outducting' them. The term 'outduction' was coined by Geoff Layer (2007) from the University of Bradford. Outduction activities for final-year students are already being developed by some forward-thinking universities, whether they be embedded or delivered on an extra-curricular basis.

Case study 4 shows how the Faculty of Engineering at the University of Kingston has introduced induction programmes for returning students and uses them as a vehicle through which to identify and deliver outduction activities as required by its students. A major two-year project funded by the Higher Education Academy is also being undertaken by Kingston University, looking at the importance of outduction activities.

Case Study 4:
Induction for Year 2 and Final-Year Returning Students
in the Faculty of Engineering at Kingston University

This one-hour activity brings together a range of key players involved in the life cycle of a student in year 2 or the final year. Direct entry students who had a comprehensive initial induction programme in Freshers' Week (see Case Study 3) join existing returning students for the general year induction for returners. The teaching timetable is extensive for engineering students, so incorporating outduction activities into the timetable is not possible. However, outduction activities are scheduled to avoid teaching clashes.

Welcome Back by the Dean

The welcome by the dean is used to celebrate the success of students continuing the transition between academic years and is an opportunity to reinforce in our students a sense of self-belief that started in the previous year about their capability and why they are undertaking a degree.

Study Expectations and Introduction to Academic Rules and Regulations for the Coming Year

Each of the academic years requires a different set of skills and expectations. All too often, it is assumed that students will automatically find and understand the information relating to their new year of study. This session is designed to outline what is required of them academically and give advice on how to succeed in their studies in the coming year.

Academic and Personal Support Available in the Faculty

In this session, we remind students of the academic and pastoral support available in the faculty. This includes personal tutoring, the peer-assisted learning scheme and support provided by the Faculty Student Support Officer. Returning students are given a 'who's who' guide to support services for the coming year.

Central Services Support

This session reminds students of the support that central services can provide, such as dyslexia support, health and counselling, and academic student support. Students may not have needed faculty or central support services in the previous year but there may be services they will need to utilise in the coming year.

The Importance of Personal Development Planning

Personal development planning is an activity in which students are required to participate in year 1. In year 2 and the final year, students are offered the opportunity to continue engaging in the activity to support their study and career advancement.

Placements and Careers

In this session, we remind students of placement options, part-time job availability and careers advice and support by the Careers Service.

continued

Students are given a booklet containing useful information and advice. We have found that this is an important activity in helping students enhance their employability upon graduation, especially in an environment where there is a pool of graduates seeking work.

Reflection on the Previous Year and What Extra Support is Required This Coming Year

At the end of the programme, we ask students to reflect on their previous year of study and identify what modules they enjoyed and found most useful. Students are asked to identify any extra academic or support sessions they would like in the coming year. For year 2 and final-year students, extra activities requested commonly include careers advice on CV writing, completing application forms and attending interviews, presentation skills, and report writing.

The Future

In the next five years, the HE sector has a number of challenges to meet. They include further increasing student diversity, improving excellence in learning and teaching, meeting the needs of a knowledge-driven economy, improving the sustainability of the HE sector, and enabling excellence.

Increasing student diversity will be particularly challenging for institutions. In the past, when there has been a downturn in the economy, education has fared well as people have put stock in education, hoping that once they have graduated, the job market will have improved. However, now that students in England pay high variable tuition fees, it is unclear whether education will be viewed as the good investment it was in the past.

What is clear is that many universities are going to have to adapt and evolve to the marketplace, rather than students adapting to the products universities have been prepared to offer. There is little clarity at present on how institutions are going to deal with the new 14–19 diplomas or how the points system for international students is going to impact on UK student numbers. In addition to retaining students by providing a high-quality student experience that covers orientation and induction, higher education is going to have to be delivered in modes that students can afford. This will mean developing work-based learning, providing flexible learning opportunities and embracing blended learning. The challenge for us is to deliver a high-quality welcome, orientation and induction for all our students.

Conclusions

In this chapter, we have aimed to provide some practical advice on how to improve the student experience in the area of welcoming, orientation and induction. We conclude by offering some basic guidelines and advice gleaned from our own experiences of supporting welcoming, orientation and induction in our own institutions:

- The welcome, orientation and induction process is part of a larger picture that starts with first contact and continues until the end of the course or degree.
- Induction is a process, not an event, and support for students does not stop when Freshers' Week (or fortnight) is over. Students need to be very clear about where to go for help, and to feel confident about seeking it throughout their life at university.
- Orientation and induction should be inclusive and support and embrace diversity. Involve students in the debate on what to offer. They are the most likely to know what help, support and advice they need and are likely to be able to guide organisers on acceptable options. It is best not to try to second-guess what they do or do not need.
- All categories of staff need to be involved in induction, from porters to car park attendants to receptionists. Receptionists are often the first faces that new students come into contact with, and can often make the difference between a good or a poor start to university life.
- Universities should consider developing a public document that sets out expectations and good practice for all its student experience activities. This might take the form of a student and staff charter laying out what is expected by both parties, so as to avoid confusion and disappointment.

References

Adnett, N. and Slack, K. (2008) 'Are there economic incentives for non-traditional students to enter HE? The labour market as a barrier to widening participation', *Higher Education Quarterly*, 61 (1): 23–36.

Bekhradnia, B. (2005) 'Postgraduate education in the UK: trends and challenges', paper given at conference 'The Future of Postgraduate Education: Supporting the Students of Today and Tomorrow', 17 March, London.

Cline, F. W. and Fay, J. (1990) *Parenting with Love and Logic: Teaching Children Responsibility*, Colorado Springs, CO: Piñon Press.

Department for Education and Skills (2003) *The Future of Higher Education*, Cm 5735, London: The Stationery Office.

Department of Trade and Industry (1998) *Building the Knowledge Driven Economy*. Online, available at: www.dti.gov.uk/comp/competitive/main.htm (accessed 30 November 2008).

Directgov. Online, available at: www.direct.gov.uk/en/Governmentcitizensandrights/Livinginthe UK/DG_10012517 (accessed 12 December 2008).

Four Counties Group of Higher Education Institutions (2002) *Retention: A Practitioners Guide to Developing and Implementing Pre-entry, Induction and Ongoing Retention Tactics,* Chelmsford: Anglia Polytechnic University.

Higher Education Academy (2005) *Guide for Busy Academics No. 1: Personal Development Planning.* Online, available at: www.heacademy.ac.uk/PDP.htm (accessed 2 May 2007).

Ipsos MORI (2008) National Student Survey 2008. Online, available at: www.ipsosmori.com/ researchspecialisms/publicaffairs/socialresearchinstitute/higher-education/nss.ashx (accessed 8 January 2009).

Kantanis, T. (2002) 'Attitude and interaction: crucial factors affecting the influence of academics on first-year undergraduate students' satisfaction and persistence', paper presented to the 15th International Conference on the First Year Experience, 1–5 July, Bath.

Layer, G. (2007) 'The final year experience', keynote address at the Course Directors' Conference, Kingston University, January.

Morgan, M. and Lister, P. (2004) 'The changing face of induction', in D. Saunders, K. Brosnan, M. Walker, A. Lines, J. Storan and T. Acland (eds) *Learning Transformations: Changing Learners, Organisations and Communities,* London: Forum for the Advancement of Continuing Education.

MORI (2001) *UNITE Student Living Survey 2001.* Online available at: www.unite-group.co.uk.

MORI (2007) *UNITE Student Living Survey 2007.* Online available at: www.unite-group.co.uk.

NUS Student Experience Report 2008. Online, available at: www.nus.org.uk/en/News/News/ NUS-published-first-major-study-into-student-experience-/ (accessed 5 December 2008).

Oblinger, D. G. (2002) 'From connections to community', in D. J. Burnett and D. G. Oblinger (eds) *Innovation in Student Service: Planning for Models Blending High Touch/High Tech,* Ann Arbor, MI: Society for College and University Planning.

RaPSS (2007) *Responses and Prevention in Student Suicide: The RaPSS Study.* Online, available at: www.rapss.org.uk/pdf/summary_pdf.pdf (accessed 5 January 2009).

Richardson, D. (2003) 'The transition to degree level study'. Online, Higher Education Academy Resource pages, available at: www.heacademy.ac.uk/resources.asp?process=full_record& section=generic&id=506 (accessed 8 January 2008).

Stuart, M. (2005) 'What price inclusion? Debates and discussions about learning and teaching to widen participation in HE', in G. Layer (ed.) *Closing the Equity Gap: The Impact of Widening Participation Strategies in the UK and USA,* Leicester: NIACE.

Stuart, M. (2006) 'My friends made all the difference: getting into and succeeding at university for first-generation students', *Journal of Access Policy and Practice,* 3 (2): 162–84.

Wilcox, P., Winn, S. and Fyvie-Gauld, M. (2005) ' "It was nothing to do with the university, it was just the people": the role of social support in the first year experience of higher education', *Studies in Higher Education,* 30 (6): 707–22.

Yorke, M. and Longden, B. (2004) *Retention and Student Success in Higher Education,* Maidenhead: Open University Press/McGraw Hill Education.

Yorke, M. and Longden, B. (2008) *The First-Year Experience of Higher Education in the UK,* York: Higher Education Academy.

CHAPTER 5

Establishing and Running a Scholarship Programme

JAMES FORSHAW

Liverpool John Moores University

Why Develop a Scholarship Programme?

Universities in the United Kingdom have long had scholarship programmes but they have tended to be small-scale by comparison with, say, US scholarship programmes – localised and often the result of personal benefactors. In the United States there are many well-developed scholarship programmes that can be either specific to a particular course or general. Usually, scholarships are offered on the basis of merit (academic or sporting excellence), need (where the student's family's financial situation is taken into account) or sociological factors (i.e. related to the student's ethnicity, race or religion), or are institutional (scholarships that are awarded by a particular university).

In the United Kingdom we have numerous bursaries and scholarships from external sources to offer students financial assistance, sometimes with very specialised eligibility criteria. An example of this is the Leverhulme Trade Charities Trust Bursary: eligibility for this award is based on need but also on other, more arcane criteria, in that a student must have a parent who is or has been a greengrocer or travelling salesman.

After the UK Dearing Report (National Committee of Inquiry into Higher Education, 1997) was published, it was clear that the HE sector was going to change significantly in the light of new proposals on paying for higher education. The Higher Education Act 2004 brought a fundamental shift in who paid for university education, from government to families. A direct result of this was that universities, among others, began to look at what could be done to counter this new financial burden facing students and how they could make themselves more competitive in the marketplace.

The beginnings of Liverpool John Moores' Scholarship Programme stem from 'The Excellence Challenge', an initiative from the United Kingdom's then Department for Education and Skills in 2001 that was intended to address the under-representation in higher education of students from financially disadvantaged backgrounds and increase participation. The notion was to raise aspiration levels in potential students from low socio-economic and disadvantaged backgrounds and increase their future earning potential. In the government White Paper *The Future of Higher Education* (Department for Education and Skills, 2003) the then Secretary of State for Education and Skills, Charles Clarke, described university as 'a vital gateway to opportunity and fulfilment for young people', saying that 'it is crucial that they continue to make real and sustained improvements in access'. The White Paper set out the government's aim to open up access to university to students from disadvantaged backgrounds, while at the same time giving universities the freedom to set their own tuition fees.

The Aimhigher programme sought to provide bursaries for young students from low-income families who had the ability to benefit from HE but did not have the confidence or financial capability to apply. In addition to offering financial incentives, Aimhigher encouraged activities aimed at bolstering and increasing the expectations of school pupils. These would typically take the form of visits to universities, summer schools, master classes and mentoring schemes.

The Opportunity Bursary scheme was introduced to target areas where participation rates in HE were low: 'Excellence in Cities' and 'Education Action Zones'. The scheme was intended to address the perceived cost of studying in HE and to remove financial barriers to participation. This initiative was further backed up by the offer of additional financial support on a targeted basis.

The provision of these Opportunity Bursaries would appear from subsequent research to have been a success. Typically, recipients were less concerned about getting into HE-related debt and more confident about the long-term investment in their future. They reported lower actual levels of debt on graduation and were more likely to progress normally through their course.

In *The Evaluation of Aimhigher: Survey of Opportunity Bursary Applicants 2001/02: Preliminary Findings* (West *et al.*, 2003), the suggestion is made that receiving the bursary may have made the recipients view their experience of HE more positively. This did seem to be borne out among recipients with whom I had contact during the lifetime of the Opportunity Bursary scheme. As part of reviewing our practices at Liverpool John Moores University for

Opportunity Bursary recipients, and subsequently scholarship recipients, we asked recipients to fill in a feedback questionnaire. Some replies mirrored these findings. For example, one student told us:

> As with the vast majority of students at University, finance is a main aspect of day-to-day life. I am very grateful to Liverpool John Moores University for providing me with additional funding to help me throughout the year. I purchased a laptop with the first payment, which was valuable for completing essays and reports. This has made a big difference to my studies.

Widening participation at Liverpool John Moores University has always been slightly different for us as compared with many other UK universities, as 24 per cent of our students are recruited locally and often come from low-income backgrounds. Nevertheless, there were a lot of important lessons learned through this scheme, although, given Liverpool John Moores' demographic profile, the allocation year-on-year was arguably too small. The Opportunity Bursaries were oversubscribed each year, normally with a substantial waiting list of students. This high demand for bursaries in the first year of operation led Liverpool John Moores to formulate a similar offer using our own funds. The Gateway Bursary was an attempt to offer financial support to students from low-income families after the Opportunity Bursary fund was exhausted.

A History of Student Funding at Liverpool John Moores University

During the years when Opportunity Bursaries were in operation, it seemed clear that the higher education sector was changing radically. We had been discussing these changes since the Dearing Report (National Committee of Inquiry into Higher Education, 1997) and looking for ways in which we could be responsive to this changing agenda. At this point in Liverpool John Moores University's bursary/scholarship history we began to expand this process and move it forward by looking to local businesses to become partners and invest in the future of our student body. The thinking behind this was that students contribute substantially to the local economy both during and after their studies and so one might expect local businesses to reciprocate. This was a very positive experience for us, though there was one issue that arose from these discussions: questions arose about what Liverpool John Moores University itself was doing as an institution. Businesses queried why they should contribute when the university was not doing so.

There was also a moral issue here. The majority of staff currently in post who had studied at higher education level and attained an undergraduate degree were likely to have done so when education was free. After much discussion, senior management came up with the suggestion of a 'staff contribution scheme', which was then put to staff around the university. This became our 'Give as You Earn' scheme (GAYE). Staff were asked to support our students and they did so. The contribution scheme was put in place and staff made a donation to the fund each month. This proved to be a major boost to the funds for scholarships and brought a lot of external companies into partnership with the university.

The culmination of our experiences of managing these funds and securing these partnerships led to the development of the 24/50 Scholarship in 2003. These scholarships were aimed at people who made significant achievements, academically or otherwise. Merseyside traditionally had a very low participation rate in higher education, so tackling this issue became a major aim at the university in line with government policy. A secondary aim of this programme was to use it as a recruitment tool to increase the quality of applicants to Liverpool John Moores and also as a means to assist retention. This proved to be very successful, with over 85 per cent of recipients graduating with a 2.1 degree or better, and less than 1 per cent of recipients failing to complete their courses.

Over the two-year period the university raised enough money to disburse scholarships to the value of £2,000 to more than 60 students for the three years of their study. This came at a politically sensitive time, as the introduction of variable tuition fees was imminent.

With the introduction of variable tuition fees and the concomitant changes in student finance, we realised we could develop these experiences into something more significant that could have an even greater impact on a larger number of students. We resolved that if we were serious about addressing the issue and removing financial obstacles, we should find the means to release additional targeted funds. Certainly in our interactions with sixth form colleges, schools and Connexions events (organised by a government-funded body that offers advice and guidance for young people between the ages of 13 and 19 and co-ordinated at local government level, normally through schools), it became apparent that the perceived cost of education was off-putting for some students coming into higher education. Getting involved with Connexions at this particular level has been helpful in alleviating financial concerns and getting the message across to potential students that it is in essence an investment in their own future.

Our presentations on the current statutory support available and its repayment were (and still are) generally met with many different responses. While there are students who see higher education as a natural progression from school and will go on to study at university regardless of the funding situation, others tend to see debt in any form as a negative thing, a belief that is often reinforced by parents. As a result, this risk-averse group will frequently attempt to get through university without taking out the loan element of the funding available, which can often lead to other financial or study-based issues. Lastly, there are those students who do not consider funding issues at all, for a variety of reasons.

Subsequently, with increased income now coming from tuition fees, we have been able to offer a much more substantial range of support, based loosely on the US model of student aid. We are looking to build support packages using internal and external sources in a bid to fulfil the wider Liverpool John Moores University aims in recruitment, retention, performance and alumni relations.

Issues of Probity

Liverpool John Moores University has a Scholarship Board to develop, monitor and review the policy framework for the management, allocation and distribution of funds and bursaries to support students. More specifically, its duties include ensuring that donations made by individuals and companies for specific reasons, such as student hardship, are allocated appropriately. If, for instance, a donor makes a donation to alleviate student hardship, then we as an institution must be sure that we spend it on this and can clearly demonstrate that we have done so. It is essential that all procedures are clear and transparent. In addition to this, the Board establishes criteria for the assessment of applications for different scholarships; monitors and reviews the management, allocation and distribution of scholarships; identifies gaps in provision; and makes recommendations on any matters affecting the distribution of scholarships. Its annual report also provides a mechanism for report to and liaison with donors through the Development and Alumni Relations Office. The composition of the Board reflects the teams concerned with the delivery of funding to students and draws upon the strengths of staff with experience in marketing and funding distribution. Typically it includes the Director of Corporate Services, the Director of Marketing, two Deans of Faculties, the Senior Adviser from Equal Opportunities and a representative from Student Welfare. In addition it includes two members external to the university, specifically a representative from the Students' Union and a lay person. This Board reports to the Strategic Management Team and also the Board of Governors.

The Office of Fair Access (OFFA) was established in the Higher Education Act 2004 and is a national independent, non-departmental public body that has been set up to promote and safeguard fair access to higher education for under-represented groups since the introduction of variable tuition fees in 2006. It is also expected to monitor how universities will spend the additional income generated by variable tuition fees. All scholarship and bursary programmes have to be approved by OFFA and thus our strategy to reward different types of excellence with scholarships was so approved with the bursary scheme aimed at financial need.

To this end, we established three levels of scholarships described in the box below: Achiever's, Dream Plan Achiever's and the Vice-Chancellor's Scholarship. The general feeling was that if the fees are going to change, then we should make the most of it and provide the most support we can to students.

Liverpool John Moores University's Targeted Bursaries

The Achiever's Scholarship
- Students must be able to demonstrate an area of commitment, achievement and excellence beyond their peers.
- Priority is given to students who attend a school in the Liverpool John Moores University schools and college network.
- These awards are intended to remove any financial barriers to studying for students who show potential.

The Dream Plan Achiever's Scholarship
- Students must achieve a minimum of three grade As at A level or the equivalent.

The Vice-Chancellor's Scholarship
- Students must achieve a minimum of three grade As at A level or the equivalent.
- Students must be able to demonstrate an area of commitment, achievement and excellence beyond their peers.
- Students will be required to attend an interview.

Who Benefits from Bursaries at Liverpool John Moores?

Although we do still administer scholarships, bursaries and prizes donated to us by philanthropic donors, since the changes in funding arrangements in 2006 the money used to fund these scholarships has come primarily from additional fee income.

In accordance with our agreement with OFFA, we have robustly sought to redistribute this money to students who can demonstrate an area of excellence that sets them apart from their peer group. We operate three scholarships with different criteria, though there is some overlap between the categories. In terms of general eligibility, only students who are eligible to pay variable tuition fees are eligible to apply for these additional bursaries. This is necessary as the funds are supported via tuition fee income. What this means is that all full-time students, both 'home' students (i.e. UK nationals) and students from the European Union, can apply. Furthermore, applications are invited only from students commencing the first year of a first undergraduate programme of study. This is designed to support our approach to widening participation and give everybody the chance to study at higher education level.

Communicating the Message to Potential Students

In earlier academic years, application forms were sent out by staff dealing with the assessment of scholarship applications to all students who had accepted a place on a course at Liverpool John Moores University. We felt that this was the most effective way to market and solicit applications to improve the quality of applications. Having taken time to reflect on this process and what we were trying to achieve, we considered how best to do this prior to the scholarship cycle beginning for 2008–9 starters. We looked around the university to see who else was sending out mail shots at around the same time. We found that accommodation packs were being posted out to all students, typically from early January onwards. Therefore, rather than post out applications to all students who had received an offer from us, we decided to take advantage of this process to send application forms to all students who had expressed an interest in coming to the university.

In addition, we have a very proactive student recruitment team who attend schools and Connexions events around the United Kingdom. An essential aspect of their role is to get the message across about scholarships and the benefits of being a scholarship student at Liverpool John Moores. A further marketing strategy is to provide the students with such a positive experience that they will in turn cascade this information to their friends. We are attempting to create a virtuous circle so that, in effect, students are coming to us to ask for additional information, rather than us doing all the work of promotion.

This has proved to be very satisfactory. In terms of the administration involved in allocating scholarships, staff are now able to focus on assessing the forms and writing to prospective students for more information. The new strategy has also proved significant in terms of increasing the quality and amount of applications for these scholarships year-on-year.

Managing the Scholarships Programme

The key purpose of the information sought from prospective students in their application forms is to allow them to demonstrate a level of excellence above and beyond that of their peers. There are two main aspects to the excellence we seek: academic excellence and commitment in a variety of areas beyond academic achievement.

Academic excellence is fairly straightforward to measure. Essentially we are looking for 360 UCAS (Universities and Colleges Admissions Service) points from three units – that is, three A levels at grade A or the equivalent.

Slightly more onerous to evaluate are the other areas of excellence and how to judge evidence of achievement. The second section of the application form contains a supporting statement that is required to be completed by a tutor, teacher or mentor. This person should be in a position to state whether the student is part of the 'gifted and talented' scheme or can demonstrate any other verifiable skills or level of commitment. The 'gifted and talented' scheme is a programme that aims to maximise the potential of students from traditionally low HE-participating neighbourhoods. In addition, there is also a section of the form dedicated to elaborating on the skills outlined previously.

This has presented a problem in previous years. Supporting statements are presented in various formats and standards, which often makes it difficult to compare them. For instance, when a statement suggests a student has taken part in athletics at 'county standard', there may be no evidence to back this up. When a situation like this arises, we will always contact the student for further evidence before considering him or her for a scholarship.

Once application forms have been submitted and the deadline has passed, applications are assessed for eligibility. Those who submit applications that do not match the general criteria are automatically sent a letter explaining why the application has been declined.

For those students who it is felt meet the 'excellence/commitment' criteria, their applications will be put forward with a recommendation for an award to the Allocations Committee, which can make any recommendations but which also has the remit to reject any applications it feels do not meet an appropriate standard. In terms of assessing applications for the Dream Plan Achiever's (DPA) awards, it is a very simple process as it is based on a student's predicted examination results at A level and the associated UCAS tariff. The teacher or tutor or headteacher should have completed the reference section detailing any skills and including predicted grades. At this stage we would provisionally approve an award to any student whose predicted grades were in line with this. However, failure to achieve these grades would mean withdrawal of the scholarship.

For the Achiever's Award, students need to be able to demonstrate an area of excellence or commitment to any given field. This again utilises the reference supplied by a member of the teaching staff at the school or college. More in-depth information is required than for the DPA and it should be backed up by additional documentation.

The Achiever's Awards are very competitive and also very broad-ranging in terms of skills that we recognise. Some of the most common areas of excellence revolve around the world of sport and volunteering, though we have also recognised musical and journalistic achievements, among a multitude of others. Often a student will have attained a certain level of development and will want to put something back into the school or wider community. For candidates who do not follow this traditional route it can be somewhat difficult to evidence, and indeed the layout of the form can be off-putting, particularly for mature students. This also applies in relation to the DPA scholarship as most mature students will not go back to college and study A levels or other courses that attract a UCAS tariff. The most popular route into HE for such students is an Access course, which has no tariff. We are currently reviewing the application form to encourage more applications from non-traditional students.

We regard non-traditional students as ideal candidates for the Achiever's Award; since they are so active generally, it is likely that when they arrive at university they will continue to develop further. We have certainly found that the students who have achieved scholarships for sporting or coaching excellence have taken part in their sports at BUCS (British Universities and College Sport) level. Students who are active prior to attending university do seem to continue in a similar vein. This means that the students are feeding back into the university their positive experiences and relaying good messages to their peers. This also has the benefit of showing Liverpool John Moores University in a positive light. An example of this was our recent graduate Beth Tweddle, who has made steady progress in gymnastics since joining the university and won the World Championships in 2007 as well as graduating successfully.

We are looking for students who are going to put something back and make a difference to our university and to the wider community. The Achiever's scholarship holders are superb in this respect. They have the confidence, leadership and organisational skills required to excel in their chosen field. These types of students encourage others and often have an impact on their peers when they get to university. An example of this was a student awarded a scholarship who within his first year had been elected chair of one of the larger societies within the Students' Union.

This is a reciprocal relationship; there is clearly a benefit for the student from this scheme in that they will have real life skills to offer an employer, putting them ahead of undergraduates with no such experiences. In turn, the university benefits from their enthusiasm prior to, during and after their higher education experiences that can be used to provide a better system for our student body.

Pastoral Care of Scholarship Recipients

If being a student were 'all sunshine and blue skies', then there would be no real need for teams like the Student Welfare team, other than to assess discretionary funding. Unfortunately, this is not the case and students will need to access the service with a myriad of problems. Students moving away from home for the first time can present with a variety of problems. These might include homesickness, which is very common in the first few weeks as students try to assimilate into their new surroundings and make friends. There is always a preponderance of financial problems, typically from students who have not applied for funding on time. Once students are in halls of residence and in attendance on their courses, they will have to cope with the behaviour of those around them and any resulting personality clashes. University is of course not all about formal education; it is also a character-building experience where individuals learn life skills that they can utilise for the rest of their life.

The scholarship programme can be viewed as a microcosm of Liverpool John Moores University's approach to supporting students in higher education. Scholarship students have traditional support systems in place via the personal tutor system, with the addition of the scholarship administrator, who acts as the equivalent of a 'key worker' within local social services that would deal with any issues that may arise. Student services staff, including the scholarship administrator, are not just available to scholarship recipients when there is a problem. Through the assessment process we would hope to have selected high-achieving and capable students who will want to get involved in university life, just as they did in their school communities. We aspire to facilitate this and provide additional opportunities for scholarship recipients to put on their CVs details other than the straightforward grades they achieve on graduation.

We encourage students to think about mentoring new fellow students. For a new student, observing the way somebody works and plays successfully can offer excellent opportunities to emulate skills and behaviours likely to result in success for them too. Scholarship recipients have also begun to visit sixth form colleges and schools with our staff to help with budgeting and other information sessions.

Case Study:
Dealing with Multiple Support Issues

'Anni' was part of my first scholarship cohort following the introduction of the variable tuition fees. She applied for a scholarship in May 2006 and was made an award on the basis of her exceptional achievements within the world of fashion and design. In addition to this background she was also the first person in her family to attend university. Her achievements at the time of application included national awards for her fashion design and setting up and running charity catwalk events. She was also considered to be at great risk of not fulfilling her potential, owing to the low income of her family. 'Anni' was a natural choice for the committee to support.

Scholarship awards are normally paid in two instalments. The first instalment is presented at the vice-chancellor's welcome reception for scholarship students. The second instalment is released in January once the student has attended a short informal interview. This is to encourage a sense of community within the scholarship cohorts and encourage channels of communication with me so that if any problems arise in the academic year they can be dealt with while they are still manageable. Working in Welfare Services, we too often see students who come in when a problem reaches a critical point, rather than earlier on, when the problem first presents. This can mean that one problem becomes several, affecting an individual's study, which is ultimately what we are trying to prevent and so improve retention.

In January 2008 I sent all scholarship recipients an email to ask them to contact me so I could check on their bursary status. 'Anni' did this, and when I began looking into it, what should have been a straightforward matter became very complex. First, holds had been placed on her account, disabling her computer usage and placing sanctions on her library loans. Second (and more crucially), she had been dropped from her course without her knowledge. The impact of this was significant: her statutory support had been cancelled; her bursary had not been processed and her debt was about to be passed to a debt-collecting agency.

---

continued

Incorrectly, she had been allowed to re-enrol in September 2007 for her second year, because students who are in debt to the university are not allowed to continue studying, and she was carrying a tuition fee debt of £3,000. She had simply not understood the need to take out a tuition fee loan and her course had been discontinued owing to the debt. She had had a very smooth and positive experience in her first year, but now her academic and personal life were in tumult. Resolving the majority of these issues centred on an appeal to her local authority to have the tuition fee loan released for the previous year. I formulated a letter for the student to submit and provided a letter of support to back this up. The appeal was successful and the associated issues were resolved.

On top of this, 'Anni' was experiencing some difficulties in her personal life. She had been involved in a car crash and was experiencing some difficulties with her memory. Furthermore, her father had become violent towards both her and her mother. A direct result of this was that she had fallen behind in coursework. These coursework assessments were deferred and have since been completed.

Support from the Outset

The starting point of the pastoral care for scholarship recipients takes the form of an informal meeting and reception with our vice-chancellor. It is vital that students develop a sense of commitment to the university in order to assist their integration into higher education. Meeting and chatting to the vice-chancellor in a relaxed atmosphere contributes to this sense of belonging and potentially increases the retention rates of this group. Certainly, speaking to the recipients prior to this occasion, I find they are often more excited about meeting the vice-chancellor than they are about receiving their cheque. The reception also offers recipients another social experience and a chance to make additional friends. Building better friendship cohorts is not something that happens by chance. Individuals need opportunities to meet, and to make friends and contacts – and for such opportunities to recur so that they can bond further.

Following the presentation of the cheque at the vice-chancellor's reception, in previous years the second instalment was paid via bank credit transfer. However, it proved hard to motivate students to come in for a chat on their progress. It was decided therefore to pay the second instalment as a cheque at an appointment with the administrator in order to promote more contact time. This entails a short chat about how the student's experiences have been and how we can further improve them. Should any problems come to light in these discussions, they can then be dealt with immediately by the administrator, who is likely to have experience in dealing with the whole range of possible issues a student may face throughout their study. In this way, students are afforded the opportunity to develop a professional relationship with the administrator, which aids their continued progress throughout the student experience.

Conclusions

Throughout the development of Liverpool John Moores University's Student Welfare team and my own professional experiences I have realised that simply handing money over to a student is not an enriching experience. Therefore, the development of the pastoral side of any scholarship programme should be seen as being as important and as integral as providing a cash benefit for students, as illustrated by the case study.

Retention is clearly a complex issue, and one that affects all universities. One significant aspect of this problem is that students can fail to develop attachments to their university. This could relate to friends, lecturers, the campus or the actual city or town. To this end I have developed the scholarship programme so that this sense of community and spirit of cohesiveness evolves as the students evolve – our very own 'institutional habitus' (Thomas, 2002).

This is facilitated by a reception held by the vice-chancellor aimed at highlighting any exciting new developments within the university. We maintain regular contact with the students throughout the calendar year rather than the academic year. The fact that they are not on campus because they have finished for the summer does not mean that we should forget about them. The net result is a group of over 300 students who feel part of the university.

We offer financial support to students and they in turn can make a contribution to university life. With our scholarship programme we cannot change the world but we can make positive outcomes more likely.

References

Aimhigher. Online, available at: www.direct.gov.uk/en/EducationAndLearning/UniversityAnd HigherEducation/DG_073697 (accessed December 2008).
Department for Education and Skills (2003) *The Future of Higher Education*, Cm 5735, London: The Stationery Office. Online, available at: www.dcsf.gov.uk/hegateway/strategy/hestrategy/word/hewhitepaper.doc.
National Committee of Inquiry into Higher Education (1997) *Higher Education in the Learning Society* (the Dearing Report), London: The Stationery Office.

PART **II**

Managing Throughout the University Year

CHAPTER 6

The Students' Union Year

MARK GRAYLING

Nottingham Trent Students Union

and **GAIL STEPHENS**

Sheffield Hallam University Union of Students

Students are given self confidence by their university appearing high up in the league tables. But another influence is the students' union which is often unconsciously influenced by attitudes in the centre of the university: successful universities usually have successful students' unions which sponsor large numbers of student societies and social activities.

Yet universities ignore the student voice, difficult as it is to identify, at their peril. From a position of distrust, if not fear, of students' unions universities have come to accept them as professional organisations that assist the university in the provision of necessary services. The president of the union, once the spokesman from the barricades, has become a partner in the management of the university and in at least one of the most successful universities is a member of the central steering committee of the university.

(Shattock, 2003)

Origins

Students' unions in many nations are the democratic membership organisations that represent the views of the student body at a particular university or college. This chapter will particularly focus on students' unions in the United Kingdom and includes two detailed case studies.

Unions organise extra-curricular activities (clubs, societies, entertainments, volunteering, etc.) and provide advice and advocacy for individual students. Many are involved in mutual trading on campus in shops, cafés, bars and similar. They add value by building and rebuilding vibrant student communities. Unions have a crucial role to play in the initial offer to prospective students and in the retention of recruited students. They help cement lifelong affinity with universities, and this has the potential to help build active alumni associations. Civic and community engagement is an increasingly important area of work as the sometimes transient student population expands in certain wards of university towns and cities.

There are also unions attached to colleges in the further education (FE) sector, but this chapter concentrates on those associated with higher education (HE), which is the principal focus of this book. Student involvement in the government of universities has a heritage that can be traced to Bologna University during the European Renaissance, and the origins of UK students' unions date back to the nineteenth century. The oldest, Edinburgh University Students' Association, has been in continuous existence since 1884. The generic term *students' union* is used to include organisations that might alternatively be called *guild* or *association* at universities in England, Wales and Ireland, whereas in Scotland the *union* usually refers to the building housing a *students' association* as the equivalent organisation. In many of the pre-1992 universities, provision for a students' representative organisation is included in the institutional charter. Since 1994 there has been a statutory requirement for such arrangements to be made at all universities. 'All learning starts with conversation' (Seely Brown and Duguid, 2000) is an observation rooted in the Vygotskian view of learning as a social activity (Pass, 2004). A union can generate conversation, and contribute to learning, by being a focal point for the student community in terms of both space and organisation.

Students' unions have traditionally been organised as autonomous, unincorporated associations, sometimes with trading operations set up in a company limited by guarantee (CLG). However, following the passage of the 1994 Education Act, and on the basis of some fiercely debated legal advice, a handful of unions converted fully to CLGs, so becoming incorporated, and until recently one union was configured as an Industrial and Provident Society (Co-op). Since the turn of the twenty-first century a number of reviews have seen a revival in the popularity of deploying CLGs to limit the liability of elected officers in their roles as trustees of unions. There has also been some interest in appointing external trustees to bring in additional skills and experience in line with arrangements more usually found in benevolent society model charities. However, unions in the United Kingdom probably owe as much to the tradition of self-help and mutualism as they do to nineteenth-century paternalism.

Students' unions have long been treated, in UK law, as exempt charities, deriving charitable status both from their own constitutions and from their close relationship with their partner universities, which are also exempt charities. However, the UK 2006 Charity Act abolished exempt charities, requiring unions with an annual income greater than £100,000 to register with the Charity Commission. This brings an external regulatory framework to bear on unions alongside the scrutiny of the university under the provisions of the 1994 Education Act. The 2006 Charity Act also introduced the new charitable incorporated organisation (CIO) as a possible vehicle by which unions can limit the liability of their trustees. CIOs in the United Kingdom do not need to register with Companies House and so avoid the need to make an additional set of annual returns apart from those required by the Charity Commission.

By Students for Students

Students' unions draw on a collectivist tradition and, from induction to graduation, aim to enhance the student experience as well as provide a credible representative voice. The union is the part of university life that students run for themselves, and provides a place that they can call their own.

In order to succeed, a students' union has first to organise a large, heterogeneous membership and create, develop and then recreate a community that fully turns over every few years. An increasingly varied range of jumping on and jumping off points in the university or college calendar may mean there are a number of starts, but the traditional UK academic year still begins in late September or early October and the preceding summer vacation is a period of preparation for the arrival of new members for week 1: freshers' week, induction week, welcome week or whatever the first few days are called at a particular university. This is a crucial period for the union.

With automatic enrolment (although there is a legal right for a student to opt out of membership but still to be able to access services and activities, without being entitled to take part in union democracy and governance), there is no recruitment drive but rather a programme of activities designed for new members. There will be a round of fairs, taster sessions, advice surgeries, entertainments and peer support available as the union helps new students settle in to new surroundings. For many students, this will be in a new town or city; for others, increasingly, even a new country. There is substantial evidence that students who stay for the first couple of weeks of term are far more likely to go on to complete their course and graduate (Allen, 1999; Tinto, 1988), so this period is central to the union helping to maintain or improve retention rates for their partner university.

At the other end of the student life cycle the union will be involved in helping to celebrate achievement and a major life event for its members about to begin their careers beyond the university. So, an event such as a graduation ball is likely to be a high point in the union's social programme.

During the period between induction and graduation, the union will touch the lives of its members in numerous and various ways. Levels of involvement will vary, and a diverse membership, running into tens of thousands, means that the union will be under pressure to do more and more with only limited resources.

Young, full-time undergraduates who have moved away from their home town to study tend to be the students most associated with the union, but great effort is made to provide for all the other sub-groups of students. The Open University Students' Association (OUSA) is a shining example of how a union will reach far beyond the traditional cohort of 18- to 21-year-olds who have progressed straight from school into HE. Tens, even hundreds, of societies and clubs are supported by the students' union to sustain hobbies and special interests and to form the basis of a social group that is easy to belong to.

The Financial Year

UK students' unions draw funding from three main sources: a grant, or subvention, from the university; surpluses from mutual and other trading; and, increasingly, the sort of grant funding usually associated with other charities and voluntary-sector organisations.

For unions that operate significant trading services (shops, cafés, bars, entertainments, etc.), there is a seasonal pattern that follows the activity of the academic year rather than that of the high street. Most income will be generated in the first half of the year, with October as the peak month. This is the period when students have both the most free time and the most disposable income. From March through to the start of the new academic year, cash holding may deplete as trading falls away but spending activity continues. Universities often phase the payment of the union grant to alleviate this seasonality. In many unions it is possible to forecast the year-end results, with some confidence, as early as January.

There are often matters of union policy that influence the way in which trading is organised: soft drinks may be priced to be cheaper than alcohol in bars; there may be a boycott of companies regarded as politically or ethically objectionable; and fair trade products will often be given prominence. Fair Trade Fortnight, the last week in February and the first in March, is an important event for many unions. NUS Services Ltd (NUSSL) was established to negotiate purchasing deals at a national level, and the value of these collective arrangements is independently audited for an annual benefit statement. Up to 2006, NUSSL was outperforming the overall deals available through other purchasing consortia by a significant margin.

It is worth dwelling on two sales statistics obtained by NUSSL. First, beer sales in unions have declined in volume by 46 per cent from 1996 to 2006. Second, 25 per cent of students do not drink alcohol; a good coffee and food offer is eclipsing traditional bar sales. The recent period has also seen changes in union retailing with growth in food-on-the-go and souvenir clothing more than replacing the decline in sales of stationery. The union offer is changing to meet new market conditions; for instance, the union at Goldsmiths College, University of London, recently converted a bar into gallery space for the use of members in response to changing demand.

The financial cycle begins with setting the budget for the following year. Unless a longer-term agreement is in place, this annual exercise will also establish a bid for the university subvention or grant. Unions are likely to bid for capital funding separately from the recurrent grant. The budget will then be implemented under a new elected leadership team, from the start of the next academic or financial year. At year end, external auditors prepare the accounts and returns for the period. As registered charities, unions will prepare financial statements using the charity Statement of Recommended Practice (SORP), and trustees are required to file annual reports with the Charity Commission. If the union is configured as a CLG, or uses a CLG for trading activities, then a report must also be filed with Companies House.

Union Staff

The greatest single area of union expenditure is on staff, both those on permanent contracts and seasonal or student employees. The norm is for unions to employ their staff directly, but in a few cases some or all of the contracts are held by the partner university with staff effectively seconded to the union on a permanent basis. Employees report, through a line structure, to a senior member of staff, usually called the General Manager, Chief Executive or Permanent Secretary. The senior member of staff reports to the trustees via the President, or another nominated elected officer, and usually has full delegated responsibility for staffing matters on a day-to-day basis.

Typically a UK union may employ staff to deliver the following services and activities:

- organising advice centres providing welfare support with both generalist and specialist advisers;
- providing 'job shops' or employment agencies;

- supporting democracy: elections, committees, referenda, representatives and civic engagement;
- undertaking research: providing briefings and information for elected officers and other staff;
- engaging in marketing activity: promoting union activities and services, selling advertising or sponsorship and providing market information;
- supporting activities: sports, volunteering, cultural- or subject- or religious- or hobby-based societies, charitable fund-raising and giving (RAG);
- supporting media: websites, print, radio and TV;
- organising training and personal development;
- providing student ambassadors;
- offering retail services (including general grocery shops, international food shops, stationery shops, post offices);
- managing cafés, bars, catering, nightclubs, live music venues;
- organising entertainments, including major events such as summer or graduation balls;
- administering other trading activities (box office, travel agency, print shops);
- providing office support: reception, administration, IT, finance and human resources;
- managing facilities: building services, maintenance and small works, vehicles (minibuses, etc.), cleaning.

Some smaller unions employ only a handful of permanent staff, whereas a few of the larger ones may have an establishment running into hundreds. The mix of staff will include some on permanent contacts and others on fixed tenure. The seasonality of union activity will require year-round and term-time attendance as well as both full-time and part-time posts. Most unions employ students alongside other staff, typically in term-time roles that can be organised around course commitments. Often they will be in member-facing jobs in shops, cafés and bars, in promotional teams, as door security staff and on reception desks. Many unions work with their university to generate income from the summer conference trade. Flexible employment arrangements suit time-pressed students, providing important basic skills training and a regular income, and giving international students the opportunity to work and improve their spoken English. Such arrangements also allow for greater control of staffing costs through the peaks and troughs of the year's activities.

Elected Officers

The life cycle of the elected officer is an expression of the students' union year. It has become accepted that student leadership is most effectively delivered by the union having officers elected by the membership, with at least some of these taking on the role full time. Borrowing the tradition from academia, this is a sabbatical year and the roles undertaken are usually referred to as sabbatical officers, shortened to 'sabbs', who are paid an allowance to support them through their term of office.

The 1994 Education Act requires that the major office bearers of the union be elected by cross-campus ballot: in other words, an election in which all members can participate. Officer elections usually take place in February or March each year. The law allows a tenure of a maximum of two years as a sabbatical officer; a few unions make a single term of office the limit.

Handover takes place during the summer, with an overlap as one set of officers leave and the new team takes over. This period is a busy one, with various team-building and training courses, provided in-house and as part of a programme organised by the National Union of Students (NUS); a round of introductions to key people in the university and in the local community; and planning for activities and campaigns for the new academic year. Successful candidates will have been returned on a manifesto. The manifesto, as a political programme, will need to be reconciled with existing strategic plans. The preparation and planning, during the summer, is a bit like the long climb at the start of a roller-coaster ride before the rest of the term of office rushes by.

An elected officer's role comprises some, or all, of four distinct elements. He or she:

- is a representative of the union;
- is a lead member, akin to holding a cabinet or ministerial portfolio;
- is a trustee and/or company director (where a CLG is deployed);
- has some hands-on duties akin to those of a volunteer.

These combine into an exceptional leadership development opportunity for those who are elected. It should be no surprise to find ex-union officers occupying positions of significant influence, power and responsibility in later life, whether that is in public service, the media, commerce, industry, education, or in other parts of the voluntary sector. Politicians such as Tobias Elwood (Conservative), Jacqui Smith (Labour) and Lembit Öpik (Liberal Democrat) all started their careers in students' unions, as did journalist and broadcaster David Aaronovitch, former consumer champion Sue Slipman and Equalities Commission chief Trevor Phillips.

Activists, Volunteers and Members

Unions depend on activists and members who take on the voluntary duties of running society committees or sports clubs, or act as delegates to the union council (parliament or assembly) or as representatives for the students on their course or in their hall of residence. In return, the union provides development opportunities and the chance to contribute to the running of aspects of a student's own organisation. Hundreds, sometimes thousands, of students will be involved in a voluntary capacity in a particular union at any one time.

After the intense activity at the start of the academic year, the main point of contact with members, for the union, is often via one of the union's trading operations. These are metaphorically and, in the case of retail outlets, literally the union shop window and the first level of engagement (SHUUS, 2007). Some students may find the union because they want to pursue a hobby or a special interest, or through sport; some will come looking for employment and some will need support with a welfare issue. Others may have arrived at university having been active on their school council or in the union at their FE college or elsewhere and are already motivated to get involved.

Levels of involvement will depend on other competing demands and pressures on the individual student, as well as on how much interest has been generated. Unsurprisingly, the first and second terms tend to be the busiest as deadlines and assessments are still a long way off. By contrast, the third term (or the second half of the second semester) is usually the quietest because of the proximity of exams and assessment deadlines.

Welfare Support, Advocacy and Advice

Unions are involved in providing advice and advocacy services on a range of student welfare issues. The bare minimum will centre on academic appeals. The union's university would face an enormous conflict of interest, the possibility of students going to solicitors more frequently and the likelihood of more cases ending up with the ombudsman service for UK higher education, the Office of the Independent Adjudicator (OIA), if there were not an independent service available to students, provided by the students' union. Agencies such as Citizens Advice Bureaux (CABs) do not have expertise in university course regulations and so the union is uniquely placed to provide this service. Although the union cannot bring cases based on academic judgement, there can be mitigating circumstances or lapses in procedure sufficient to justify supporting students in appeals and complaints against the university.

Beyond the absolute basics, provision varies from institution to institution, with the university and union developing sometimes complementary, sometimes overlapping services. For instance, housing issues are usually the province of the union, where the university is the landlord. Other issues on which the union may advise include debt, aspects of consumer rights and money management, and the support offered may include negotiating with the university where it is the creditor.

On immigration issues, such as applying to extend visas for international students, some unions undertake the work and some is done by universities.

Enriching Student Life

Unions provide the organisational support and allocate funds to provide for some or all of the following:

- sports teams;
- societies (course-related, cultural/religious, political/campaigning, hobby and special interest);
- charitable activity/RAG;
- community volunteering;
- peer-led personal development or training courses;
- media (print, radio, TV);
- entertainments.

All of this adds to the overall offer to students, and much of it has become an expectation as the choice of university is considered by a prospective student. Involvement in these activities can contribute to the career choices that a student might make, and all give the opportunity to enrich a CV.

Some union activities have taken on a significance that goes beyond the union movement and contributes to society more widely. For instance, the union entertainments circuit has a strong heritage and remains highly important to the music industry. Perhaps the most famous union concert in the United Kingdom was recorded as a seminal live album by The Who in 1970 at Leeds University Union, where a blue plaque has been mounted on the union building to mark the occasion.

The tradition of community action volunteering based in unions also sits well with the citizenship agenda. Student Volunteering Week is organised by unions, co-ordinated by Volunteering England (VE), and takes place in February each year.

Many journalists and broadcasters cut their teeth in student media, and prestigious national awards, sponsored by organisations such as the *Guardian* newspaper, are dedicated to union newspapers, radio stations and TV. Union drama groups take their shows to the Edinburgh Fringe Festival, and public service includes many graduates from student political and debating societies.

Case Study 1:
A Year in the Life of Sheffield Hallam University Union
of Students

July–September 2007

When the new Executive Team took office, in July 2007, the union had as its interim general manager the Director of Estates and Facilities, seconded from the university, supported by two Acting Assistant General Managers, one from the university and one from within the union. The first priority therefore was to recruit a new General Manager, and this was done at the end of July. At this point also, the union embarked on a review of all its staffing and management arrangements.

Of equal significance, in July the union met as a cross-departmental team of staff and officers to determine the mission, vision and values of Hallam Union, which resulted in a very clear statement and understanding of direction. Put simply, Hallam Union's mission is to support and enrich the experience of all Hallam students.

The mission was bedded in over the summer, and in September the union saw its most successful Freshers' Week ever, with over 8,000 students attending the Fairs.

October–December 2007

The new General Manager joined the team midway through October. At this stage, the immediate priorities were to produce a strategic plan for the union and to initiate a governance review in the light of changes to charity law. By the end of October a Strategic Planning Group, comprising senior managers and executive officers, had produced a vision statement for the union and had started the strategic planning process.

A Governance Review Group was formed, again comprising staff and officers, which with the sanction of the Union Representative Council embarked on a review of governance arrangements. It was decided that the review would be wide-reaching and would also encompass arrangements for democracy and representation. A timeline and a consultation methodology were established.

Operationally, this was a hugely significant time for the union. Trading activities went from strength to strength, and appointments made over the summer to support societies and the student learning experience made a demonstrable difference in terms of the numbers of students who engaged with the union. This period also saw the launch of SHU Media in October, giving students the opportunity to become involved with *SHU-Life* (a monthly magazine), SHU-Radio (a podcast radio station) and SHU-Box (a promotional video production society).

The union held its AGM in November, which although not quorate saw its best attendance for many years. The Executive Officers engaged with the NUS's Strategic Conversation and participated in the Extraordinary Conference in early December to decide upon the NUS's Governance Review.

January–March 2008

The Strategic Planning Group continued with its work, producing the first draft for consultation in January.

Early February saw the Students' Union launch its Love Your Union Campaign, in which students and staff talked to over 500 students at one of the university's satellite campuses, resulting in increased awareness of the work of the Executive Officers and involvement with the union, Hallam Volunteering and societies. The start of the year also saw the launch of the Faculty Involvement Groups, which brought together student faculty representatives with staff from their faculty to co-ordinate the student voice and work together to resolve issues.

For the first time, students standing for election in February had their manifesto speeches filmed by SHU-Box and broadcast throughout the union and the university, thus significantly raising the profile of both SHU Media and the elections process. This resulted in an 18.5 per cent increase in votes cast, with almost 10 per cent of Hallam students voting in contested elections.

The review of staffing arrangements continued, resulting in the rationalisation of some posts and the creation of others. The union has taken the opportunity to investigate new ways in which the staff can support the work of the elected officers, and increase engagement with the union by a wider number of students.

April–June 2008

April saw the formal approval and publication of Hallam Union's strategic plan, *The Sky's the Limit* (SHUUS, 2008), which sets out the union's vision for the next five years. Work is now under way to

continued

consolidate the plan into an annual business planning process, in turn informing staff objectives and key performance indicators.

Hallam Union elected a full contingent of delegates to NUS Annual Conference. The first consultation phase of the Governance Review has been completed and an outline structure approved by the Union Representative Council, thus enabling the new officers and staff to continue developing this work over the coming months.

At a time when, traditionally, unions and universities start to slow down for the summer period, Hallam Union has started a period of redevelopment of the space within the union building, to ensure that its physical resource is best used to support students.

The current executive team stand down on 30 June and the new team take up office on 1 July; the journey continues.

Outcomes: What has the Union Achieved?

The year has been particularly productive for Hallam Union. It has campaigned on issues ranging from sexual health to student safety. Twelve new societies have been created, taking the total number of societies to 43, with 586 students actively engaging with the union in this way. Hallam Volunteering has over 500 active volunteers working on more than 30 projects. The union won the Higher Education Active Community Fund Outstanding Project of the Year for its Monday Club project, which works with young people with Asperger's syndrome, and one of its students scooped the Student Volunteer of the Year Award for her work in the community. The union won a Silver Sound Impact Award for its work on ethical and environmental issues, and working with the Carbon Trust has significantly reduced its carbon footprint. One of our elected officers became the first student member to be appointed to the board of the Quality Assurance Agency for Higher Education (QAA).

Commercial services have seen an increase in turnover of 11 per cent year-on-year, and are forecast this year to make a net contribution of £126,500 – an increase of 43 per cent on the previous year. Over 150 student staff are employed by the union across all of its activities. The opening of a new coffee and juice bar in September means that the union will be able to engage with significantly more students by attracting them into the building.

The union has made an active contribution to the university's Corporate Planning Process and Estates Plan, and working with the newly formed Faculty Involvement Groups has ensured that the student academic voice is heard. The union has established informal and formal links with key partners in the university and the community, and through the Strategic Plan and Governance Review is working to ensure that its direction and focus truly support and enrich the Hallam student experience.

Gail Stephens

General Manager, Sheffield Hallam University Union of Students

The UK National Infrastructure

The collective of students, organised in their unions, is often referred to as the UK student movement. The glue that binds this movement together and maintains a national community of elected student leaders is provided by the National Union of Students (NUS). Founded in 1922, the NUS has a name that is something of a misnomer in that it is really a national federation of students' unions. The NUS has two main aims: to represent the interests of students at a national level and to strengthen and develop students' unions. The NUS (with a 25 per cent share) and over 200 shareholding unions own NUSSL, which is a student-led, not-for-profit company providing collective purchasing, central billing and business development services to support union trading activities. Only NUS-affiliated unions are eligible to own shares in NUSSL. Most unions with permanent employees also belong to the Association for Managers in Students' Unions (AMSU), which aims to bring together the diverse community working in the movement with specialist networks for different sub-groups of staff. The AMSU works collaboratively with both the NUS and NUSSL, and plays a role semi-analogous to that of the Association of University Administrators (AUA).

A number of unions are working with the Students' Union Evaluation Initiative (SUEI) as a way of benchmarking against a national organisational quality standard. The SUEI has its origins in the European Foundation Quality Model (EFQM) but has been developed specifically for the movement. In 2007 the UK Department of Innovation, Universities and Skills (DIUS) allocated funding, via NUS, to encourage uptake of the scheme.

Along with other charities, and alongside their partner universities, UK students' unions face new challenges as the twenty-first century develops. In 2012 there will be a significant demographic shift as the proportion of 18- to 21-year-olds in the UK population falls off dramatically. Patterns of attendance may change, with a greater proportion of students opting for courses nearer their permanent address and with more flexible modes of study. Unions will need to respond to this change with changes in service design and with different forms of access to those services. The impact of higher energy costs coupled with the opportunities afforded by rapid developments in information technology may also make new demands on unions. Old-fashioned buildings are being replaced by flexibly designed space as universities refresh their estates, and there is increasing potential for unions to provide informal meeting and study areas, as well as all the traditional services and activities, in a place that students can still call their own.

Case Study 2:
Leeds Metropolitan University Students' Union

Sometimes it takes a crisis to make people reflect fully on current practice rather than continuously evaluate progress and perform-ance, as they perhaps should. Leeds Met Students' Union had almost to go bankrupt before the urgency of the situation made the executive officers seriously compare what the union *should* be doing with what it actually *was* doing.

The Students' Union team in 2007–8 realised that unless sub-stantial changes in focus were made, the union would go bankrupt and become increasingly irrelevant to students and thus powerless when issues arose. At that time, the focus on core business was what allowed the union to continue; the union team agreed that repre-sentation, campaigns, activities and development were the main things the union should be doing, moving away from traditional students' union activities such as organising club nights and gigs, and selling produce in shops.

Students' unions in the United Kingdom have to some extent been populated in the past by students who became distracted by the operational business when they should have been more concerned with the strategic importance of enhancing the student experience and working in those core areas. Officers elected on a manifesto centring on cheaper beer are increasingly a thing of the past as students' unions nationally have recognised that their role is predominantly about hearing both the voice of the individual and the collective voice of the whole community, and acting upon them.

The first thing an organisation should do in a time of crisis is to look to its core principles. What are the things we hold dearest?

From these will come our mission, vision and other characteristics of the organisation, which may be markedly different from those of the current organisation. This may take some time, but if the crisis is of a systemic nature then it is most likely worth the time spent asking these profound questions. Difficult decisions will have to be made, but with a set of core principles for guidance, at least you can always be assured that you are on the right track.

Tough decisions have been made in the last year: to transfer the business of running shops to the university, to make staff redundant where there was no longer a business need for the Students' Union to employ them, and to recognise that the bars and clubs in the city can offer today's students better deals than our bars can, owing to economies of scale. In our Students' Union the principles are that we are always student led, democratic, independent, open and accountable while realising that we exist in a diverse student community. This is helping us to survive and thrive in a highly competitive environment and to concentrate on what we do best: campaigning for the issues we hold dear, developing core areas and representing students.

Lewis Coakley
President of Leeds Met Students' Union 2008–9

For More Information

This chapter has been written as a primer to introduce the reader to students' unions in higher education. In these days of easily accessed internet-based publications, much more information is available from sources such as www.nus.org.uk or www.sueinitiative.co.uk, and each UK university-based union has its own website as a first port of call.

References

Allen, D. (1999) 'Desire to finish college', *Research in Higher Education*, 40 (4): 461–85.

Pass, S. (2004) *Parallel Paths to Constructivism: Jean Piaget and Lev Vygotsky*, Charlotte, NC: Information Age Publishing.

Seely Brown, J. and Duguid, P. (2000) *The Social Life of Information*, Boston, MA: Harvard Business School Press.

Shattock, M. (2003) *Managing Successful Universities*, Maidenhead: Open University Press/McGraw Hill Education.

SHUUS (2007) *Student Engagement Model*, Sheffield: Sheffield Hallam University Union of Students.

SHUUS (2008) *The Sky's the Limit*, Sheffield: Sheffield Hallam University Union of Students.

Tinto, V. (1988) 'Stages of student departure: reflections on the longitudinal character of student leaving', *Journal of Higher Education*, 59 (4): 438–55.

CHAPTER 7

Managing Course Administration

CHRISTINE CHILD
London School of Economics

SUE KING
Glyndŵr University

RACHEL LANDER
University of Westminster

and **JOHN RYAN**
University of Worcester

A student with multiple problems in tears in a course leader's office; the course leader's frustration with processes that have contributed to the distress; and the administrator's struggle to ensure that all students, including this one, are being treated fairly. This is one scenario illustrating how the management of course administration impacts directly on the student experience. This chapter, which has been written by both administrative and academic staff, examines their different perspectives and highlights the importance of different groups of staff working together effectively with mutual understanding and respect for each other's expertise. The aim is shared: good course administration supports a good student and staff experience.

Context

The nature of course management in higher education is a complex one, and an institution's senior executive team (administrators in US parlance) necessarily has a close interest in ensuring its effectiveness. This is a result both of the prominence it receives in external inspections and audits by quality assurance agencies, such as the UK Quality Assurance Agency for Higher Education (QAA)[1] and professional accrediting bodies, and of its impact on students', employers' and other stakeholders' satisfaction. Arrangements for feedback, course organisation, timetabling, the provision of accurate information and infrastructure are all essential aspects of course management; their quality influences student feedback and, ultimately, satisfaction levels as evidenced by the UK National Student Survey and other measures. This means that most institutions have put in place a high degree of regulation relating to course management. But how does this impact on the day-to-day experience of staff, both administrative and academic, who are charged with managing the student experience of their courses and how this might be improved? Here we are using the UK term 'academics' for what are known as 'faculty' in the United States, and 'administrators' for what are termed 'support staff' in the United States. This chapter, written by administrators and academics in three UK universities, unpacks some of the key issues in these areas and proposes some pointers for others in similar contexts.

Introduction

In reviewing course administration practices in our own and other UK higher education (HE) institutions, we discovered that course (or programme) administration requirements across institutions were surprisingly similar. Nevertheless, on the basis of our findings we argue that managers should review the dimensions of trust and institutional character to tailor course administration systems for their own institution. We recommend positive approaches to course management to allow professional, administrative and academic staff to concentrate on activities suited to their roles and so improve the learning and teaching experience. This will require senior management to provide leadership and encouragement to generate confidence and trust, which will allow a reduction in the bureaucracy that is often embodied in the term 'course management'. Our findings draw upon research conducted using a literature search to identify issues, a review of course administration practices and a programme of semi-structured, exploratory interviews in three institutions. This assessed whether these same issues are being experienced by staff currently working in higher education. Quotations and examples from these interviews will be used to illustrate our points, together with reflections from the chapter authors. We found that the following key themes have a significant impact on the management of course administration:

- *the nature of the institution* as defined by its internal processes and procedures, its size in terms of student numbers, the types of students and its use of technology;
- *how far staff are trusted* – often demonstrated by how prescriptive and bureaucratic the processes are and whether staff feel it is safe to raise the issues they think are important;
- *workloads and how these are managed*, and whether there is clarification about roles and responsibilities, for example the extent to which academic staff are responsible for course management and the kinds of processes that are the responsibility of the student.

These themes are closely interlinked and impact on each other, but we conclude that the most effective institutions have taken all these factors into account and tailored practices to their own situations, rather than just accepting examples of others' good practice without adaptation.

Typical Institutional Problems and Approaches to Tackle Them

The Nature of the Institution and its Internal Processes

The size and complexity of the institution affects the choice of processes for course administration. In large universities with complex modular courses there can sometimes be several hundred students on a single module. In such situations, home or international students who are unfamiliar with UK university contexts can struggle to deal with regulations and new environments. Those from non-traditional backgrounds can be in particular need of guidance on the rhetoric of higher education and may need support from both academic and administrative staff to deal with the fundamental processes with which they need to engage in order to progress successfully through their studies.

For students, once they have been accepted for a course, their first experience of course management systems is probably at enrolment, also known as matriculation, which is the act of registering to join the university as a student. The purpose of enrolment is fairly straightforward: to check that:

- the student enrolling is the same person the university accepted on to the course;
- entry criteria have been met;
- student details are correctly held;
- adequate arrangements for fees and living costs are in place.

Most of these processes have been transformed by the use of information technologies, which mean that enrolment processes can be done remotely by students themselves or by administrators outside the enrolment hall.

Long, snaking queues of anxious students clutching various pieces of paper may not be a thing of the past just yet, but the time is fast approaching when most paper-based processes can be avoided.

Once the students are enrolled, the same approach can continue, with much course administration being undertaken by students through student portals which give them easy access to course handbooks, timetables and assignment results, and which allow them to update their own records and request information. However, although sophisticated systems provide most of the administrative information students need, the challenge is to get them to use them, since many are happier confirming information by talking to a live person. We need to check rigorously that our systems are usable, the training we provide is effective and that students understand the specialist language we speak. If they do not know the difference between induction and enrolment, for example, they will miss crucial information even before they have started their course. A survey at one of the universities included in our research showed that some students found the website difficult to use and one commented on a particular web page, 'A lot of people are struggling to find it in the first place'. Obviously these issues need to be addressed if students are to be more independent in terms of their administration.

Course administration should have a minimum impact on students' academic study, in that most systems should work smoothly without students being aware of them. Some student engagement in aspects of course management is unavoidable, such as checking results and receiving timetables, but the important point is that when they need help with their progress or when something happens out of the ordinary, they know where to go and are confident that those who can advise them are accessible and speak a language they can understand. Referring a student to a handbook is not enough. Students will often need a conversation with staff to help them understand the applicability of regulations to their specific case.

Effective course management also includes activities that are almost impossible to separate from other quality management procedures in higher education. The paperwork, data collection and interaction with students required for administration of courses potentially involve a wide range of staff across almost every department in the institution.

Development of administrative requirements within overall quality procedures in the United Kingdom is usually closely aligned with QAA guidelines. One course leader reported that 'standardised procedures are developed in the belief that there is one best way, to simplify and to bring everyone into line'. Academic and administrative staff reported feeling that there is now an overwhelming amount of regulation in higher education, such as programme specification templates.[2] A number of course or programme leaders suggested that standardised course administration reduces their autonomy and their ability to use their professional judgement. Staff value the freedom to do the right thing rather than just following procedures, reflecting the continual trade-off between local flexibility and a centralised approach to procedures that ensures equity of treatment across an institution. Increasing regulation is justified by the need to manage external requirements such as performance targets linked to funding, and QAA audit, and to cope with litigation when students complain about mal-administration. Examples from our research illustrate the problem. Annual monitoring in one institution was perceived as a mechanistic box-ticking exercise where, as a member of staff put it, 'Staff have become adept at writing for the quality systems rather than addressing the actual issues'. One administrator further noted that she might see the same piece of paper two or three times during approval of a transaction but she didn't know why.

Some courses (e.g. professional programmes) may also be subject to additional external regulation that is not in line with institutional requirements, resulting in extra work for course teams and administrators. Stephenson (2004) warns that external agencies will 'stultify diversity and creativity in the classroom' if they are not sensitive to the environment in which they operate, and urges them to 'evolve as circumstances change'. This applies equally to their validation and accreditation processes and to their control over course content.

Robust and measurable systems and processes are as essential in course management as in any other area of university administration. The theoretical side of methods to aid development of these, such as Total Quality Management (TQM) and Business Process Reengineering (BPR), is well understood; there are many business texts documenting good practice (see, for example, Jeston and Nelis, 2008), and there is much discussion of applicability to and examples from education (see, for example, Sahney et al., 2004; Allen and Fifield, 1999). TQM focuses on incremental improvement of existing processes through an emphasis on the quality of the products of that process, whereas BPR takes a more radical approach with work process redesign underpinning wider organisational transformation. Valentine and Knights (1998) provide a useful comparison of these two methods. A number of vendors of process design tools and technologies are also targeting the education market (see, for example, Triaster's or QuASK's websites, listed in the references), and the professional administrator bodies such as the Association of University Administrators (AUA) (www.aua.ac.uk) in the United Kingdom and the American Association of Collegiate Registrars and Admissions Officers (AACRAO) (www.aacrao.org) regularly organise events on these topics. However, the lesson from practice in HE institutions is that implementation of these can be problematic; for example, Allen and Fifield (1999) found that 'the organisational culture and structure of HEIs limit the degree of change sought from a BPR project'. Allen (2003) then goes further, suggesting that change management techniques employed must 'reflect the complex nature of HEIs' and citing Sporn (1999): 'successful processes and structures for adaption can only be implemented through joint activities of administration and faculty'.

Building and Using a Climate of Trust

Course management and administration, at a basic level, consist of the operation of a series of processes that interface with different groups throughout the life of the course, from initiation through development into operation. The starting point is validation of new courses using quality management procedures, and it is here that a chorus can frequently be heard from academics and administrators about burdensome, controlling processes that stifle creativity and professionalism and, by doing so, restrict freedom and display a lack of trust. Szekeres (2004) notes that the rise in managerial control means that '[n]ot only is there a need for constant detailed reporting, but senior managers have to be able to successfully account for all activities in the organisation' (p. 9).

Quality assurance processes in most UK universities are governed by the Quality Assurance Agency (QAA, www.qaa.ac.uk), and while its codes of practice covering academic standards and quality assurance are not prescriptive, in practice the procedures the QAA recommends are usually adopted by universities. Institutional arrangements will vary but it is a certainty that academic staff will perceive that the 'centre' has an over-developed interest in establishing and retaining the bureaucratic processes that underpin course management. Stephenson reports that

> critics of QA in the UK claimed that it had invaded the life of academics, created significant workloads, and impacted negatively on the quality of the student experience in that academics had less time available for their core business of teaching and research.
>
> (2004: 64)

In response to this, the QAA has changed its audit processes and there is evidence that many institutions are responding positively to this, encouraged by an apparently genuine desire on the part of the quality agencies to shift the dynamic of inspection in favour of enhancement rather than assurance (or 'ticking boxes', as it is usually described). During our research we heard examples of course validation procedures that openly acknowledged the importance of providing guidance and establishing thresholds, but identified and involved only those staff with the necessary expertise, the documents essential to the process, and checks to ensure that the process had been followed. The last element of the process meant that the validation committee did not need to see all the documentation only to be sure that it existed.

The University of Worcester's Strategic Plan is another example that includes the strategic objective of applying the principles of better regulation to all internal processes. It was written with the university's quality assurance procedures, which derive from and still rely heavily on the classic Council for National Academic Awards (CNAA) model,[3] very much in mind. The process of change is under way but there is often a nervousness and reluctance to embrace change. Instead of a 'let's do things differently' mentality, concerns about potential criticism or failure in any future inspection regime can easily lead to scenarios where people say, 'what if we don't continue to do this, we'd better not change'. There is comfort in a box-ticking approach to course management, and persuading people to leave their comfort zones is a challenge. Another oft-quoted reason for retaining existing regimes is a belief that the QAA, for example, is not really serious about introducing a lighter touch to institutional audit, or at least that its auditors may have not caught up with its new approach.

Dimensions of Trust

Trust emerged as a key issue in our research interviews with staff. To encapsulate these findings the authors have produced a matrix (Figure 7.1) to represent the range of system types found in course administration. The dimensions of size and trust were identified, as these appear to have substantial correlation with the types of course administration systems observed in the institutions participating in the research.

A 'high trust' organisation will allow distributed light-touch management. One manager interviewed in our study recommended that academic staff should be 'given ownership of the process but guidance on time limits, noting that processes can be abbreviated if they focus on what is new'. Tight bureaucratic control was previously demonstrated in one institution in our study by requiring students to complete several forms when they submitted their projects. This was ultimately reduced to just one when no purpose could be found for the others.

We also found examples of staff who indicated that they never reported real problems because of the difficulty of resolving issues in a very formal and overly bureaucratic quality system. We found many staff who held the view that they were writing for the quality system rather than addressing real concerns. One staff member noted that they had 'become expert in rhetoric which doesn't change anything'. This is a serious concern as it suggests that problems are going unreported that might have major implications for course quality. It can be addressed only by improving trust levels so that staff have the confidence to report real problems.

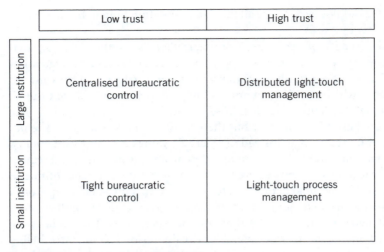

Figure 7.1 Approaches to Course Administration.

Reflections on Trust

Sue (Academic): I had not realised how equally powerless and frustrated the administrative staff felt about the bureaucracy involved in course management. I was forced to consider for the first time exactly what the various groups of administrative staff were responsible for and what factors (including my actions) affected their workloads. Prior to the case study I was only able to see academic and non-academic staff and only really valued the contribution made by academics and school administrative staff. I also feel more confident to challenge unnecessary bureaucracy as I feel my administrative colleagues may share my views. As with all misunderstandings relating to people from different cultures, I know the only way to work better together is to spend time getting to know and understand the perspective of the other group.

Christine (Administrator): Writing this chapter and working more closely than usual with academic colleagues provided me with explanations about why some things that seem obvious to administrators cause problems for academic staff. I now question assumptions that our requests for information are simple and straightforward, and realise that this is not always the case. I question the need for standardisation. Higher education is complex, and processes must take account of people. Simplicity might be attractive but we can be more sophisticated than that. If we trust our colleagues and they trust us, we can work together to provide clever, creative solutions to organisational and procedural problems.

Rachel (Academic): I now see course management as a good indicator of overall institutional 'health'. The factors that influence systems and processes are related to 'people issues' in the institution, including work culture within groups of staff, effectiveness of communication between academic and administrative staff, and management issues, notably support and effectiveness in introducing information technology to support staff. Overall, management willingness and ability to establish participative reviews of work processes is critical, as it is in these that an understanding of different roles in institutions, and development of trust between work groups, can be established.

John (Senior Manager): I am now more convinced that effective course management must be based on partnership and trust between academics and administrative staff. Managers have a responsibility to ensure that institutional procedures do not endanger that trust and that the respective roles of all professional staff, academic and administrative, are well articulated, clearly understood and respected. Managers must also be prepared to listen and respond to feedback on the quality and effectiveness of the systems and procedures in place, to explain satis-factorily why the system is as it is, and to champion changes if this can lead to increased trust and more successful partnership working. Managers must balance external requirements with their responsibility to provide an outstanding student experience and to ensure that bureaucracy does not detract from the quality of that experience and the professional satisfaction of staff in discharging their responsibilities.

Clarity of Roles and Responsibilities and Workload

One of the most striking findings from our investigations was the deep cultural divide between central administrative staff and academic staff. There was an apparent ignorance on both sides of the roles, priorities and pres-sures experienced by the other group of staff. Respondents used expressions to describe one another that included 'difficult', 'unreasonable', 'tail wagging the dog' and 'they don't do as they're told'.

In many institutions, academic and administrative staff exist in two separate hierarchies. Unchecked, this can lead to the existence of two quite separate and distinct groups of staff. This encourages mutual lack of respect and trust, and provides considerable scope for misunderstanding. This can severely limit the scope for partnership working across a range of activities, including course administration. It is quite common for administrators to be referred to as 'non-academic staff', ignoring the fact that many are as highly qualified as their academic colleagues, sometimes more so. One interviewee in our study described administrators as being regarded as 'second-class citizens'. Administrators become the bureaucrats, whose purpose is perceived to be obstructive; they are classified as non-creative, barriers to the effective pursuit of excellence in teaching (and research). Szekeres (2004) notes that administrators seem to have been elevated to a more managerial role as the quality assurance practices and managerialist style in higher education make these workers more visible and seemingly more powerful. In turn, many administrators perceive academics as mavericks, bent on circumventing processes and procedures designed not only to satisfy external requirements, but also to assure the quality of academic provision and the student experience. Academic staff are often perceived as rule breakers, and dismissive of the need to have in place regulations and procedures that are necessary and valuable in ensuring equity and consistency.

Individual academic staff are professionally recognised by their achievements in research and scholarly activity. This can require a level of autonomy that clashes with hierarchical, team-based central control systems (Davies *et al.*, 2007). It appears that some of the tension we noticed between administrators and academics is caused by perceived non-compliance with standardised systems and processes by academics and subsequent 'policing' by administrative staff. It was noted by one academic that 'if one person does something wrong, a new rule is invented for everyone'. Shortfalls are often blamed on lack of competence or commitment (Trowler *et al.*, 2005) rather than on alternative reasons such as irrelevance, detrimental impact on staff and students, unnecessary administrative burdens, and so on. These phenomena are present in all institutions, but are in our view greatest in larger universities and can have a negative impact on the commitment of staff to their institutions, which in turn affects efficiency and effectiveness. Smeenk *et al.* (2006) report that '[a] vast amount of studies suggest that the conflict in universities between hegemonist organization values and professional employee values leads to unintended behaviour of the individual employees, such as lower organizational commitment' (p. 2036). They go on to describe the feelings caused by the attempts to reduce autonomy and draw a direct negative link between this and performance.

Advice and Guidance for Others

Developing Systems, Processes and IT to Meet Individual Needs

Effective course management requires continuous adjustment of processes to local needs. A process that works for a small professional course with mature students is almost certain to need some adjustment to work well for a large modular course with several hundred students on a single module. University managers, teaching staff and administrative staff all need to review how students learn best, not just with regard to academic studies, but also in relation to learning processes. For example, online enrolment and student module registration may be best demonstrated by existing students, as confidence may be built by seeing other students using the system rather than just being told what to do by an expert.

By and large, the academic course manager (or course leader) should not need to worry about the detail of many of the processes necessary to ensure effective course delivery. Enrolment, for example, should be an invisible process; IT systems should be used as fully as possible to ensure that the submission of assignments, the collection and transmission of marks to students, and the monitoring of attendance should not require the personal intervention of the course manager, although the important responsibility of helping students to understand and use feedback should still remain with academics. In a team-based approach there should be a clear delineation of responsibilities so that staff and students know who is responsible for key operational aspects of course management, where to go for information and, of increasing importance, where to go to complain. Simple diagrams included in course handbooks can help here, such as flow charts showing what students should do when they have a problem.

We found that academic staff involvement and the scale of the use of information technologies in these processes can vary a great deal between institutions. Encouraging student independence in utilising technology and dealing directly with administrative departments can save students and staff time. Processes need to be reviewed but, as Allen and Fifield (1999) note, process changes involve 'shifting responsibilities', and the introduction of technology does not herald a reduction in workload but shifts it to new areas. For example, students now have greater access to their records and learning resources via technology and therefore have greater responsibility for their own learning and management of their studies. They may also have higher expectations than previously about the amount and speed of access to information to which they are entitled. In this context, there must be effective management of workloads to maximise the advantages of technology.

Staff in HEIs working on developing improvements in course management structures and process need to understand the complex nature of the institution and its staff and not just employ standard formulae of project management standards, methods and systems without careful reflection on the nature of their particular HE institution. In one case study of change to campus administration (Child and Lander, 2008), the initial step of recognising problems in work processes involved more than just superficial identification of inefficiencies and potential improvements. It appeared that underinvestment had caused a specific work culture to evolve to cope with poor processes and understanding, and addressing this through joint project management, careful collection of evidence, and facilitation of administration and faculty communication was fundamental in delivering successful change.

Confident Quality Assurance

Using the right staff with the right skills sets and expertise can influence processes designed to ensure and enhance the quality and standards of courses. Course and curriculum development remains a core academic entity, but ensuring compliance with the regulatory framework should be recognised as an important but ancillary process best carried out by expert professional staff. Similarly, the effective design and implementation of arrangements for managing the assessment and feedback process should be undertaken by administrative members of the team, and arrangements for course monitoring should also recognise that much can be done to ease the administrative burden on course managers and leaders through reducing the bureaucracy associated with it.

In HE institutions, problems of perception of the audit culture and quality systems implementation (Watson, 2006) continue to militate against delivering the improvements all stakeholders want. A start in good practice here is to recognise the problem of trust and address it through creating structures and processes that improve communication between staff involved in course management. Staff need to listen to each other's viewpoint and suppress the tendencies on all sides to dismiss the concerns of the others. Academics may lack understanding of why administrators need a full set of reports tabled before annual course monitoring, for example, and administrators may be seen to be stifling academic innovation through blocking proposals that do not conform to perceptions of required standards. Smaller institutions can be better at creating an environment supportive of mutual understanding. The issue of scalability of practice relates to wider questions of appropriate structures and governance models in HE institutions (Bassnett, 2005). Part of the answer, in our view, lies in grassroots-level practice in course management. There are often good working relationships between academic course managers and those involved in administrative support for students, but the interaction is frequently informal, so good practice may be missed in audit trail approaches. For example, staff may meet pre- and post-enrolment and before and after assessment boards to jointly pick up problems, but these would not be documented as essential to the process. We heard in our study an example of a school administrators' forum that meets a couple of times a year to share practices. This could easily be catalogued in annual monitoring reports under 'good practice', but more often such things are omitted and thus overlooked. We were told by academic and administrative staff we surveyed that they felt powerless to change things and were not usually asked how they thought things could be improved. Induction at the start of the course provides one of the best opportunities for academic and administrative staff to work together to provide students with an introduction to what is expected of them.

In course management, quality managers, course administrators and academics need to work together to effect improvements. We argue that central to this is the development of trust in these working relationships. In their discussion of an ideal 'identification'-based trust in work relationships, Lewicki and Bunker (1996) state: 'trust exists because the parties effectively understand and appreciate the other's wants; this mutual understanding developed to the point that each can effectively act for the other' (p. 122).

Across HE institutions, trust is an issue between administrative and academic cultures. We acknowledge its importance in more general management–staff relationships in HE institutions, but that is not the focus of this chapter. What is important is better appreciation of the roles and concerns of those involved in course management. In reporting implementation of a Total Quality Programme (TQP), Sitkin and Stickel (1996) quote a telling remark from a manager in their case study: 'the scope of TQP should be carefully limited to those things for which it is useful. It should not be seen as a way of creating uniformity, but as a way of creating understanding' (p. 207).

Roles, Workloads and Mutual Respect

A change of culture, a willingness to embrace new ways of working, and an environment that values partnership working and an equal relationship between academic and professional support staff are all required if this is to work well. This is not without its risks, and, as with any period of change, it will need to be carefully managed and monitored. People need to be assured that reducing the levels of bureaucracy and working differently will not expose individuals and course teams to unnecessary risk; the fear of the failed inspection or a poor external examiner's report remains a powerful emotion and a potential barrier to change. However, if there are to be gains, and a real and measurable reduction in the traditional and bureaucratic approach to course management, these risks must be faced and people moved on from their comfort zone of reliance on tried and tested, command

and control type approaches to the management of courses. The barriers may be real, but the prospect of freed academic time to concentrate on enhancing the quality of teaching and the students' learning experiences should make their removal an attractive proposition.

How then can university managers ensure that this integration happens? One key requirement is using appropriate terminology. We need to reposition course management as a shared responsibility in which academic staff work alongside and receive high-level support from professional administrators. There can be significant development needs for administrators, to give them the skills and confidence to undertake new ways of working with academics, and for teaching staff, to develop team-based working skills that will give them the confidence to trust administrators and to cede to them overall responsibility for course administration. There will also need to be concrete and specific examples of how a reduced burden of bureaucracy will enable academic staff to concentrate on those interests and activities that brought them into an academic career in the first place. Funding may be an issue, but our research included a school where this had been directed into a new administrative post, which had released the course leader from daily student enquiries and administration. The new arrangement worked well, but it is worth noting that the administrator said she had to build trust so that the course leader would let go of the detail and forgo some of the personal interventions he was used to making on behalf of his students.

This will not be easy, particularly in large institutions, where trust levels may be low. There remains a reluctance, which is particularly prevalent in former CNAA-validated institutions with heavy bureaucratic traditions, to relinquish to professional support staff some of the responsibilities that have traditionally been the exclusive preserve of the academic course manager unless it is made safe to do so. The answer is to shift the focus in favour of a partnership approach, with clear definitions of relative responsibilities and an acknowledgement that course teams, which comprise academic and administrative staff, share and contribute to the achievement of a common goal. This approach will increase mutual understanding of the respective roles of the academic and the administrator, increase awareness of the rationale for ways of working, and move course management and administration 'beyond bureaucracy' and towards an approach that has at its core quality and standards, and an excellent student experience.

Conclusion

Our research found variations in practice across and within institutions, and there is evidence that as institutions mature and become more confident, trust develops and a lighter touch is possible. Barriers to this type of growth appear to be feelings of powerlessness at grassroots level. Senior managers of universities need to send clear messages to all staff about the importance of the contribution of all concerned to developing a culture of co-operation, mutual respect and trust. Problems associated with course administration seem to come from strong subcultures that reinforce misunderstandings, confusion about roles and an inability to see issues from each other's perspective.

Professional managers in administration could evaluate, as a minimum, what structures and systems are in place in their institution to address process improvements specifically related to the administrative–academic interface. Is this done only through academic standards committees or are there additional working parties? What are the different problem perceptions of administrative and academic staff? What priority is given to these problems? Is there sufficient trust between parties and, if not, how can better working relationships be built?

A different approach to course management may be required if the energy and time invested in it by many academic staff are to be released, to enable them to concentrate on activities better guaranteed to improve the learning and teaching experience. This would require new approaches and new kinds of partnerships between academic and administrative staff, the formation of team-based approaches where professional administrative skills are highly regarded; and a shift of emphasis of responsibility for the management of courses. Ideally, academic staff should be freed of the responsibility for routine administrative tasks and given incentives to trust professional support staff to discharge this responsibility on their behalf, allowing teachers to concentrate on delivering, through inspirational teaching and learning, a truly outstanding student experience.

Notes

1   'The QAA is an independent body funded by subscriptions from UK universities and colleges of higher education, and through contracts with the main UK higher education funding bodies. Its mission is to safeguard the public interest in sound standards of higher education qualifications and to inform and encourage continuous improvement in the management of the quality of higher education. It does this by working with higher education institutions to define academic standards and quality, and we carry out and publish reviews against these standards' (www.qaa.ac.uk).

2   Programme specifications are required as part of validating and revalidating named awards in UK universities. They describe the learning outcomes and how these are achieved and assessed. Templates are available from www.qaa.ac.uk/academicinfrastructure/programSpec/default.asp.

3   The Council for National Academic Awards (CNAA) was the body that awarded degrees in the then non-university sector in the United Kingdom, mostly comprising polytechnics, from 1965 to 1992.

References

AACRAO (2008) American Association of College Registrars and Admissions Officers: Meetings Calendar. Available at: www.aacrao.org/meetings.

Allen, D. K. (2003) 'Organisational climate and strategic change in higher education: organisational insecurity', *Higher Education*, 46: 61–92.

Allen, D. K. and Fifield, N. (1999) 'Re-engineering change in higher education', *Information Research*, 4 (3): 12. Online, available at: http://informationr.net/ir/4-3/infres43.html.

AUA (2008) The Association of University Administrators Events Calendar. Online, available at: www.aua.ac.uk/events.

Bassnett, S. (2005) 'The importance of professional university administration: a perspective from a senior university manager', *Perspectives*, 9 (4): 98–102.

Child, C. and Lander, R. (2008) 'Managing successful change in an overwork culture', *Perspectives*, 12 (2): 38–43.

Davies, J., Douglas, A. and Douglas, J. (2007) 'The effect of academic culture on the implementation of the EFQM Excellence Model in UK universities', *Quality Assurance in Education*, 15 (4): 382–401.

Jeston, J. and Nelis, J. (2008) *Business Process Management*, 2nd edn, Oxford: Butterworth Heinemann.

Lewicki, R. J. and Bunker, B. B. (1996) 'Developing and maintaining trust in work relationships', in R. M. Kramer and T. R. Tyler (eds) *Trust in Organizations: Frontiers of Theory and Research*, Thousand Oaks, CA: Sage.

National Student Survey, HEFCE. Online, available at: www.hefce.ac.uk/pubs/circlets/2007/cl28_07/.

Quality Assurance Agency (2008) Online, available at: www.qaa.ac.uk.

QuASK (2008) *Workflow and Business Process Automation*. Online, available at: www.quask.com/workflow/home.asp.

Sahney, S., Banwet, D. K. and Karunes, S. (2004) 'Conceptualizing total quality management in higher education', *TQM Magazine*, 16 (2): 145–59.

Sitkin, S. B. and Stickel, D. (1996) 'The road to hell: the dynamics of distrust in an era of quality', in R. M. Kramer and T. R. Tyler (eds) *Trust in Organizations: Frontiers of Theory and Research*, Thousand Oaks, CA: Sage.

Smeenk, S. G. A., Eisinga, R. N., Teelken, J. C. and Doorewaard, J. A. C. M. (2006) 'The effects of HRM practices and antecedents on organizational commitment among university employees', *International Journal of Human Resource Management*, 17 (12): 2035–54.

Sporn, B. (1999) *Adaptive University Structures: An Analysis of Adaption to Socio-economic Environments of US and European Universities*, London: Jessica Kingsley Publishers.

Stephenson, S. (2004) 'Saving quality from quality assurance', *Perspectives*, 8 (3): 62–7.

Szekeres, J. (2004) 'The invisible workers', *Journal of Higher Education Policy Management*, 26 (1): 7–22.

Triaster (2008) *Process Improvement Company*. Online, available at: www.triaster.co.uk.

Trowler, P., Saunders, M. and Knight, P. (2005) *Change Thinking, Change Practices: A Guide to Change for Heads of Department, Programme Leaders and Other Change Agents in Higher Education*, York: Higher Education Academy.

University of Worcester (2007) *University of Worcester Strategic Plan 2007–2012*. Online, available at: www.worc.ac.uk/documents/Strat_Plan_FINAL.pdf.

Valentine, R. and Knights, D. (1998) 'TQM and BPR: can you spot the difference?', *Personnel Review*, 27 (1): 78–85.

Watson, D. (2006) 'Who killed what in the quality wars?', *Quality Matters*, QAA Briefing Paper, December. Online, available at: www.qaa.ac.uk/enhancement/qualityMatters/QMDecember06.pdf.

CHAPTER 8

One Great Day

Organising Graduation Ceremonies

PAM FEARNLEY
Leeds Metropolitan University

RACHEL FROST and **MAZ BROOK**
University of Essex

and **JAMES ARTHUR**
University of Bath

Introduction

The day has finally arrived. Months of careful planning, negotiation, diplomacy and angst all come down to these ceremonies at which your students will celebrate and receive the fruits of their labours. Everything is in place; all that is required now is for the students and their guests to arrive and enjoy the celebrations. Graduation is a crucial milestone in the academic year, and this chapter outlines some thoughts on how to make this day one of the best of the graduating student's life.

Higher education (HE) is increasingly competitive, and higher education institutions (HEIs) have to demonstrate that they can satisfy student needs in order to maintain and increase student numbers. An important aspect of this is customer satisfaction, crucial for the success of any business, and this applies equally to higher education throughout the academic year from registration to graduation. Even when the customer has had multiple interactions with a business, each individual encounter is important in creating a composite image of high quality (Zeithaml and Bitner, 1996: 87). For family and friends in particular, graduation is one of the times they will witness your institution in action. Everything you do on this day will tell a story about your university, a narrative crucial to your current and future success.

In this chapter we will discuss the strategies employed by three HEIs and examine the practical implications of organising graduation ceremonies and the logistics involved in the planning process. We will also consider key issues, illustrated through case studies of how they have been tackled by our respective institutions, and provide guidance and candid advice on how to stage a successful event both in the United Kingdom and internationally. The universities referred to are:

- The University of Bath (Bath), a campus-based university in south-west England. Graduation ceremonies are held in the winter at the historic Assembly Rooms in Bath, and in the summer at Bath Abbey.
- The University of Essex (Essex), located at multiple sites in Essex in south-east England. All its graduation ceremonies are held during the summer in the Ivor Crewe Lecture Hall, at its Colchester campus.
- Leeds Metropolitan University (Leeds Met), located at multiple sites in and around Leeds in Yorkshire. Its historic campus at Headingley is where the UK graduation ceremonies are held. Leeds Met also holds overseas ceremonies in Hong Kong, Tanzania and Zambia.

We recognise that it has not been possible to cover every aspect of organising graduation ceremonies and have therefore concentrated on the critical areas. A process diagram showing the key activities is shown in Appendix A and forms the basis of our deliberations.

Graduation Strategy

The graduation strategy adopted by a higher education institution evolves over time and adapts to changing needs, as demonstrated throughout this chapter. Three of the key issues covered by a graduation strategy include the overall approach and purpose (strategic analysis and direction), the choice of venue, and the cost and charging policy (strategic choice), which align with identified strategic management processes (Viljoen and Dann, 2000: 47).

In addition to being an occasion to celebrate achievement, graduation also provides an important opportunity for the alumni team to meet graduating students and promote their alumni association and activities, encouraging graduates to maintain subsequent links with the university. It also offers the HEI the opportunity to promote itself with businesses locally, nationally and internationally. It is therefore important that the delivery of graduation reflects the university's service positioning, as this plays a large part in influencing customer perception (Zeithaml and Bitner, 1996: 84). Graduation also provides an opportunity to recognise the achievements of others through the careful selection of VIP guests and the granting of honorary degrees. At Bath, Essex and Leeds Met, nominations for honorary degrees are accepted from all members of the university and are considered by a committee. Nominations might typically include nationally or internationally recognised figures, those who serve as a role model to young people, or academics with an international reputation – or they may be made in recognition of achievements not previously recognised. The majority of nominations are likely to have links to the institution or the local area.

Determining what makes up the overall approach and purpose of graduation for an HEI, therefore, is an essential starting point in the planning process. The structure for managing graduation across HEIs can vary; however, the effective formulation of actions and activities addressing all areas involved is critical in ensuring the successful implementation of the graduation strategy (Viljoen and Dann, 2000: 447). At Bath, responsibility is split between the Student Records and Examinations Office, which is focused on the student element of the ceremonies, and the Events and Ceremonies Office, whose personnel manage the venue and all staff matters. At Leeds Met, graduation is managed centrally from the Awards, Examinations and Graduations Office and supported by event co-ordinators in the faculties, while at Essex the overall management of graduation rests with the central academic section, with receptions and publicity being co-ordinated by the Communications Office. Where the responsibility for graduation is shared, an appropriate mechanism is essential to avoid fragmentation of the strategy and an inconsistent delivery. At Essex a Graduation Planning Group was formed in 2007 to oversee the strategy and organisation of graduation. This allowed the key people involved to agree collectively the approach to be taken, and has proved successful. At Leeds Met the graduation team has regular group meetings with faculty co-ordinators to ensure consistency in the message communicated to students, in addition to meetings with the registrar and the secretary, who has overall oversight of the process, to ensure that the graduation strategy is communicated throughout the planning process. Appendix A provides details of the key areas to be addressed by graduation planners.

The location of the ceremonies and the time of year when they are held are important factors in the graduation strategy, as both have a significant impact on the planning process. In terms of venue choice, different approaches will be taken according to the circumstances and what is to be achieved. At Leeds Met, when its external venue became unavailable and there was no viable alternative, the decision was taken to build its own. The ceremonies were moved to the summer and a marquee was constructed on campus specifically for graduation each year, providing a garden party atmosphere. This is a radical solution, but one that allowed the university to create a venue that would specifically meet its needs. At Essex the construction of a new, larger lecture hall allowed a reduction in the number of ceremonies held each year and an increase in the number of guests invited to each ceremony, an important factor in improving the graduation experience for students. At Bath, two external venues are used, the Assembly Rooms in the winter and Bath Abbey in the summer. Each venue has its own benefits and drawbacks. Bath Abbey, for example, is a venue with grandeur appropriate for such an event but, being a large stone building, can become hot should the sun choose to shine. Having used a variety of venues in the past, both on and off campus, the university considers the current venues the most appropriate for ceremonial occasions such as graduation – and feedback from graduates confirms this to be the case. In each of these examples the venue chosen provides a different type of environment for the graduation ceremony, and the way in which it is used in conjunction with what the university wants to achieve will determine its success.

Linked closely to venue selection is the cost and charging policy. In an age of increased tuition fees and students being considered as customers, the question of whether or not to charge for graduation, whom to charge and how much is of great importance. So too is the overall cost and budget provided by an HEI to support graduation, which again links to the purpose and importance placed on graduation and what it is trying to achieve. The costs and charging model adopted by an HEI are critical in terms of what can be delivered. The price of a service can influence the perception of quality (Zeithaml and Bitner, 1996: 75).

Many institutions, including Bath, do not charge, but at Essex and Leeds Met charges are made for guest tickets. At Essex, guest ticket charging was first introduced in 2005, and in 2008 the costs stand at £15 per guest ticket. It was determined that changes to the format of the ceremony, the improved location and use of technology, along with enhancements to the receptions and a higher standard of entertainment and facilities across campus during graduation, could be implemented by using the increased income from guest ticket sales. Leeds Met kept the cost of guest tickets at £15 each in 2008 despite the increased cost of building the marquee. The Higher Education Act 2004 (Part 3, Student Fees and Fair Access, para. 41) states that fees in relation to undertaking a course include graduation fees but exclude 'fees payable for attending any graduation or other ceremony'. This indicates that institutions can legitimately charge students for attendance at a graduation event should they wish to do so.

A vital factor affecting both the formation and implementation of a graduation strategy is the culture and traditions of the HEI. These will vary according to the age, size and type of institution and cannot be ignored, as they have been recognised as having an impact on the performance of the organisation (Wood *et al.*, 2001: 391). For example, the University of Cambridge Congregation for the conferment of degrees takes place in the university's purpose-built Senate House and is conducted in Latin (University of Cambridge, 2006). It seems unlikely that either the location or the language used during the conferral process would be changed in the short term, but it may be appropriate to review other areas.

It is essential for an HEI to have a clear idea of what it wants to achieve and deliver through graduation. This must be championed by senior staff and those implementing graduation and clearly communicated to all involved, and should align with the overall mission and culture of the HEI. Uniformity of service standards and approaches in the delivery of graduation ceremonies, particularly when the responsibility for graduation is split across different areas of the organisation, is vital, and adoption of a formal mechanism for unifying all the separate parts is a valuable method of achieving this. Finally, it is important to continually review and enhance the strategy in order to keep it up-to-date, relevant to students and in line with the evolving focus and mission of the HEI.

Logistics

The logistics of organising graduation are complex, involving multiple stakeholders: students, their families and friends, university staff, and internal and external suppliers. So how do you begin to manage the endless requirements and deliver graduation successfully? The key issues involve planning, co-ordination and communication and can be considered by looking at areas that affect the graduation ceremony itself and those that affect the supporting activities.

The nature of the graduation ceremony will be governed largely by the venue. Whether it is internal or external to the institution, the location, size and layout of the venue will affect how the ceremonies, students, guests and processions are organised. For example, a need to review the seating of students arose following a change of venue for Essex. The Ivor Crewe Lecture Hall has tiered seating throughout, which resulted in the need to relocate the students to the back of the auditorium (in the previous venue they had been located on a flat area at the front of the room). This ensured that students did not block the view of guests when leaving their seats to be presented to the chancellor and then returning. Consideration of special requirements, such as disability access for both students and guests to every aspect of the ceremony, should also be addressed. A recent case in the United Kingdom (*Potter* v. *Canterbury Christ Church University*, 2007) in which a graduate took legal action against the institution, emphasised the need to ensure that all reasonable adjustments have been made so that no graduate feels disadvantaged. In this particular case the ceremony involved the graduates ascending steps onto the dais in the cathedral to be greeted by the chair of governors. The graduate concerned, being in a wheelchair, was unable to do so and believed this to be less favourable treatment (a view upheld by the judge). Within the United Kingdom the Disability Discrimination Act 1995 and, in particular, the Code of Practice (revised) for providers of post-16 education and related services (2007) need careful consideration.

Other areas to be addressed can include the location of cameras for filming the ceremony, graduation photographers and musicians. Additionally, a university needs to consider how many support staff are required and where they are to be located. In the case of Leeds Met the venue holds more than 2,000 people, therefore a lack of staff to usher the students and guests could have serious implications as well as adversely affecting their experience. Other considerations include the location of robing and photography, and, in particular, what entrances and exits are to be used. Finally, the structure of the graduation ceremony itself – the duration, format and speeches – is another point to be considered.

Other activities outside the graduation ceremony itself are of equal importance in terms of the graduation experience as a whole and involve careful consideration, for example ticket collection and registration. The co-ordination of other facilities – such as the location of alumni teams and students' union stands; the sale of gifts, DVDs and other memorabilia; catering outlets; and music and entertainment – needs careful planning. The post-graduation receptions should be co-ordinated and aligned with the ceremonies. Leeds Met provides a buffet; therefore, careful consideration has been given to special dietary needs and also taken into account where hospitality is provided outside the marquee.

Support service issues such as transport, security, parking arrangements, venue presentation, adequate clear signage, and management of other non-graduation activities are all of equal importance to the delivery of a successful ceremony. For some universities, transport and parking are a major consideration; at Leeds Met a transport strategy specifically for graduation has been developed, which required close liaison with the local council and careful consideration of the needs of local residents who are affected by increased numbers of vehicles in the vicinity (see the case study). At Essex and Leeds Met, all building works, non-essential deliveries and conference activities are suspended throughout the days of graduation. At Bath the summer ceremonies include a procession through part of the city centre, which requires traffic to be stopped for short periods throughout the day. At campus-based universities, great care and attention is paid to the appearance of the campus itself, and grounds staff work hard in advance to make it look attractive. Regular inspections and maintenance activities, ranging from providing decorative hanging baskets to clearing litter throughout the day, aim to ensure a pristine and immaculate campus.

When one is organising an event such as graduation, it is essential to ensure that all services provided are consistent in quality, style and professionalism. Once a benchmark is set, consistency across all services is expected by the service providers and can have an effect on staff morale and thereby the quality of service if not addressed. The strategy adopted needs to be flexible and responsive to changing demands, and capable of dealing with the unexpected. Each year will provide its own individual challenges in a different area. Security at Essex, for instance, has rarely been an issue, except for the year when the partner of one of the honorary graduands was Nelson Mandela. Similarly at Leeds Met, security had to be tightened in 2005 when reporters for national newspapers entered the campus and attempted to 'doorstep' graduating Asian students and parents for comments when it became known that one of the 'London Bombers' was a Leeds Met alumnus.

Unfortunately, the weather is beyond the control of event organisers. While the winter ceremonies at Bath are self-contained within the Assembly Rooms (including gowning and photography), the procession in the summer has on occasion required the addition of umbrellas to the standard regalia. Bad weather also resulted in last-minute changes to parking arrangements at Leeds Met. Furthermore, a comprehensive risk assessment should always be included in a university's pre-planning processes, covering health and safety and emergency evacuation issues, and reviewing any changes to the format to ensure compliance with relevant legislation.

Case Study:
Leeds Met Transport Strategy
Throughout the four days of graduation at Leeds Met, the area where the graduation marquee is located is designated a traffic-free zone. Parking in other areas of the campus is limited to guests and staff with special needs, VIP guests and event organisers. On the day, the campus is accessible only to vehicles with a permit.

A shuttle bus is in service for staff travelling to the university's Headingley campus from its city centre campus throughout the four days of graduation.

continued

> Students and guests attending the event are offered parking on Beckett Park, adjacent to the campus and managed by Leeds City Council. Spaces on this car park are secured by the university for staff who normally park at the Headingley campus.
>
> The traffic management strategy put in place by Leeds Met during the graduation ceremonies ensures that staff as well as students and guests have a safe and enjoyable experience.

Academic Planning and Preparation

All of the processes outlined form the basis of the planning strategy for a graduation ceremony. However, possibly the most important part of the process, and at the centre of graduation, is the academic planning, from student invitations through to the conferment of degrees.

The first stage of the planning process is to determine the schedule by allocating departments to ceremonies. This will normally involve considering the expected numbers of students, placing related departments together if applicable, and the assignment of appropriate honorary graduands. The ceremonies are scheduled according to numbers, and therefore at the three universities mentioned, students are not given a choice of which ceremony to attend. However, a student may be moved to a different ceremony in exceptional circumstances. For example, at Leeds Met a Jewish student was unable to attend a Saturday ceremony for religious reasons and was offered an opportunity to attend an alternative ceremony. At Leeds Met and Bath, honorary graduands are given a choice of dates and times, but on occasions their choice does not align with their faculty's ceremony. At Essex, honorary graduands are asked for their preference of date, and the final schedule is released once these preferences are known, to ensure that departments can be scheduled on an appropriate date with a relevant honorary graduand. This is carried out before working out a 'best fit' of departments to ceremonies within the constraint of the venue capacity and finally deciding on what day each faculty or department will attend. Large departments may have to be split; smaller faculties and departments, and centres or schools, have to be fitted in with others where capacity allows.

Once allocation is complete, many institutions publish the relevant information on their website, and invitations are issued. At Essex the graduation schedule is published on the website at the beginning of March and students are advised by email that it is available. At Leeds Met, invitations are sent out around the end of March and a response is expected by the end of April. The academic calendar is confirmed and published about 11 months in advance. This provides 4 months' notice in some cases for students and their guests to make necessary arrangements, for example for travel and time off work.

Most universities will issue a formal invitation to students eligible to graduate, although some, such as the University of British Columbia, in Canada, and the University of Queensland, in Australia, require their students to submit an application to graduate (www.graduation.ubc.ca and www.uq.edu.au/graduations). The institution's student records system will be utilised, where possible, to record ceremony and certificate information, and can thereby allow the invitation process to be revised from a paper-based postal method to a web-based invitation form. The invitation form or letter allows those eligible to indicate whether they will be attending the ceremony, request guest tickets, provide details of any special requirements and ensure that their personal details are accurate. Where an institution charges for graduation, payment processing will also be included. For those institutions that have an online invitation form and link to their student records database, this will streamline processes significantly, removing the need for manual data processing and thereby reducing the risk of error.

The allocation and provision of student and guest tickets can be an area for concern, both for the administrators and for the students and their guests. Normally, a maximum of two to three guests per student is allowed, with the flexibility to allow further tickets to be issued where available. Many students request additional tickets, for example for siblings, step-parents, children or partners, and this can be an emotional time. It is important to ensure a consistent and fair approach to ticket allocation and to publicise the procedure clearly. At Leeds Met a 'ring-in day' is publicised for those ceremonies where tickets are available. Essex and Leeds Met provide a free live screening of the graduation ceremonies in a separate location on campus. This allows guests without tickets or those with young children (aged under 5) to watch the ceremonies and be part of the occasion. At Leeds Met a live webcast provides families of students overseas with the opportunity to enjoy the ceremonies. The University of Bath summer ceremonies were webcast for the first time in 2008. While this was not a live webcast (it was available 24 hours after each ceremony), it allowed many more guests, such as those unable to travel, to watch the ceremonies. Though a live webcast might be considered ideal, it was considered that many 'viewers' would be overseas, where the time difference would make simultaneity less important.

At all three universities, tickets are collected on the day of the ceremony, ensuring that they are not lost in the post or forgotten on the day. Where the ceremony venue has a limited capacity, it is critical that the number of tickets issued is monitored. This process also allows for reallocation of uncollected tickets, as at Bath and Essex. Seating is allocated to students, but guests are normally given unallocated seats.

Some students who have applied to attend graduation may not be able to do so; therefore a procedure needs to be put in place to ensure that the names of non-attendees are not read out. At Bath a registration session is held prior to the ceremony, which provides an opportunity for the presenter's list to be checked and returned before the ceremony commences. At Essex and Leeds Met, students are issued with a name card, which includes their details and seat number and is checked by ushers before being handed to the presenter. This process also allows for the inclusion of late arrivals.

Arguably the central focus of the graduation ceremonies is the conferment of awards – the moment at which the student becomes a graduate. Where an institution requires its students to apply to graduate, it is often the case that conferment takes place at the ceremony, both in person and *in absentia*. Others will have conferred awards pre-ceremony, with the chancellor's conferral speech reflecting the chosen process. Some universities present the actual certificate at the ceremony, as is the case at Bath and Leeds Met, which requires highly effective systems, while others will require certificates to be collected following the ceremony, as happens at Essex.

The timing of ceremonies has a significant impact on planning and preparations. If an institution holds its ceremonies in October for those who have completed in May or June, there is significantly less time pressure than when the ceremonies are held in June or July. Institutions may consider separating postgraduate and undergraduate ceremonies, and two of our institutions (Bath and Leeds Met) hold some ceremonies at different times of year, with summer ceremonies being a common factor. Essex previously held postgraduate ceremonies in April and undergraduate ceremonies in July. These were brought together in July 2006 for operational and cost reasons. This change aligned with the immediate conferral of postgraduate awards, eliminating the need for postgraduates to wait until a graduation ceremony to receive their award. Where summer ceremonies are held in late June or early July, there is a period of intense activity between the boards of studies or equivalent, at which awards are approved, and the ceremonies themselves; this interval can be as little as a few days. Once pass lists are received from the boards, these have to be processed: at Bath they are sent to the vice-chancellor for conferment; at Leeds Met and Essex the pass lists are signed by the chair of the board of examiners. The details are added to the ceremony brochure or programme so that it can be printed; all certificates have to be produced and checked, and the detailed lists of awards provided to the chancellor and the presenters (usually deans of faculty or school, or heads of department) have to be finalised.

Provisional lists of graduating students will have been prepared. However, it is vital that the final pass lists are cross-checked against any other lists held to ensure that they correspond. For example, the presenters require their lists well in advance to allow time for familiarisation and to ensure they are versed in the pronunciation of all names. It can be upsetting for students and guests if the presenters stumble through lists of unfamiliar names, undermining the dignity of the occasion.

There is little that can be done to ease the time pressure without delaying the ceremonies, but careful preparation can ensure that the quantity of work is minimised. Streamlining processes and regular communication with all involved will provide additional time for quality checks.

Co-Ordination and Communication

Effective co-ordination and communication are critical in ensuring that everyone involved in graduation understands their role and knows where they are expected to be. This will involve liaison with a number of different internal groups, such as marketing and communications teams, audio-visual or technical teams, students' union services, catering and other services with which good relationships are crucial to ensure smooth running of operations on the day. Graduation receptions also need to be co-ordinated to align with the duration of the ceremonies so that students and guests can enjoy the whole event without feeling rushed.

The two main groups of staff to be co-ordinated are academic staff (for processions) and support staff assisting with activities during graduation. At Essex, all departments are asked to provide the names of a specified number of academic staff for the processions, and a request is also issued to university staff for volunteers to assist with graduation. At Bath, academic staff have the opportunity to join the processions if they wish to do so. Departments ask administrators to assist with the registration process, but support is predominantly provided by Central Registry staff. As a result of the support staffing approach used at Essex, it has become an unofficial team-building event, allowing people from all areas of the university to mix and work together who may not ordinarily have the opportunity to do so, while contributing towards delivering a high-quality experience for students. This is also the case at Leeds Met, where there is a very strong expectation that all academic staff attend their own students' graduation and that cross-faculty support is provided to ensure celebratory graduations.

The effective communication of plans is essential in terms of ensuring that everyone knows and understands what the graduation strategy is, why it is being implemented and what impact it will have on them. At Essex, changes to the format of the ceremony following the move to a new venue included the presentation of students to the chancellor by heads of department in place of deans and the introduction of an announcer (or master of ceremonies) role, its purpose being to introduce each speaker and briefly outline their role or activity, to ensure that all students and guests know who is about to speak and what is about to happen. This change needed to be communicated clearly upwards to the chancellor, vice-chancellor and senior staff of the university, in order to ensure support and successful implementation of the changes. Clear communication is also required with all internal and external suppliers, for example to ensure that they are familiar with their location during graduation, expected student and guest numbers, ceremony times, and opening hours for support services. Any subsequent changes need to be communicated in sufficient time, and major changes may require a site visit by external suppliers.

It is also important to ensure that adequate training is provided to support staff to enable them to carry out their roles effectively and consistently; the use of guidance notes and briefing sessions may prove useful in assisting with this. It is essential to match customer wishes and needs with employees' ability to deliver (Zeithaml and Bitner, 1996: 96); therefore, it is crucial to ensure that staff are fully trained regarding their role prior to and during graduation. Communication with support services such as estates, catering and conference teams must be completed in sufficient time to allow full dissemination across teams, particularly where the suspension of non-essential and conference activities is involved.

Communication to all graduating students must be timely, relevant and clear, and provided in an accessible way, for instance on a website. Information about policies, for example in relation to the purchase of guest tickets and the cancellation policy, must be clearly available, along with details of facilities and services, since disappointment can have a negative effect on students' perceptions of their university. It is better to manage their expectations in advance, so they know what they realistically can and cannot expect.

In addition, since students sometimes find the formality of the ceremony daunting in prospect, clear information should be provided about what will happen during the ceremony, especially where, for instance, students may be required to walk up and down stairs or on and off a stage. It should also be clearly communicated to students and guests that if they require special arrangements, they must notify the HEI in advance to ensure that these can be put in place; this does not always happen in practice. It is important, particularly in the United Kingdom, to comply with disability legislation and to accommodate any requirements students or guests may have. Event co-ordinators need to work closely with colleagues, for example disability support officers or academics in the faculties.

The university should have clear plans in place for what it wants to deliver. This includes co-ordinating the activities carried out by internal and external suppliers, academic staff and support staff to ensure clarity about the end result. It is a good idea to seek to promote graduation from the top down and where possible encourage involvement from across the HEI, since graduation belongs to all staff and there are many opportunities for individuals to play their part. Staff leading graduations should ensure that clear, timely communications are provided without assuming that people will know or understand what they need to do. It is important to acknowledge everyone's contribution after the event in an appropriate way, for example by circulating a note of thanks.

The Ceremony

Ceremonies commonly last between one and two hours. It is important to take into consideration the needs of all those attending the ceremonies, including guests of all ages, who may become uncomfortable or restless during a long ceremony. The length of each ceremony may dictate the number of ceremonies per day. While three ceremonies per day appears to be the norm in our three universities, with careful co-ordination Bath has been able to incorporate a fourth ceremony on one of the graduation days (with each ceremony lasting approximately an hour).

Students and guests are generally required to be seated at least 15 minutes before the ceremony, therefore careful management of the crowds is required and specific attention must be paid to the seating of students and guests with special requirements.

Seating arrangements may be varied according to preference, but most institutions aim to ensure that guests are seated with a clear line of sight to the stage; students are often seated to the side or rear of the venue, with VIPs allocated front-row seating. In all three universities either a stage or a platform area is used, upon which the academic procession and the officers of the university sit, and over which the students process to have their awards conferred or presented.

Background music is played at the ceremonies of all three universities while guests and students take their seats, often by a brass band or string quartet, and large screens may display a montage of the university's events throughout the year. These screens can also be used to provide an additional view of proceedings throughout the ceremony for those with a restricted or distant view, and to allow close-up images as students are presented. The musicians also provide the processional and recessional music.

The ceremonies in each of the three universities begin with the entrance of the academic and officers' procession into the venue, comprising staff in formal academic dress, followed by an opening speech, often by the most senior member of staff present: At Bath, Essex and Leeds Met this is the chancellor of the university, the chancellor being the lay head of the university who carries out ceremonial duties such as presiding over graduation. The students are then usually presented to receive their awards, often individually as in the case of Leeds Met, Bath and Essex, though sometimes at larger ceremonies held at other institutions, students have their awards presented in groups. This is often followed by the conferral of any honorary degrees, although the order is sometimes reversed, with the honorary degrees being presented first. At Essex, students were presented by their head of department for the first time in 2007, the head of department using the occasion to make a brief speech about the achievements of the department. Frequently the assembly or congregation is also addressed by any honorary graduates and the vice-chancellor during the ceremony. A critical factor in ensuring that ceremonies run to time is effectively managing the duration of all speeches in order to prevent an overrun, although this cannot always be achieved. There is a balance to be maintained between making it a meaningful, dignified and celebratory occasion, and keeping the throughput of ceremonies to time.

At the end of the ceremony, recessional music is played as the processions exit. At Bath and Essex the graduates follow by forming a procession out of the venue, while at Leeds Met the procession, led by the vice-chancellor, forms a 'guard of honour' to recognise the graduates with applause as they leave the marquee.

Post-Event Review and Measuring Satisfaction

It is essential to hold a post-event review incorporating feedback from staff and students to examine what went well in addition to identifying areas for improvement in future ceremonies. This will also form the basis of the planning process for the following year.

Student satisfaction is an increasingly important factor for HEIs, and the ceremonies should be a memorable occasion (for the right reasons) for all those attending them. A survey of students can provide a useful insight into the ceremonies, and can focus attention on areas that might otherwise have been overlooked. Bath and Leeds Met conduct such surveys annually, covering the process from initial contact to the day of graduation. Any suggestions and criticisms are fed through the appropriate channels for consideration. It is important to pass on all feedback as part of the process, including thanking those involved in the success of the ceremonies.

Overseas Ceremonies

For HEIs that deliver courses overseas, organising graduation can be challenging. Hong Kong Football Club is the graduation venue for students who study Leeds Met courses at the Vocational Training Council in Hong

Kong. The successful model of graduation that had already been established in the United Kingdom since 2004 was the starting point for organising the event in Hong Kong.

Putting students at the centre of planning means that the focus must be on the student, therefore any cultural differences should be taken into account and practices adapted as necessary to the local context. For example, the graduation team from Leeds Met travelling to Hong Kong in 2007 was provided with language and culture classes before working on the event. This helped staff to identify and address some of the issues and gain a better understanding of the additional complexity of organising ceremonies overseas. In Hong Kong, guests have a more casual approach to the ceremony and frequently stand up to take photographs and chat among themselves. Staff learned a few polite words in Cantonese to enable them, without causing offence, to ask guests to sit down. Additional photo opportunities were provided for families after the event.

Any change to planning as a result of working overseas can have a serious impact on the occasion. For example, at Leeds Met a 'no charge' policy meant that students could take only two guests to the ceremony in Hong Kong. Strict controls had to be put in place to check tickets as, in their enthusiasm to celebrate graduation, students tried to bring additional guests on the day, which was problematic for catering and seating purposes.

In managing overseas ceremonies, a number of processes may be different: for Leeds Met in Hong Kong, the process for hiring gowns and hoods differed significantly from that in the United Kingdom. Students in Hong Kong hired their own gowns from a choice of suppliers, which led to some inconsistencies in quality. Logistics like this should always be considered and factored into the planning process in advance, as far as possible.

With ever-increasing changes to export regulations, event organisers can find themselves trying to beat the clock if early familiarisation is not carried out. No amount of begging, pleading or negotiating can speed up the processes of transportation of ceremonial gowns, programmes or marketing material to another country where practices are significantly different from those in the United Kingdom.

Locating a key local person in the host organisation with whom you can liaise on such details is crucial when working on overseas ceremonies. Someone who knows the local conditions and regulations, speaks the language and knows the area and, in some cases, the students can often save the day and hours of work.

A survey of students about their experiences of graduation is an important tool to enable planning for future graduations. Just because a model of graduation works well in the United Kingdom, that does not necessarily mean that it will work overseas. Leeds Met benefited greatly when it asked students to rate their graduation experience, leading to a change in a number of processes for future occasions.

Summary

It is vital throughout the planning and preparation for the graduation ceremonies not to lose sight of their purpose and, crucially, whom the day is for.

Throughout this chapter, clear advance planning has been shown to be crucial, and flexibility should always be built in to accommodate the unexpected. Different emphasis will be put on each aspect depending on the institution's mission or objectives and its graduation strategy. Whether it is choosing the venue, setting the price or simply deciding on seating arrangements, universities should not lose sight of the fact that the student must always be the primary consideration. Although a university may choose this great day as an opportunity to showcase its activities to a wider audience for the benefit of future students, it is important to keep graduating students at the heart of the experience. Staff work hard to develop and manage the many complex processes involved, therefore it is important that they do not get too wrapped up in the detail of bureaucracy to the point that they distract students and their families, diminishing their enjoyment of what for them is one great day.

Further reading

Bitner, M. J. (1993) 'Managing the evidence of service', in E. Scheuing and W. Christopher (eds) *Service Quality Handbook*, New York: AMACOM.

References

Disability Discrimination Act 1995. Online, available at: www.opsi.gov.uk/acts/acts1995/ukpga_19950050_en_1.
Higher Education Act 2004 (c.8) (2004) *Part 3 Student Fees and Fair Access, Supplementary*. Online, available at: www.opsi.gov.uk/acts/acts2004/ukpga_20040008_en_4#pt3.
Potter v. *Canterbury Christchurch University* (2007) Online, available at: http://83.137.212.42/sitearchive/DRC/the_law/transcripts_of_key_judgments/potter_v_canterbury_christ_chu.html.
University of British Columbia (2008) *Graduation at UBC*. Online, available at: www.graduation.ubc.ca.
University of Cambridge Office of Communications Services (2006) *University of Cambridge: The Way it Works*, 2nd edn, Cambridge: Cambridge University Press.
University of Queensland (2008) *Graduations at the University of Queensland*. Online, available at: www.uq.edu.au/graduations.
Viljoen, J. and Dann, S. (2000) *Strategic Management*, 3rd edn, Frenchs Forest, NSW: Pearson Education Australia.
Wood, J., Wallace, J. and Zeffane, R. M. (2001) *Organisational Behaviour: A Global Perspective*, 2nd edn, Milton, Queensland: John Wiley.
Zeithaml, V. A. and Bitner, M. J. (1996) *Services Marketing*, New York: McGraw-Hill.

Appendix A: Key Activities Involved in Organising a Graduation Ceremony

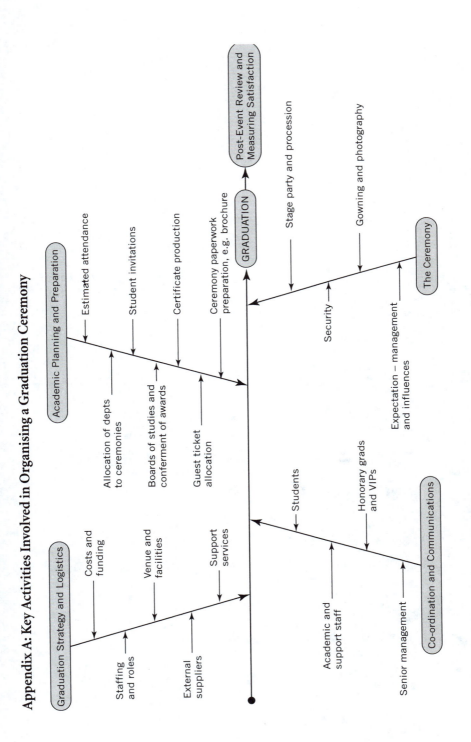

PART III

Assuring the Quality of the Student Learning Experience

CHAPTER 9

Managing Assessment Systems and Processes

SANDRA MIENCZAKOWSKI
University of Nottingham

PAUL KELLY
Northumbria University

CHRISTINE BEXTON
University of Nottingham

and **IAN HAMLEY**
University of Nottingham

Introduction

The aim of this chapter is to provide an overview of the key challenges facing higher education institutions (HEIs) in the twenty-first century in relation to the management of assessment systems and processes, and describes how two English universities have responded to these challenges. The first section outlines the key issues to be addressed, with a discussion of problems faced in the past and anticipated in the future, as well as internal and external constraints. The second section describes how these issues have been addressed, by comparing and contrasting approaches. The third section provides examples of good practice, advice and guidance. Issues surrounding the academic practice of assessing students are not covered here, although we recognise that 'trends in assessment policy and practice' and the 'consideration of the purposes of assessment' (Leathwood, 2005) are topical debates.

Northumbria University, formerly Newcastle Polytechnic, was awarded university status in 1992, becoming the largest higher education provider in the north-east of England. Located in the heart of the city of Newcastle upon Tyne, Northumbria has a student population of around 31,000, with over 3,000 overseas students on the Newcastle campuses and a further 4,000 studying Northumbria programmes in their own countries. The university is organised around nine academic schools, supported by a range of professional support departments, and employs over 3,000 staff, 58 per cent of whom work in central and school-based support services.

The University of Nottingham was awarded a royal charter in 1948. Located in the East Midlands, the university is situated to the west of Nottingham city centre and has a student population of around 30,000, with over 7,000 overseas students on the Nottingham campuses. It has two international campuses, one in Semenyih, south of Kuala Lumpur in Malaysia, with a student population of over 3,000, and one in Ningbo, China, also with a student population of over 3,000. The university is organised around academic schools supported by a range of professional support departments, and employs over 6,000 staff.

Key Issues in Managing Assessment Systems and Processes

When one considers the main challenges faced in managing assessment systems and processes, the keywords 'fair' and 'consistent approach' are at the forefront, and this is supported by the UK Quality Assurance Agency publication *Outcomes from Institutional Audit: Assessment of Students* (QAA, 2008). In recent years, radical changes have taken place within higher education in the United Kingdom. There has been increased national government intervention, with initiatives like the introduction of a National Qualification Framework (NQF), which sets out the levels against which a qualification can be recognised in the United Kingdom; the research assessment exercises (a peer review evaluating the quality of research at UK universities); subject benchmarks (expectations about the standards of degrees in subject areas in the United Kingdom); and the Quality Assurance Agency for Higher Education (QAA) codes of practice and institutional audits. However, universities also need to take account of proposed national developments, including the Burgess Review of degree classifications (finally reporting in 2007, the 'Burgess Group' was established to consider the measuring and reporting of student achievement in the United Kingdom), and international developments such as the Bologna Agreement (an agreement made in 1999 in Bologna, Italy, to construct a European higher education area, including the adoption of a system of comparable degrees and a transfer system of academic credits).

In addition, there have been major increases in student numbers; a commitment to a mass higher education system, with the UK government pursuing policies intended to result in 50 per cent of students remaining in education through to the completion of a university degree; the introduction and raising of tuition fees; and moves towards student self-service, with a growth in electronic communications. Many of these trends are also evident elsewhere in the world.

Newby (2003) identifies 'students today [as having] much higher expectations of the quality and professionalism in the provision of university amenities and services . . . and of high academic standards'. Increases have also been seen in recent years in the United Kingdom in the numbers of academic appeals, data protection subject access requests, and requests under the terms of the Freedom of Information Act as students seek to support such appeals.

The diversity of learners, too, has increased in the HE sector, with more students following varied patterns of study. While classroom-based tuition on campus may still be the most common form of learning, increasing numbers of students are studying programmes or modules off campus, some based in the workplace, and many with the aid of online tools and learning materials.

This has implications for the management practices of both academic and non-academic individuals within an institution. Central service divisions, while retaining their role in supporting schools and faculties in their business, must also ensure that students are provided with high-quality services to support their learning and achievement of successful individual outcomes, catering for non-traditional students and satisfying 'helicopter' parents – that is, parents who, having invested strongly in their progeny's education, hover in the background in a way unprecedented in previous years.

Managing Assessment Systems and Processes

Among the many challenges faced by those managing assessment systems and processes, the following are significant and subject to much current debate:

- ensuring the integrity of assessment data, in particular the accurate capture and reporting of student marks or grades and progression and awards outcomes;
- managing the increasing volume of assessment data as student numbers grow and high summative assessment loads continue to be built into curricula; also, managing the assessment loading on staff and students at peak times in the year, especially around each semester end;

- managing assessment exceptions such as reassessment after failure, and claims for personal extenuating circumstances or allegations of academic misconduct;
- ensuring that assessment systems and processes support the increasing diversity of learners;
- achieving fair and consistent processing of assessment outcomes through examination boards and their reporting to students.

Systems Problems and Constraints

With increases in student numbers, the range of modules available and the complexities of scheduling a large number of examinations into a defined period of time, inevitably issues arise that require resolution by the administrative team. Examination timetabling systems need to be sufficiently flexible to be able to deal with these complexities, and it is crucially important to develop IT solutions to streamline the process as much as possible while retaining the ability for manual intervention and manipulation as required.

Students Requiring Reasonable Adjustments for Examinations

In order to treat all students with equity, a consistent approach is required, as institutions need to make reasonable adjustments for all disabled students (including students with dyslexia and/or dyspraxia) and students with long-term medical conditions as well as those unable to take exams on particular days or at particular times for religious observance reasons. Adjustments may also need to be made at short notice for students who have been affected by an accident or short-term illness. Arrangements for such adjustments must, however, be balanced by ensuring the smooth running of examinations, and this is a growing challenge for the staff of the examinations office.

Communication

How information is communicated to students is an important consideration to ensure that students are kept well informed, so it is imperative to ensure the robustness and reliability of systems used. A further issue to be addressed is how best to communicate with the student population through methods relevant to them in their day-to-day lives, for example through text messages or emails, rather than methods previously used, like noticeboards and letters mailed to their homes.

Assessment Processes

Key challenges in managing assessment processes include the increasing diversity of learners and their needs, taking into consideration different modes of study, including on-campus and off-campus learning and blended approaches. International students may be studying on-site or in their home countries, with delivery by home nation and international partners.

The notion of the 'standard' or 'traditional' student is increasingly inappropriate, even dangerous, if systems and processes continue to be geared towards what may become a minority of learners: it is unwise to premise administrative systems based around 18-year-old, full-time undergraduates from the United Kingdom, studying 120 credits in each academic year on campus. Processes and systems need to recognise, understand and support this diversity. We need to maximise each student's opportunity to achieve the best possible assessment outcome and, ideally, to learn through the assessment process.

It is important to create, where possible:

- a good spread and balance of assessment workload, pacing assignments to maximise student engagement;
- clarity in specification of assessment activity, expectations and marking criteria, so that students and staff are clear about what is to be achieved and how it will be graded;
- clear information on the resources available to support student learning prior to assessment;
- an awareness of how feedback will be given;
- an understanding of what learning can be achieved through the assignments set, expressed in terms of learning outcomes to be demonstrated.

Issues Concerning the Assessment of Postgraduate Taught Students

In recent years the handling of assessment issues for postgraduate taught students has become more complex. There are a number of reasons for this, including an increasing proportion of international students on full-time courses, an increase in the number of part-time students and a growth in the number of courses studied by e-learning or at a distance.

In the academic year 2007–8, both universities had a significant proportion of full-time postgraduate taught students classified as international or from the European Union (EU) for fees, over 60 per cent at Nottingham and more than 35 per cent at Northumbria. Unlike undergraduate international students, who normally have at least three years to adjust to a new environment, these students come to take a 12-month course of study, at very high cost and with very high expectations of success placed upon them. A UKCOSA survey (2004) highlighted a range of issues affecting this group of students, such as cultural alienation, financial difficulties, and gender and religious issues. They may have little time to adjust, but before long they are expected to hand in assignments, and in less than four months on some programmes they are sitting examinations that will count towards the classification of their award. Study methods will often be very different from the methods to which they have been accustomed, and this makes it all the more possible that they will fail, or even find themselves accused of academic offences such as plagiarism, since conventions on quotation and referencing vary from nation to nation.

It is likely that numbers of part-time students at postgraduate level will continue to increase, given that postgraduate recruitment is likely to suffer as a result of the numbers of undergraduate students graduating with a high level of personal debt, and a levelling off in recruitment of international students to the United Kingdom, owing to economic recession and the introduction of the points-based immigration system, which will apply to all students who require student visas in order to study in the United Kingdom as from 2009. In 2007–8, around 30 per cent of Nottingham's postgraduate taught students were registered on a part-time basis (at Northumbria the corresponding figure is around 60 per cent), taking their courses over a period of between two and four years. Different factors affect part-time students, many of whom, for example, have work commitments, or young children and/or elderly parents to care for. These external pressures may make it difficult for them to attend taught sessions on a regular basis, and can make their attendance at examinations very problematic. Course completion rates may suffer as a result.

By contrast, in recent years a number of schools at both Nottingham and Northumbria have started to run postgraduate taught courses by distance learning. These courses have the worst completion rates of all, doubtless owing to the isolation of the students, the heavy dependence on reliable IT systems, and the difficulties of self-motivation without the friendly support of fellow students face-to-face, the lack of availability of university study facilities, and a less obvious shared learning experience.

Certification: Transcripts/Diploma Supplements

Graduates are entering an increasingly competitive employment environment and not only seek clear and accurate information about their academic achievements, but also want recognition for all HEI-sponsored activity outside their accredited programme of study as well as comprehensive background detail on that programme for third parties, especially concerning content and approaches to learning, teaching and assessment. As the Burgess Report (Universities UK, 2007) recognised, a large majority of UK universities provided students with increasingly detailed background information and performance detail through the European Diploma Supplement and Transcript (see below), but broader individual achievements, such as non-accredited placement or work experience, local or national awards, volunteering, and so on, largely went unrecognised in formal award documentation.

The Diploma Supplement, introduced throughout the European Union in 2005 as part of the Bologna Agreement, gives information about students' academic achievement and also gives more information on their programme of study, how awards have been made and the national education system. The information contained within the document gives employers and other institutions abroad the ability to assess applicants without further reference back to the university or the student for clarification, following a common template that is instantly recognisable.

Although challenges still face universities in ensuring accuracy, clarity, currency and validity of certification, particularly in the international context, sector-wide use of the Higher Education Achievement Report (HEAR), proposed by Burgess, is expected by 2010–11 and this should provide students and interested third parties with a consistent and reliable evidence base. It is expected that the HEAR will provide a rich picture of student achievement. The HEAR will include not only the academic transcript, but additional information about a student's academic and non-academic achievements during their period of study, verified by the university. It will probably also include contextual information about the university and UK higher education qualifications frameworks and processes, currently presented in the Diploma Supplement.

Award of Credit and Exam Boards

The servicing of assessment boards has been typically a heavy process, being time-consuming both in preparation (to ensure accurate marks entry, provide administrative support for marks entry and support report production) and in operation (the volume of documentation required, lengthy discussions of cohort and individual student performance, undertaking module review alongside confirmation of marks or outcomes). Issues may arise regarding inconsistent practice within and across schools, departments and faculties, and in the past, wide discretion may have been used in the application of regulations.

It is important for universities regularly to review assessment board processes, openly questioning approaches currently and traditionally in use. It is useful to query how best to reduce the paperwork, for example, by asking:

- Do we need all the data we ask for?
- Can we find paper-reduced ways of presenting the information?
- Do we need multi-tier boards?
- Can we combine and thereby reduce attendance time for internal and external examiners?

- Does everyone need to attend?
- Can we safely leave more decision-making to the system and to smaller pre-board groupings?
- Can we reassess the role of external examiners at boards to make better use of their limited time in supporting broader review discussions?

Approaches taken to exam boards are outlined further later in the chapter.

The volume and timeliness of feedback continue to be the most significant concerns raised by students in local and national surveys. We need to explain clearly the various forms of feedback, which are vital for diverse learners (including written feedback, oral feedback, critiques, model answers, online responses, and so on), and build this explicitly into approval processes.

Anecdotal evidence suggests that students (and potentially some academic staff) do not generally treat referrals (the requirement to retake an assignment or resit an examination) as seriously as they should, especially where any reassessment period is distant from the initial assessment and there is limited academic guidance or support available.

Late Approvals and Extenuating Circumstances

Challenges arise in managing late approvals, where a student asks for permission to submit an assignment without penalty beyond its stipulated deadline date. These include:

- ensuring acceptable reasons and quality of evidence provided;
- student understanding of relevant processes;
- inconsistency in academic and administrative roles in the processes.

Universities are noticing an increasing volume and diversity of claims being made for special circumstances to be considered in mitigation of student assessment. This can lead to more time being spent scrutinising each claim, and increased system complexity to enable extenuating circumstances to be reported to assessment boards. It may also lead to inconsistent practice across boards in applying regulations to extenuating circumstances. At Northumbria, for example, boards have discretion either to disregard modules subject to extenuating circumstances claims or defer the student in those modules, depending on individual or local circumstances. Some view this practice as providing useful flexibility in the application of the regulations which is to the benefit of individual students, but evidence shows that, because of the difficulty in tracking decisions made, it can very easily lead to inequitable decision-making.

Should assessment processes keep the scrutiny of personal extenuating circumstance claims simple by determining only whether they had 'no effect' or 'an effect' on a student's performance? Some institutions will consider how seriously a student's performance has been affected by the claimed extenuating circumstances and grade the outcome of the claim accordingly, e.g. 'no effect', 'some effect', 'serious effect'. This is reported to the examination board for its use in determining progression or award outcomes. Calibrating each extenuating circumstance claim in this way can be a very time-consuming task. Should we consider practice elsewhere to help reduce the volume of claims for examinations, such as 'fit to sit' (which requires students, before sitting an examination, to declare themselves fit to take the assessment; they would then be unable to submit an extenuating circumstances claim for the period leading up to the examination itself)?

How These Issues Have Been Tackled at the Two Universities

Proactive approaches to resolving issues have been taken in both universities. At the University of Nottingham the approach also has to take into consideration the university's international campuses.

Managing Assessment Systems and Processes

SCHEDULING OF ASSESSMENTS

At the University of Nottingham, exams running during the main university exam periods are centrally scheduled. The university examines at the end of each semester (January and May/June), with a resit exam period in August/September each year. The number of examinations to be scheduled necessitates the running of three exam sessions each day. Saturdays are included as examination days.

In 2008, exams were scheduled for around 18,500 students, equating to 69,000 desk spaces, with 1,200 papers being produced in each exam period. Reasonable adjustments were arranged for around 1,200 students in each exam period, and overseas exam arrangements were made for around 300 students in the resit period. Information about student module enrolments is held on the student record systems and is downloaded to an exam timetabling system to schedule exams.

The Exams Office liaises with school exams officers about the schedule of examinations that are to be timetabled in a given semester. At this point, the schools also indicate other scheduling constraints that they would like to be taken into consideration when producing a timetable. The Exams Office then produces a timetable, which is initially generated electronically and then 'drilled down' manually to provide the best timetable for students, taking into account scheduling constraints. Students are not normally expected to sit more than two exams in a day, and where possible these will not be consecutive exams. Student feedback suggested that taking an evening exam followed by a morning exam was problematic, particularly during the January exam period, and is taken into consideration where possible. The completed timetable is circulated to schools for comment and checking that all expected exams have been included approximately one week before being published to the students as the definitive timetable.

The timetable is published to students via the university electronic portal six weeks before the start of each exam period. To avoid confusion, room locations and seat numbers are withheld at this stage while arrangements are made for students requiring reasonable adjustments for examinations. Students can be added to or removed from exams up until the point when room locations and seat numbers are published, three weeks before the start of each exam period for all students.

Once room locations and seat numbers are published, it is not possible to add students to exams. Students not on the register are permitted to take an exam following a 'green card procedure' whereby they sit the paper at their own risk, with registration issues being resolved after the exam.

The examination scheduling processes are very similar at Northumbria, with the same challenges being faced.

The Academic Calendar

Northumbria University is set to reorganise its academic calendar from 2009–10, and similar issues have been considered at Nottingham. Plans for immediate change and further discussion at Northumbria include:

- the removal of the summative assessment period (typically, formal examinations at each level) at the end of semester 1, in part to remove the long break in learning and teaching activity over the Christmas and New Year period;
- encouragement to review assessment strategies, for example consideration of alternative assessment methods, particularly those enabling assessment more closely aligned to learning;
- reconsidering the volume, timing and spread of assessments on study programmes, including specification of assessments against programme rather than module learning outcomes to highlight unnecessary duplication;
- rethinking assessment at level 4, with the possibility of progression based on pass/fail and greater assessment focus on formative feedback, integrative assessments, assessment for learning, and so on;

- consideration of scheduling referrals closer to the point of failure, at a minimum bringing forward the formal examination resit period to before the summer, within three to four weeks of original sitting.

STUDENTS REQUIRING REASONABLE ADJUSTMENTS FOR EXAMINATIONS: DISABLED STUDENTS AND THOSE WITH LONG-TERM MEDICAL CONDITIONS

Disabled students who require reasonable adjustments for examinations are assessed by staff of the Academic Support Services team at the University of Nottingham. Academic support tutors are able to communicate adjustments to the Exams Office via an electronic form, which adds the student and his or her requirements.

The Exams Office makes the adjustments for the students, and these are communicated to the students via the portal, together with their timetable. Exams for students with adjustments are held in rooms other than the main location to allow for extra time and individual requirements. Similar support and communication processes operate at Northumbria.

Streamlining through electronic solutions has enabled this group of students to be managed through inclusion into processes already in existence, meaning that students requiring reasonable adjustments for their exams, with the exception of a note of the adjustments being made, see exactly the same information at the same time as non-disabled students.

REASONABLE ADJUSTMENTS FOR STUDENTS FOLLOWING AN ACCIDENT OR SHORT-TERM ILLNESS

Owing to the short-term and 'last-minute' nature of accidents and short-term illnesses, time constraints normally mean that there is no time for students to be assessed by Academic Support for adjustments to their exam arrangements. The University of Nottingham has introduced a process whereby an agreed standard set of arrangements may be put in place for a student without the need for an assessment, and similar adjustments for such students are in place at Northumbria.

Up until three weeks before the start of each exam period, the Exams Office will make temporary adjustments. After this time the volume of examinations and large number of arrangements being made for disabled students preclude this. Academic schools or departments may decide to make an alternative arrangement for a student's exams 'in-house' from the standard set of arrangements at this point, or, where this is not possible for logistical reasons, may consider setting an alternative form of assessment or deal with the student under the university's extenuating circumstances procedures.

RELIGIOUS OBSERVANCE

At the University of Nottingham, students who are unable to take examinations on particular days for reasons of religious observance (for example, Orthodox Jewish students who do not wish to take exams on Friday evenings or Saturdays) complete a Religious Observance Form, which is authorised by their personal tutor and submitted to their school exams officer by a specific deadline each semester. The school exams officer makes the Exams Office aware of these at the scheduling stage, and every effort is made to accommodate requests. However, owing to the logistical difficulties of scheduling a large number of examinations involving many thousands of students in a limited number of days, this may not always be possible.

In circumstances where it is not possible to schedule examinations to take students' requests into account, and the student has completed the Religious Observance Form by the published deadline, the school concerned may make the following alternative arrangements:

- setting an alternative examination paper to be taken on another day;
- permitting the student(s) to take the examination as an alternative assessment candidate at either an earlier or a later start time, on condition that the student is able to provide a chaperone acceptable to the school, who will accompany the student in the intervening period;
- setting an alternative form of assessment.

Schools make every effort to ensure that an alternative arrangement for a student is made, but in exceptional circumstances they may need approval to permit the student(s) to take the examination 'as if for the first time' during the August/September resit period under the university's extenuating circumstances policy. Similar adjustments for such students are in place at Northumbria.

THE ASSESSMENT OF POSTGRADUATE STUDENTS

The University of Nottingham has many facilities to help international students acclimatise (for example, Welcome Week, the provision of support staff in the International Office, in schools and in the Student Services Centre, and the provision of academic support, in particular for study skills). There is also a need to consider the needs of part-time students, for example whether teaching and assessment should take place outside the traditional nine to five Monday to Friday schedule, and whether forms of assessment should be modified, perhaps replacing timetabled examinations with different forms of assessment that could be taken more flexibly. Given the size of the University of Nottingham and the numbers of students involved, central systems may not be flexible enough to support the different learning and assessment needs of such diverse groups of students. The University of Nottingham's assessment policies allow schools wide discretion in the format of assessments, and allow them to timetable examinations locally. In addition, in 2007–8 the university took the step of devolving responsibility for decision-making on extenuating circumstances to school level, hence schools can be more flexible in considering the many different sorts of circumstances that can affect postgraduate students, including work commitments (after all, in many cases part-time Master's degrees are being taken for work-related reasons).

If a module is assessed either solely or partly by examination, then, unless a school chooses to set examinations locally, the timing of those assessments will tend to be the same (in many universities this is in January for the autumn semester and May for the spring semester) regardless of whether a student is taking the course full time or part time. Part-time students with work commitments can find this extremely inflexible: for example, the University of Nottingham Procedure and Guidance for Dealing with Extenuating Circumstances for Students on Taught Courses states that paid employment or voluntary work is an example of an unacceptable circumstance for missing an examination or an assessment deadline, stating, 'It is the student's responsibility to ensure that any paid employment or voluntary work does not interfere with their ability to engage with their studies or assessments. This includes unexpected work commitments and/or deadlines'.

For convenience, the Central Registry at Nottingham uses the same processes for giving and collecting information on assessment results for all postgraduate taught students. However, this does raise issues for a number of reasons. For example, courses may have been taught in blocks rather than by weekly lectures and may not have fitted in with the university's usual teaching schedules, and exam boards may meet at different times of the year for some courses (e.g. cohorts based overseas).

Furthermore, for distance learning courses, there are often no standard start dates, which means that coursework deadlines have to be set on an individual basis, making it difficult for all students' performance to be considered by school examination boards. This can mean that student records are left in limbo, because the results from part-time courses are received at a different time from those for full-time courses, leading to operational difficulties in, for example, arranging reassessments for these students in the usual August/September reassessment period.

Another issue arises from the University of Nottingham Regulations for taught Master's degrees, postgraduate diplomas and postgraduate certificate courses, which permit students who have failed to have 'a right to one re-assessment in each failed module at a time to be specified by the admitting School but normally by the end of the following academic year or equivalent for part-time students'.

The flexibility open to schools in setting the timing of their reassessments can mean heavy extra financial costs for students who are expected to take reassessments as external candidates in the following academic session.

Award of Credit and Exam Boards: How Exam Boards are Managed at the University of Nottingham

For the majority of the university's taught programmes, each school will hold two formal examination boards per academic year. One of their main responsibilities is to apply both the university's and the course regulations to each candidate in the school, including those studying at the China or Malaysia campuses, and provide a progression decision to the Registry. Upon receipt, the Registry staff carry out a number of semi-automated processes to update the student records system with the board's decisions.

The recorded progression data not only serve to complete each student's academic record, but also drive a number of portal channels through which each student can see their module marks, progression status and, where applicable, the classification of their degree. The student record also drives the university's online registration system and graduation proceedings. Thus, ensuring that the student record is correct is of paramount importance to the integrity of a number of processes.

Over recent years, the Registry has worked hard to streamline and improve the way in which boards submit their decisions. In advance of the board meeting, central Registry staff populate a 'decisions template' with the names of the students who are expected to require either a progression or an award decision. After or during the exam board, the board's secretary can then record the board's decision for each student using a drop-down menu. The university has deliberately limited the kinds of decisions that the board can record to those that are encoded in the university's assessment regulations, although the board may still recommend a course of action that is not covered by the university's published regulations if presented with a particularly complex case that cannot be dealt with under existing regulatory provision.

Standardising the process of submitting decisions has produced a number of significant gains for both central administrative staff and school staff:

- The time needed for central processing is significantly reduced by having all schools using the same electronic mechanism for recording the board's decisions.
- The submission of electronic decisions allows data to be quickly

and accurately uploaded into the student record system, without the need for large amounts of data entry or rekeying.

- Once the board's decisions have been submitted, the communication of the outcomes does not rest with the school, allowing its staff more time for providing one-to-one feedback to students.
- Establishing an institution-wide mechanism for submitting the board's decisions has removed much ambiguity from the process. This, in turn, has reduced the probability of central administrative staff misinterpreting the board's decision and conveying incorrect information to students.

How Exam Boards are Managed at Northumbria University

Previously, Northumbria's information systems would produce basic student profiles for assessment boards, presenting component marks and an overall outcome for each module, and a percentage-level average against which progression or award decisions would be made. Although regulations would guide boards in determining overall outcome, including classification, there would typically be much discussion about individual and cohort performance, the impact of extenuating circumstances, the significance of exit velocity and other factors that board members felt to be important. Boards, too, were used to review delivery during the year.

Boards had significant discretion in determining outcomes based on the profiles but were criticised for their subjectivity and inconsistency. As student numbers grew, it also became impractical to review modules and programmes. With the greater volume of board activity, tracking decisions to ensure consistent application of the regulations and use of discretion became extremely difficult.

Northumbria's current information system generates richer reporting for assessment boards, crucially recommending progression or award outcome for each student based on rules defined by university regulations and approved local variations. Once module outcomes have been approved at the first-tier module assessment boards, the second-tier progression and awards boards confirm the system-generated recommendations for each student. Extenuating circumstances claims are considered before the board, their impact already having been taken account of by the system when progression or award outcomes are recommended. The impact of academic misconduct is also taken into account and applied according to university rules and approved local variations. The final assessment boards have little work to do apart from rubber-stamping the recommendations already made. With its embedded rules applying the regulations and decisions of preliminary module boards and extenuating circumstances and academic misconduct panels, the system should generate objective, accurate and consistent recommendations, with, as a consequence, less time needed post-boards to adjust and correct the data. Time spent in preparing for and attending boards should also reduce with the declining need for discussion and use of discretion.

The effectiveness of this approach, and its credibility with staff and external examiners, relies on maintaining accurate core assessment data, valid regulations and embedded rules, and a reliable information system. The key challenge for administrative and academic managers is to establish an infrastructure that can ensure the quality of the base data and the integrity of the automated processes. It is also important to ensure transparent and participative processes for reviewing regulations, and the operation of boards and related decision-making bodies.

Dealing with Extenuating Circumstances at the University of Nottingham

Students' claims of extenuating circumstances are considered by key members of the school's board of examiners, normally before the main meeting of the board. Their role is to determine whether the student's absence or under-performance in an assessment took place with 'sufficient cause'. In order to demonstrate sufficient cause, the student must demonstrate, with third-party supporting evidence, that attempting the assessment would not have been a reasonable expectation in the light of the student's circumstances. If the claim is upheld by the examiners, any marks associated with the first attempt are discarded (irrespective of whether the mark was a pass), and another assessment is offered once the extenuating circumstances have ceased, or at least abated. Conveying the board's decision to the Registry is done through the decisions template at the end of each stage of a student's degree course and communicated to the student through the portal.

When considering the validity of the student's claim, the board seeks to find answers to the following questions:

- *Timing.* How do the claimed extenuating circumstances relate to the timing of when the assessment was offered?
- *Severity.* Were the claimed circumstances severe enough to make any mark (or absence) unreliable?
- *Evidence.* Is there any third-party, independent evidence that is supplied by a credible source? If so, does it support the student's claim?
- *Impact.* If there is supporting evidence, does it just recount the facts of what happened, or does it explain the impact the circumstances had on the student's ability to undertake an assessment?

To allow the board to make an informed decision, the most useful evidence is that which independently outlines the impact that the circumstances have had on the student at the time that they were expected to present themselves for assessment. Typically, this is a note from a doctor, counsellor or other professional – generated at the time of the event rather than retrospectively. Of course, there are sometimes valid reasons why the student might not have been able to seek professional help at the time, and these are considered on an individual basis on their merits.

If the student disagrees with the board's decision, then they may appeal on one of three grounds: (1) that there was a procedural irregularity; (2) that the board made a manifestly unreasonable decision; or (3) that the board was biased or prejudiced. The burden of proof for each of these grounds lies squarely with the student, and an appeal that does not successfully make a prima facie case is unlikely to succeed.

Dealing with Late Approvals and Extenuating Circumstances at Northumbria University

Broad principles and procedures exist at Northumbria, with specified penalties for unapproved late submission and agreed processes for evidencing and scrutinising claims for extenuating circumstances.

In 2007–8 the university reviewed the penalties applied to late submission of assignment work, investigating practice across the sector and noting extremely wide variations in penalties applied. A significant number of universities allow a degree of late submission without penalty, or apply sliding penalty scales depending on lateness. Northumbria decided to retain its policy of penalising unapproved late submission with a zero mark for the assessment component. This is overwhelmingly viewed by students and staff as an appropriate and unequivocal policy, where supported by a transparent, equitable process for receiving and authorising late approval requests.

To reflect the differing requirements across programmes and subject areas, schools have established their own procedures for guiding the submission and authorisation of late approval requests. While a degree of local decision-making is useful (for example, sports science staff are best placed to determine whether participation in British University Sports Association events is acceptable evidence for a late approval request), some consistency in practice is also important.

The review revealed weaknesses in managing late approvals:

- some staff and student confusion about how to request, from whom to seek authorisation, timescales involved and evidence to be provided;
- inconsistencies in the handling of late approvals locally and across the university.

Best practice is to be shared during 2008–9, with common standards for submission and authorisation to be agreed, which will still permit acceptable local variations. Within Northumbria's highly devolved structure, with nine academic schools each with a dedicated administrative function headed by a school registrar, there exists a strong tradition and desire to share best administrative practice. School registrars meet regularly to help shape and influence university policy and to develop common administrative service standards. Using school administrative staff to receive and authorise late approvals, thereby releasing academic staff time, will be considered, and the relationship between late approvals and personal extenuating circumstances more clearly articulated in policy and procedure.

Case Study:
A Centralised Invigilation Service

Institutions can attempt to reduce the potential for students to commit an academic offence during an examination or assessment through clear communication of what constitutes such an offence, the use of plagiarism detection software for coursework and dissertation submissions, and effective penalties. At the University of Nottingham an invigilation service for centrally scheduled main university exams was introduced in 2007. Schools are encouraged to use the central service, although they may still provide invigilators for exams if they wish. Invigilators are recruited both from the university's postgraduate research students and externally (typically, retired members of staff from the university or other educational institutions). They undergo a training programme that includes discussion of regulations and procedures, and examples of 'real-life' scenarios, and culminates in a multiple-choice test that is also available online. New invigilators are paired with experienced invigilators for a number of slots, and performance is monitored by observation and feedback from staff and students. All continuing invigilators are required to attend a refresher session annually, where they are also made aware of any changes to procedure or policy. Invigilators are encouraged in providing a professional service to ensure the quality of the student experience and the operation of examinations within university regulations and following consistent procedures. All invigilators are identified by their 'Invigilator' T-shirts, making them easily recognisable to academic staff attending the beginning of their papers and students alike. A feedback session is held with invigilators annually, where issues that have arisen during exam periods can be addressed.

Marks Processing and Transcripts/Diploma Supplements

At the University of Nottingham, mark sheets are processed centrally, although the school returning the mark sheet is responsible for the accuracy of the mark returned. Mark sheets are generated and processed electronically. Once all mark sheets are returned and uploaded into the student record system, degree and progression calculations are run, taking into account university regulations. Graduation Diploma Supplements are produced in-house at the University of Nottingham and are issued to graduating students at the same time as they receive their degree certificate (normally at a graduation ceremony held at the university).

Students are able to request additional copies of the Diploma Supplement and also copies of the transcript element only. They are able to obtain interim transcripts of marks throughout their studies. The cost of production and length of document were important considerations, and the Diploma Supplement was designed to be no more than four pages in length.

The first page of the Diploma Supplement is security-printed and contains a bespoke University of Nottingham hologram on the front page. This page contains information relating to the student, qualification achieved and transcript of marks taken from the student record system. Certification of the supplement is also on this page. The second page is pre-printed and includes links to university web pages. Other pages include a description of higher education in England, Wales and Northern Ireland, together with a diagram of the higher education qualification levels in England, Wales and Northern Ireland, and again are pre-printed. The use of a centralised marks processing system, together with tested internal procedures for ensuring the quality of the data, made the transition to using the Diploma Supplement a smooth one. Proposed developments include the production of an updated version of the Diploma Supplement that will make less use of webpage references for additional information.

Guidance on Managing Assessment Systems and Processes

Within the individual university, it is essential that good communication channels are developed and maintained to allow absorption of external policy into the structure and culture of the organisation and to ensure that relevant policies and procedures are communicated clearly to the staff and students involved. All universities' systems are likely to start from common sound principles, which then vary according to the local context. Here we propose some solutions to some common pitfalls, based on our own experiences.

TABLE 9.1 Common Pitfalls in Managing Assessment Systems and Processes

Potential pitfall	*Solution*
School staff feeling unsure of how to apply complex regulations correctly	Key members of the central administration can provide regular training sessions to all staff involved in assessment. It is a good idea also to provide bespoke training to staff as and when necessary and ensure that they are automatically notified when revisions are made to the regulations.
Over-reliance on IT for delivering key student processes	Key members of the central administration can work with colleagues in Information Services to develop a schedule of critical processes that require dedicated technical support at specified times in the academic year.
Reaching different conclusions on students with similar extenuating circumstances	The publication of very clear guidelines on the minimum standard of supporting evidence can help to avoid inconsistency.
Administrative staff being unaware of how the student record is used for other processes	The production of a regularly updated procedures manual that outlines the procedural steps to follow when undertaking core operations on the records system. This can be backed up with bespoke training leading up to an assessment period.
School staff being unaware of key deadlines and the reasons behind them	A university portal can be used to communicate with groups of staff identified as 'Exams Officers' (including exams administrators) and those identified as 'Marks Processing' contacts. A monthly newsletter containing key deadlines for the forthcoming month can be invaluable, as can an annual schedule of key dates and processes published well in advance.
Students being unaware of key deadlines and what is expected of them	Effective communication means, including school/department handbooks, the university portal, targeted 'Message of the Day' announcements on data screens and by email, and regular reviewing and updating of university web pages can be effective in ensuring that students have key information and are able to act on this at appropriate times.

Conclusions

The task of managing assessment systems and processes is becoming increasingly complex, and one of the challenges is to ensure that administrators and managers are able to respond effectively to meet the demands of ever-changing environments.

Those in central services need to support not only the university's schools and faculties, but also individual students, who increasingly have more bespoke requirements during the assessment process. The need for a flexible and proactive approach in all areas of student-centric administration is essential in the modern university. The importance of robust, reliable and flexible business systems cannot be overestimated as universities seek to streamline processes and procedures, which is particularly important in the current climate of internalisation and widening participation in higher education. Visibly equitable treatment and a consistent approach to issues are also important factors as the student population becomes more demanding, with raised expectations of what the university should offer. This is likely to increase in the United Kingdom with the anticipated lifting of the fee cap in 2010, allowing universities to charge higher fees.

It is anticipated that these challenges will increase in the future as the student population changes, with the number of full-time undergraduate students potentially being the smallest cohort of students with widening participation and an increase in part-time and distance learning. In the future, the culture and structures of organisations may need to change in order to respond to the multiple challenges ahead.

Useful Websites

http://www.nottingham.ac.uk
http://www.northumbria.ac.uk

Further Reading

QAA *Academic Credit in Higher Education in England.* Online, available at: www.qaa.ac.uk.
QAA *Code of Practice.* Online, available at: www.qaa.ac.uk.

References

Bologna Agreement (1999). Online, available at: www.europeunit.ac.uk (accessed November 2008).
Leathwood, C. (2005) 'Assessment policy and practice in higher education: purpose, standards and equity', *Assessment and Evaluation in Higher Education,* 30 (3): 307–24.
Newby, H. (2003) 'The management of change in higher education', *Higher Education Management and Policy,* 15 (1): 9–22.
Procedure and Guidance for dealing with Extenuating Circumstances for Students on Taught Courses. Online, at: www.nottingham.ac.uk/quality-manual/assessment/pro-guid-ext-cir. htm#standard (accessed November 2008).
QAA (2008) *Outcomes from Institutional Audit: Assessment of Students Second Series.* Online, available at: www.qaa.ac.uk (accessed November 2008).
UKCOSA (2004) *Broadening Our Horizons: International Students in UK Universities and Colleges,* Report of the UKCOSA Survey, London: Press/SRHE.
Universities UK (2007) *Beyond the Honours Degree Classification,* London: Burgess Group Final Report.
University's Regulations for Taught Masters Degrees, Postgraduate Diplomas and Postgraduate Certificate Courses. Online, available at: www.nottingham.ac.uk/quality-manual/study-regulations/taught-postgraduate-regulations.htm (accessed November 2008).

CHAPTER 10

Dealing with Complaints and Appeals

LIZ BUCKTON
University of Sheffield

with **LIS CHILD**
Nottingham Trent University

and **JACKIE FLOWERS**
Birmingham City University

Introduction

At family occasions or dinner parties, when the conversation turns to careers it is hard enough to give an accurate or interesting description of what a university administrator does. If you try talking about complaints and appeals, then it becomes even harder to keep people's attention, yet this is a crucial strand of work for some university administrators, and key to presenting a good public face to our students. The three contributors to this chapter are university administrators with extensive experience of dealing with complaints and appeals in various universities across the United Kingdom.

So what exactly does the administration of complaints and appeals in an academic environment involve? One of the first things to note is that working in this field is challenging. It is stressful, yet the work can be rewarding. There is a great feeling of satisfaction when you know you've made a difference to someone's life or when you've managed to solve a seemingly unsolvable problem. The human element involved ensures that the work is never boring. Each complaint is different and each student or academic reacts in different ways, according to the circumstances. Change in university systems is perpetual and sometimes rapid, often brought about by drivers such as new

159

legislation, shifts in cultures and even the outcome of high-profile cases. A positive corollary is that very few people have an in-depth knowledge of the minutiae of complaints and appeals procedures, and it is possible to end up being an expert quite quickly. Training and mentoring are extremely important to help develop this expertise and to ensure continuity and consistency across an institution and within the higher education (HE) sector as a whole.

Case Study 1:
The Contract Plagiarist

Mr X, a taught Master's student, has submitted his dissertation, which has been marked. In the meantime a colleague from another HE institution has spotted a posting on an essay cheating website and recognises it as coming from a student in the department of Y. He sends an email to the course director, alerting him to this potential 'contract plagiarism' case. When Mr X's dissertation is checked, it appears to be written in rather eloquent language, totally different from his normal writing style. What is more, the dissertation title matches the one posted on the cheat website. The department is convinced that unfair means have been used, and a full investigation is undertaken.

Do you think:
- that the alleged misconduct should be formally reported for action under the institution's discipline regulations? Or
- that informal action should be taken within the academic department, following institutional guidelines? Or
- that there is anything the university can do to stop students using such cheat websites?

Mr X then complains about the way his case has been handled, saying that the course has been badly taught and demanding a refund of his fees. He doesn't like the way he is being accused of using unfair means, and lodges a formal complaint against the lecturer concerned. In the meantime, Mr X has posted a series of extremely abusive messages about the lecturer on the social networking site Facebook.

- What should you do next?

This is a very serious case of buying or commissioning an assignment, as it appears to demonstrate clear intent to deceive. For this reason, formal disciplinary action is likely to be taken, with a view to expelling the student. The institution needs to make it clear to students that submitting bought or commissioned assignments is a serious disciplinary offence (as is selling them), and must demonstrate that it will not tolerate such behaviour.

Inappropriate use of social networking sites is a form of harassment and could constitute a separate disciplinary charge in itself. In the meantime, the complaint needs to be handled in accordance with the university's complaints procedure, but it is important to have clear guidance in place to deal with such complex cases and to be aware which procedure takes precedence over another.

Training Staff in Responding to Student Complaints

As part of its risk management strategy, every university should provide training for academic and support staff in handling student complaints. The purpose of this training is to enable staff to feel confident in using their complaints procedure and to understand and apply principles of good practice. This will help them to identify potential complaints and nip them in the bud, or resolve them as close as possible to the point of origin. The training should focus on improving written and oral communication skills, acknowledging student complaints appropriately and responding positively and effectively. Staff need to be aware that students will not necessarily say, 'I want to make a complaint about . . .' but may express their dissatisfaction or concerns in a more obscure and roundabout way. Staff who can pick up these subtle signals can be very successful in fending off full-blown formal complaints. Complaints handlers should also be aware of the general worry that students often express, usually to students' union advisers, that if they complain, their grades will suffer. As part of complaints training it is useful to get some idea of the participants' personal experience of student issues and how they currently handle them. Discussing actual case studies (in strict confidence) offers opportunities to highlight and share points of good practice. Staff also need to understand that student complaints can provide useful feedback to a university, thus ensuring that improvements can be made to both teaching and services. Handling complaints effectively can enhance the student experience and aid retention.

Understanding Complaints and Appeals

As with many other areas, the terminology for complaints and appeals will vary from one country to another and from one institution to another, which is largely a result of different histories, cultures and management structures.

Some examples that spring to mind are the terms 'fitness to practise' as opposed to 'fitness for practice', 'registration' by comparison with 'enrolment' and so on, but there is a degree of commonality across universities nonetheless. In general, the term 'complaints and appeals' covers student complaints at varying levels, from informal complaints against academic or service departments through to formal grievances (or their equivalent), as well as appeals against academic decisions and appeals arising from disciplinary, fitness to practise and academic progress procedures.

Cases may be handled by schools or faculties or be administered centrally; the detail of how such complaints are dealt with is not necessarily relevant here, as the principles are essentially the same. In the late 1990s, John Gledhill wrote, 'There are very few rights and wrongs in determining the proper way to manage students . . . choose the methods which fit your needs and do it well' (1999). This still holds good. In other words, it is not so much what you do as how you do it. As long as an institution's published procedures are fair and reasonable and those procedures are followed scrupulously, then, by and large, things should be fine. The problems mainly start when procedures are not followed properly, even if such decisions are taken with the student's best interests in mind.

Complaints and appeals are often grouped together because, quite simply, it is not easy to distinguish them, since cases are often multi-layered and complex. For example, students might submit an academic appeal if they are dissatisfied with their grade (providing there are appropriate grounds for them to do so). At the same time, they might complain about a lack of supervision or conditions in the examination hall, and it can be hard to work out which is the appeal and which is a complaint; the two merge and become 'entangled', depending on individual cases. It is for this reason that the United Kingdom Quality Assurance Agency (QAA) code of practice treats the two as interchangeable:

> A 'complaint' is defined as the expression of a specific concern about the provision of a course, or a programme of study, or a related academic service. An 'academic appeal' is defined as a request for the review of a decision of an academic body charged with decisions on student progression, assessment and awards.
>
> (Quality Assurance Agency, 2000)

When putting together the second edition of the code, the QAA proposed separating the two categories, but, having listened to feedback from across the sector, decided against it.

For an example of how various complaints and appeals procedures might fit together, see Figure 10.1 (p. 164).

Case Study 2:
Complex Grievances

Miss Y was subject to an allegation that she was not fit to practise. An internal panel found no substance to the case, but raised some concerns that needed to be addressed. She had been suspended from placement pending the outcome of the panel hearing but was allowed to continue with her academic work. However, she did not hand in any assignments and received a 'fail' for not submitting her dissertation.

Miss Y put in a claim to the University Mitigations Committee, which decided that her claim for mitigation was in fact an academic appeal, since she claimed that misleading advice from her tutor was the reason why she had not submitted work. In addition, she had been very stressed by the allegations. The case was referred back to her faculty under the university's academic appeals regulations.

Miss Y then also made a complaint about the member of staff who had first raised the fitness to practise concerns and also claimed that the fitness to practise procedure had not been properly followed.

This type of case, which is not uncommon, would in many institutions be covered by four different procedures: mitigating circumstances, academic appeals, student complaints and fitness to practise – each with its own different processes, timescales and remedies. Often the responsibility for each procedure lies within a different administrative department and/or at a different level within a university.

An institution should ensure that there is discretion to deal with such complex grievances without a student having to follow a number of different procedures, deal with several different people or face unnecessary delays.

Providing Information About Complaints Procedures

As already noted, the culture relating to complaints and appeals is continually undergoing change. Up until the late 1990s, HE institutions tended to take the view that if you published your complaints procedure, then you were likely to be flooded with complaints. So, if an organisation had a procedure (and not every institution did), it was kept well hidden (at Sheffield University it was on the back page of the Students' Charter, handed out in leaflet format to first-year students at registration). Today, such practices seem difficult to understand or justify.

Even before the Office of the Independent Adjudicator for Higher Education (OIA) started up in 2004 as the new independent body for student

Figure 10.1 Flow Chart for Academic Appeals, Complaints, Discipline, Fitness to Practise and Progress.

Source: University of Sheffield, www.shef.ac.uk/ssd/squ/grid.html. Reproduced with permission.

Note: The diagrams below show the different stages in the procedures described. A procedure can complete at any point indicated by a box outlined with a bold frame or can be taken further if it is linked to another box by an outgoing arrow.

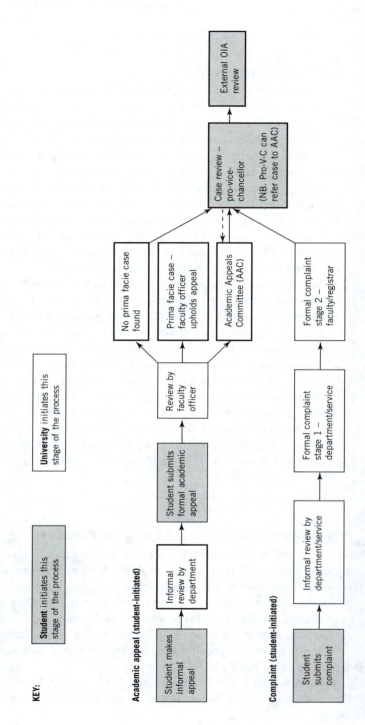

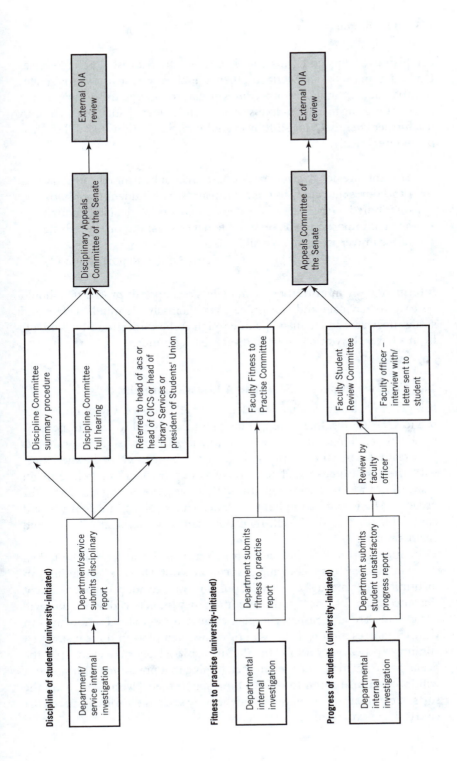

Discipline of students (university-initiated)

Department/service internal investigation → Department/service submits disciplinary report

- Discipline Committee summary procedure → Disciplinary Appeals Committee of the Senate
- Discipline Committee full hearing → Disciplinary Appeals Committee of the Senate
- Referred to head of acs or head of CICS or head of Library Services or president of Students' Union

Disciplinary Appeals Committee of the Senate → External OIA review

Fitness to practise (university-initiated)

Departmental internal investigation → Department submits fitness to practise report → Faculty Fitness to Practise Committee → Appeals Committee of the Senate → External OIA review

Progress of students (university-initiated)

Departmental internal investigation → Department submits student unsatisfactory progress report → Review by faculty officer

- Faculty Student Review Committee → Appeals Committee of the Senate → External OIA review
- Faculty officer – interview with/ letter sent to student

complaints in England (this role is termed the Scottish Public Services Ombudsman (SPSO) in Scotland), there was already a move towards greater transparency. Complaints procedures began to emerge from their hiding places, appearing in easy-to-access websites and student handbooks. The OIA has further energised this shift by encouraging institutions to publish their procedures openly:

> Students are not always clear about sources of help and the internal procedures that apply to their complaints. The Student Handbook distributed at the start of the course may not be detailed enough and it is important to place the up to date regulations on the website of the university in an accessible place.
>
> (OIA Annual Report, 2006: 14)

Information on an institution's complaints and appeals procedures should be easy to navigate and the procedures themselves should be fair and straightforward, in language plain enough to be understood by students from all over the world and from diverse backgrounds.

The Negative Impact of Failing to Address Complaints

It is generally accepted that complaints are an effective way of improving services, as wrongs that have not been put right tend to stick in people's minds much longer than good experiences. What is more, students (especially international students) tend to share these bad experiences with friends, to negative effect. Conversely, a brush-off or failure by an institution to engage with something that has gone wrong can fester for decades. The idea of 'complaints as jewels' has evolved in recent years; if complaints are handled well, then they can play a crucial role in good customer care.

In other words, if we don't learn from our mistakes and get it right, then a lot of time may be spent trying to sort things out. However, sometimes an institution does manage a case well, but students are not prepared to accept the outcome; unless they get the resolution they think they deserve, they will not give up. These persistent complainers may resort to legal action and can tie up resources for long periods of time (over ten years in some instances), running up heavy legal bills for the university. They may even 'spill the beans' to the media or via the internet, hoping that press and public interest will force an institution to resolve the issue in their favour. These are the sorts of complaints that an independent body such as the OIA and even the courts may never resolve.

One possible way of discouraging persistent complainers is to set time limits for submitting complaints. At one time, few higher education complaints procedures specified when a complaint might be considered to be out of time, but from around 2004 things began to change – possibly because institutions (including Sheffield University) have followed the OIA's lead. From the outset, the OIA's scheme rules specified that complaints were unlikely to be entertained three months after an institution's internal procedures had been completed and three years after the events complained about had happened. Introducing time limits makes it possible to reject a complaint concerning a matter that occurred several years previously, which otherwise might have been difficult to resolve after so much time had elapsed.

New Stakeholders

UK institutions are increasingly seeing complaints from parents as well as students (who can be highly embarrassed by such interference). From 2006, with tuition fees coming out of family budgets rather than government funds in the United Kingdom, increasing pressure has been put on universities to provide services of an even higher standard. What students might once have put up with, their parents (who see themselves as stakeholders) increasingly will not. Universities are now seeing demands for refunds when a lecture is cancelled and for compensation when a student is not awarded the degree they believe is deserved. Sometimes students do not give their parents the full story and blame their institution for poor teaching when in fact their failure might have been due to a lack of attendance and application. It can be difficult for parents to discover that their son or daughter has been 'economical with the truth', but even more difficult to understand that after their child's 18th birthday they become 'a third party' in the United Kingdom under data protection legislation and are no longer entitled to any information about exam results or attendance. This can lead to very complex and sensitive situations that are difficult for universities to manage.

Putting Things Right?

Another interesting area relates to the issue of apologies. In the past, administrators were advised never to offer an apology to students, mainly because of the legal implications of admitting liability. It has only fairly recently been accepted that a skilfully worded apology can be a powerful tool, and that there are ways of apologising that get round the legal difficulties. One solution is to offer an expression of remorse, going on to acknowledge that things have not gone right and demonstrating empathy with the complainant. It can also help to make the student aware that changes have been made to procedures, to prevent other students having similar difficulties.

The Scottish Ombudsman, the SPSO, has a helpful leaflet on the subject which recognises that not everyone finds it easy to say 'sorry'. It emphasises that 'a meaningful apology can have a powerful effect for both parties in diffusing emotion and moving forward to a new phase where resolution is possible' and that 'it is important to remember that an apology is not a sign of weakness or an invitation to be sued' (SPSO, 2006). It is, however, worth checking out the legal and insurance aspects before issuing any such apologies.

Example of a Letter of Apology

Dear Mr Jones

I am writing to inform you that your academic appeal against your second-year examination results has been upheld. The complaint you submitted about the way your appeal was handled has also been upheld, since the Dean accepted that the letter you were sent by the department could have been misleading and noted that you were upset by the contents of the letter.

The university is sorry that you were upset by these experiences and can see that you have suffered a considerable amount of anxiety and stress. I would therefore like to express my regret that you may have suffered distress or anxiety as a result of any aspect of your studies, or your interactions with staff.

You may like to know that the department has been asked to review the wording of its standard letters, to ensure that similar misunderstandings should not occur in the future. Thank you for bringing this matter to our attention.

We would like to wish you every success with your studies next year.

Yours sincerely

Name

Title

Some institutions now use mediation and negotiation to resolve the more serious complaints and appeals. Since most procedures are paper based, students do not necessarily get the opportunity to talk to those responsible for making a decision on their case, something that can be very frustrating and appear extremely bureaucratic to the student. Getting all parties together in the same room means that there is more scope for reaching a resolution, which is why alternative dispute resolution is growing in popularity. Of course, complex cases are harder to resolve, such as those involving supervisory issues, where the parties involved have very fixed but opposing viewpoints.

If mediation is to be considered as an option for resolving a student complaint, careful consideration needs to be given to whether this is a suitable alternative to other forms of resolution, such as negotiation or conciliation. One way is to take careful account of the particular circumstances of the complaint. In the case of an academic appeal it is unlikely that mediation can be used, since this revolves around a student's disagreement with a board of examiners' decision. Mediation is not always an appropriate option for complaints but can be particularly effective in a situation where a student has a personal grievance about a member of staff. The issue might involve an apparent misunderstanding (which might have cultural roots) or involve a clash of personalities. If this is the case, mediation can offer a means of rebuilding the relationship between the student and the member of staff, giving each party the opportunity to come to an understanding of the other's viewpoint. This is an important consideration where the staff member and student have to continue working together in an academic context. Other forms of complaints resolution are more about solving the immediate problem than about looking to the longer term. For this reason alone, mediation can have an immediate benefit.

If the complaint handler feels that mediation might help in a particular dispute, they should ensure that the process is fully explained to all parties and that their agreement is obtained. The term 'mediation' can be easily misunderstood in its everyday context, so a full briefing on what will happen during the process is vital. From mediation pre-meetings (the mediator with each party individually) to the full meeting (the mediator with both parties together), full information should be given to each party.

Once the various parties have been persuaded to agree to mediation and have been fully briefed on the process, the actual meeting needs sensitive handling. For example, the staff member must not feel that the complaint is 'their fault' or that they are being blamed. Equally, it is important that the student does not feel intimidated by the process. The complaints handler must be aware of the inequality of the power balance between the student and the member of staff; for mediation to work, each party must feel that they are on an equal footing and can take equal responsibility for any successful outcome.

It is also important to use professionally trained mediators – ideally, people from within the university, who are familiar with its ethos and culture. An advantage of mediation is that, if successful, it can resolve a complaint more quickly, and with less bureaucracy, than following the complaints procedure through to its conclusion. However, if mediation is offered as an alternative method of dispute resolution, then the institution's complaints procedure should make appropriate reference to it.

Some Important Considerations

The principles of natural justice should underpin any student procedure, to ensure that cases are handled fairly and reasonably, even in the very early investigative stages. For example, in fitness to practise or discipline cases, students should be informed of the university's concerns in advance of any interview or hearing and be given sufficient time to prepare their case. They should not have to face rows of people when they walk into the interview or hearing room and should be offered the opportunity to be accompanied by a friend or adviser. Some institutions are wary of allowing students to be represented at any stage of the process, particularly by someone legally qualified. Others actively encourage students to seek advice from sources such as the students' union, where advisers are skilled at helping students put their case together. A decision is normally safer if made when the student is fully supported and aware of the procedure being followed, particularly if procedures are not conducted in their native language (in which case the institution might wish to engage the services of an interpreter). Staff should listen carefully to a student's explanation of events and keep an open mind, without jumping to preconceived conclusions. In addition, members of committees or panels should not include anyone with prior knowledge of the case, in order to prevent any possible bias. Keeping to these fairly simple and common-sense principles should mean there is less scope for students to appeal against a decision.

Complaints practitioners also need to have an understanding of political developments, since new legislation can fundamentally change working practices. For example, following the enactment in the United Kingdom of disability discrimination legislation in the mid-1990s, cases of dyslexia need particularly sensitive handling as the condition is now a registered disability under the legislation. This means that students can claim they have been discriminated against if reasonable adjustments are not made, for instance during the assessment process. Disability issues are a specialist area that may be better handled by staff with the relevant training. Other developments that have impacted on the way we work include a new tuition fees structure in the United Kingdom, the establishment of ombudsmen such as the OIA and SPSO, and equality legislation (particularly that relating to disability, gender and race). These have become familiar over time, but when they were first introduced they needed careful analysis and discussion to ensure an institution's compliance.

Good communication necessarily plays a vital role, and one of the key principles is to ensure that all parties are kept fully informed as to how a case is progressing. If there is an unavoidable delay, then it is important to make sure that everyone knows what is happening and why, otherwise things can go very wrong. It also helps if you have a good working relationship with academic departments; they will provide the information you need within required timescales but can be confident in the knowledge that you are there to help support them. Some of the more complex cases may well involve students making intense and potentially hurtful criticisms about individual staff, something that needs careful and sensitive management.

Keeping Abreast of Key Issues

Because of the complex nature of the work, a range of complaints and appeals networks have sprung up in the United Kingdom (both regional and national). These networks provide tailored training opportunities and the chance to share experiences and good practice with colleagues facing similar challenges. They also provide useful opportunities for finding out about new initiatives and developing case law. Firms of solicitors and organisations such as the police and the OIA seem more than willing to come along and share their expertise, something that is extremely helpful.

Hot topics come and go over the decades. In the late 1960s and early 1970s in the United Kingdom there was much discussion about mass public disorder on campus (an issue which re-emerged some 40 years later); in the 1990s, personal harassment and stalking were topical issues. Ten years on it has become tuition fees and the rise of the student as consumer in the United Kingdom, with big debates about the term 'customer'. Many of these issues had far-reaching implications for institutions. For example, in the mid-1990s a high-profile rape case at King's College, London, resulted in a task force being set up under the chairmanship of Professor G. J. Zellick, Principal of Queen Mary and Westfield College, University of London. A report published in 1994 recommended changes to institutions' disciplinary procedures (which is one of the reasons why many UK universities, particularly pre-1992 institutions, now have very similar discipline regulations). One of the guiding principles was that universities should not take disciplinary action against students until the police and courts had followed due process, in order to prevent any contamination of the evidence and because of the hazards of double jeopardy (penalising someone more than once for the same offence).

Ten years later, fitness to practise issues hit the UK headlines with high-profile professional negligence cases, such as those of Nurse Beverly Allitt and Dr Harold Shipman. This prompted many institutions, including the University of Sheffield, to carry out reviews of their existing mechanisms for handling concerns about students registered on professionally accredited courses. In order to protect students as well as the public, an institution must be seen to be addressing those concerns appropriately and in a fair and timely way. Other issues engaging today's administrators include how to treat students' engagement with social networking sites (particularly where offensive allegations about staff or other students are publicly aired), the introduction of American-style academic Honor Codes setting out expected behaviours, the appointment of campus ombudsmen, terrorist activities on campus, anti-social behaviour, plagiarism and impersonation in examinations. Only a crystal ball will reveal what the next challenge might be.

Managing Expectations

One of the biggest impacts on complaints and appeals in the United Kingdom in recent years has been caused by the replacement of the various HE sector independent review systems with the OIA (in Scotland the SPSO). Some institutions were initially nervous about the idea of such public external scrutiny and resented the fact that students would have such direct access to an independent review body.

Some of these misgivings have been borne out, as there is indeed a lot of work involved in handling OIA cases, especially where a review becomes complex and involves detailed investigation. One concern is that student expectations are now much higher. For example, there tends to be a perception among students that once a case goes to the OIA, the whole matter will be resolved in their favour. This means that the fallout if students do not get the result they want can be quite difficult to manage. However, external review does make institutions look at their procedures with a more critical eye, resulting in systems that are generally more robust and transparent. Decision makers are also increasingly aware that their decisions may be open to external scrutiny and now give fuller and more focused, reasoned decisions.

However, even the OIA has changed its approach. Initially, the first Independent Adjudicator for Higher Education in the United Kingdom, Baroness Deech, advocated formal student contracts. However, by the year preceding her retirement in 2008 she had conceded that they were not really worth the paper they were written on since they were unlikely to hold up in a court of law or help an institution avoid litigation. The OIA has also had to change its attitudes towards judicial review. Initially it resisted the idea that its decisions might be open to judicial review. However, in the case of *The Queen on the Application of Siborurema v. Office of the Independent Adjudicator* in 2007, the Court of Appeal ruled that the OIA's decisions were open to judicial review, but only as a limited remedy in the courts and only if the OIA was considered to have overstepped its powers. In other words, the courts are likely to be reluctant to interfere, and only in rare cases would permission be given for judicial review of a decision taken by the OIA.

The United Kingdom is well ahead of many other countries in setting up national student complaints systems. 'The OIA is increasingly seen as a model for resolution of student disputes by overseas universities and governments' (OIA Annual Report, 2007). By way of contrast, a student at the University of Sydney might have recourse to the New South Wales ombudsman for external review under the Ombudsman Act if they were not satisfied with the way a matter had been dealt with by the university. Similarly, students in other states could apply to their own state's ombudsman, but no national independent review schemes (such as those in the United Kingdom) yet exist.

How the Media See Complaints and Appeals

Journalists seem to find good copy in complaints and appeals. When revisiting publications of the late 1990s, it is interesting to see that the media were convinced that a deluge of litigious students was waiting in the wings. Palfreyman and Warner (1998) gave dire warnings that things were about to get out of control. They quote a *Times Higher Education Supplement* editorial of July 1996 which talks about the student community getting 'stroppy', the natives being restless with 'the risk of UK HE getting mired in expensive and unsatisfactory litigation which can only undermine public confidence'.

Similar views were repeated nearly ten years later, when in August 2007 the BBC ran an article on the OIA's annual report of the previous year, in which the vice-president of the National Union of Students, Wes Streeting, indicated that he felt that universities were not dealing with complaints adequately themselves (BBC News Online, 2007). The news item reported that 465 eligible complaints were made to the OIA in 2006. This may seem a lot, but does not take account of the majority of students who were presumably happy with their university experience. Compared with the number of students attending higher education institutions each year, these do not seem to be the hordes of complaints the media warned us about. Neither do these figures take account of the number of complaints and appeals that have been handled very successfully by universities, which work tirelessly to ensure that students are treated fairly and reasonably. UK freedom of information legislation introduced in 2000 has given the press much easier access to public information, but unfortunately some of the articles do not necessarily give a true picture and can distort the statistics.

However, it is true to say that complaints to the OIA have increased annually following its establishment in July 2003, rising by 25 per cent between 2006 and 2007, with the biggest category being complaints about assessment (OIA Annual Report, 2007). Each year when the OIA produces an annual report, the media run a high-profile story on it. They might put the rise in complaints down to such factors as the growth of a consumer and litigation culture and a less deferential attitude to academic staff. Or it might be the introduction of tuition fees and the changing nature of the student population (with higher numbers of mature and international students who have made financial and personal sacrifices to enter higher education and have high expectations). We are told that students increasingly have to take paid employment at the same time as studying, which means they have less time to prepare for assessments. Our view is that the modularisation and semesterisation of the mid-1990s have increased the number of assessment points, giving more opportunities for failure. It is poor performance in assessments that drives academic appeals, but which also gives rise to more generic complaints about teaching and support issues.

Learning Points

It would be difficult to summarise in one chapter everything that a complaints handler needs to know about the resolution of complaints and appeals, but here are some practical hints and tips to think about:

Do:
- acquire a working knowledge of the law, but know when to seek professional advice;
- apply the principles of natural justice;
- use plain English whenever writing to students: do not be tempted to use legalistic or old-fashioned expressions;
- keep meticulous records of each case;
- monitor numbers of cases and report to the relevant boards, university committees (and perhaps even students);
- always try to be one step ahead and anticipate pitfalls before they occur;
- be aware that complaints and appeals make interesting news items; this may mean that you have to talk to journalists from time to time (or have to brief your publicity department);

- keep up-to-date with new developments and what might be happening in other HE institutions;
- work in collaboration with academic and other administrative colleagues (including colleagues in the students' union), working hard to earn their trust;
- think about the rehabilitation and education of students, as much as any disciplinary penalties;
- treat any student as you would want to be treated yourself;
- take advantage of any training or networking opportunities, but keep in mind that it is possible to learn more from mistakes you might make than from any training session you might attend;
- recognise that staff named in a complaint may feel anxious and be under quite a lot of stress.

Don't:
- lose your sense of humour;
- forget to keep things in perspective;
- feel intimidated by complainants who say they are taking legal advice (they may not be; this may just be a threat to get you worried);
- underestimate the impact on complainants of the power balance between students and staff;
- bottle up any stress you might feel; talk to colleagues and share any concerns;
- forget to keep a big box of tissues on your desk (for you, colleagues and students).

Conclusion

In a perfect world there would be no complaints or appeals, but perfection takes time and is hard to achieve. In the interim, there is every indication that the number of complainants, while still only a tiny proportion of the student population, will continue to increase year-on-year.

Most staff working in the area of complaints and appeals would say that they often feel like the Cinderellas of higher education administration, beavering away in a world that their institutions would rather did not exist. With an ever-increasing focus on business culture, such an area of work is not seen as income generating or exciting. This latter point is the most mistaken of all; learning lessons from complaints and appeals cases helps to improve the student experience, as well as keeping retention figures healthy.

Indeed, not utilising what we learn from complaints and appeals can in itself be very expensive in terms of damage to reputations. In addition, it can hit an institution's pocket: for example, in 2007 the OIA recommended compensation payments totalling £173,000 (OIA Annual Report, 2007). Can your institution afford to pay out such sums?

For a website giving further information on these procedures, see www.shef. ac.uk/ssid/procedures/grid.html top (accessed 31 December 2008).

References

BBC News Online, 16 August 2007. Online, available at: http://news.bbc.co.uk/1/hi/education/6948332.stm (accessed 28 August 2008).

Gledhill, J. M. (1999) *Managing Students*, Philadelphia, PA: Open University Press.

Office of the Independent Adjudicator for Higher Education Annual Report (2006). Online, available at: www.oiahe.org.uk/docs/OIA-Annual-Report-2006.pdf (accessed 31 December 2008).

Office of the Independent Adjudicator for Higher Education Annual Report (2007). Online, available at: www.oiahe.org.uk/docs/OIA-Annual-Report-2007.pdf (accessed 31 December 2008).

Palfreyman, D. and Warner, D. (eds) (1998) *Higher Education and the Law: A Guide for Managers*, Buckingham: Society for Research into Higher Education/Open University Press.

Quality Assurance Agency (2000) *Code of Practice for Academic Appeals and Student Complaints on Academic Matters*, Gloucester: QAA.

Quality Assurance Agency (2007) *Code of Practice for Academic Appeals and Student Complaints on Academic Matters*, 2nd edn, Gloucester: QAA.

Scottish Public Services Ombudsman (2006) *SPSO Leaflet 2, Guidance on Apology*. Online, available at: www.spso.org.uk/webfm_send/1538 (accessed 11 June 2009).

CHAPTER 11

Scrutinising Quality

Working with External Examiners and Others to Maintain Standards

KATIE AKERMAN
Bath Spa University

and **PHIL CARDEW**
London South Bank University

What is an External Examining System?

At its core, the external examining system in the United Kingdom presents itself as the chief means by which standards of UK awards are ensured and protected. In order to achieve this remarkable claim, individuals must be appointed who are sufficiently senior and experienced in their subject area to have a sense of the 'standards' they so assiduously maintain, yet who have sufficient 'distance' from the appointing institution to maintain a balanced perspective on the application of those standards, ensuring that they are not influenced by 'fear or favour' in making their judgements. External examiners in the United Kingdom should be able to establish a national standard through their use of national reference points, such as the Quality Assurance Agency's Framework for Higher Education Qualifications and subject benchmark statements (which describe expected content for particular subjects).

Denmark and Norway also utilise systems of external examining. In Denmark the Ministry of Education established a national body of external examiners for each study programme and for each subject in the humanities and natural sciences. More than 100 such bodies had been created and their aim was to ensure a national standard. However, Stensaker *et al.* (2008)

indicate that the establishment of a national standard in Denmark has been problematic for a number of reasons. Danish academics are somewhat doubtful about the ability of external examiners to contribute to quality development of subjects. It was expected that external examiners would simply be utilised for higher degrees. In 2008 an external examining system for undergraduate provision was reintroduced, but on a much smaller scale. The system is meant to be based on a twofold structure where the examination of student work is complemented by quality assurance mechanisms in the form of feedback from external examiners.

Stensaker *et al.* (2008) also discuss the external examining system in Norway, where there is a greater emphasis on evaluating the programme of study than student work. This has resulted in less use of external examiners at undergraduate level.

The University of Malta utilises an external examining system and defines an external examiner as 'a senior academic who is an expert in the field of study being examined and who is not affiliated to the University'. In terms of role, the University of Malta regulations (2008) include the rubric 'When an external examiner is appointed for a written Examination, the Board of Examiners shall submit the draft Examination paper and mark scheme for his advice and shall invite him to set questions of his own'. The university's Senate is responsible for the appointment of external examiners, and they are appointed for a maximum of three years. Examiners are expected to approve and moderate papers, marking schemes and other assessment exercises. They are also expected to examine the work of all students, where possible. Where this might prove unfeasible, a sample is submitted by the university. Examiners are also expected to provide a written report on their findings.

On the other hand, the United States, for example, does not utilise a system of external examiners. There is continued debate as to whether the United Kingdom needs to continue to employ such a system. Some see the system as impossible to manage in the light of the 'massification' of higher education (HE); one might ask whether it is genuinely possible for external examiners to ensure comparability of standards across around 170 higher education institutions and 270 colleges of further education offering higher education provision, plus a number of private organisations offering higher education, including employers, as is the case in the United Kingdom.

What is an External Examiner?

Harvey (2004) describes external examiners thus:

> [A]n external examiner is a person from another institution or organisation who monitors the assessment process of an institution

for fairness and academic standards. External examiners are normally academics but may also, in some settings, be employers or other professionals not employed in higher education institutions. For example, external examiners for fashion and textile degrees may be practising cutting-edge employers.

This presents a relatively 'modern' perspective on the type of individual needed to fulfil the role: someone who may be familiar with both the academic and the professional worlds and who may look at what would traditionally be viewed as 'academic standards' alongside professional competencies – with the ensuing connotations of 'fitness for practice'. It is certainly the case that such individuals are appointed within a range of institutions (particularly those which maintain a professional focus in the delivery of awards), but it is equally the case that many 'traditional' disciplines would shy away from such appointments – unless, perhaps, teamed together with a more recognisable 'academic'.

There is no question, however, that institutions view the relationship between external examiners and standards as key to their effective operation:

- The University of Birmingham (2008) states that 'the External Examiner system enables the University to ensure that the qualifications it awards are of a suitable standard, and that student performances are judged appropriately'.
- The University of Cambridge (Walker, 1997) explains that an external examiner is 'appointed from another university, to ensure that degree standards are consistent between universities'.
- Massey University, New Zealand (2008) specifies 'a highly qualified person with specialist knowledge, not employed by the University, who is appointed by the University to examine and grade a postgraduate thesis/research project or final undergraduate assessment'.
- Northern Illinois University (2008) describes an external examiner as 'an expert in the field from outside your program, usually from a similar program at another institution to conduct, evaluate, or supplement assessment of your students'.

The common themes seem to be that the external examiner is an expert in his or her subject area, and is external to the institution. There is some variability in the role, depending on the level of award under examination, and between institutions (and potentially between subject areas in the same institution).

Where did the Idea Come From?

The external examining system dates back to the nineteenth century and was largely developed in the face of the expansion of HE in the United Kingdom and elsewhere that began at this time. The system has spread with the wide influence that UK higher education has had during the past century, and thus is also found in countries whose higher education development has been influenced by the United Kingdom, such as Australia, India, Malta and New Zealand.

What Should be the Purpose of External Examining?

The main role of the external examining system is to maintain a broad comparability of standards across a national system of HE. In the United Kingdom the Council for National Academic Awards (CNAA) was responsible for the validation of programmes and for maintaining a system of external examining at public sector institutions (former polytechnics) until the Further and Higher Education Acts 1992 made changes to the funding and administration of higher education and further education within the United Kingdom. This allowed polytechnics to become universities, resulting in the dissolution of the CNAA. The appointment of external examiners was then devolved to the former polytechnics themselves, although universities had always been able to appoint their own examiners.

Precept 1 of the QAA *Code of Practice for the Assurance of Academic Quality and Standards in Higher Education* (Quality Assurance Agency, 2004: Section 4, 'External examining') states that external examiners should be able to report on:

- whether the academic standards set for its awards, or part thereof, are appropriate;
- the extent to which an institution's assessment processes are rigorous, ensure equity of treatment for students and have been fairly conducted within institutional regulations and guidance;
- the standards of student performance in the programmes or parts of programmes that they have been appointed to examine;
- where appropriate, the comparability of the standards and student achievements with those in some other HE institutions;
- good practice they have identified.

In this sense, external examiners focus on matters related to both academic standards and academic quality:

- *Academic standards.* In this respect, external examiners form a part of the assurance mechanisms of the university, which operate both within and across its individual awards. External examiners must have both the appropriate background and appropriate access to student work to allow them to exercise this crucial role.
- *Academic quality.* In this respect, external examiners play an important role within the quality systems of the university, reflecting upon the quality of student learning opportunities, the equitable application of regulations to all students, and matters relating to the student experience as a whole.

What Should External Examiners Do?

External examiners have a fourfold role in UK higher education institutions. First, they are responsible for acting as moderators of the examination or assessment process; second, they are responsible for acting as calibrators or regulators of academic standards for the awards being examined or assessed; third, they act as adjudicators or arbitrators; and finally, they act as consultants to the programme teams with whom they work.

In acting as moderators, external examiners should consider and comment upon the appropriateness of assessment practices within a given subject or programme. They have a responsibility to ensure that:

- the examination or assessment process has been conducted as the institution's regulations state;
- the examination or assessment practices have been conducted fairly;
- due regard has been given to equal opportunities and avoidance of discrimination in examination or assessment processes;
- the examination or assessment is appropriate to the learning outcomes;
- a written report is provided, usually commenting on the validity, comparability, reliability, integrity and security of the assessment process.

In calibrating or regulating, external examiners should compare academic standards with those of other institutions with which they are familiar, and they should compare the outcomes of examination or assessment with similar provision.

As adjudicators or arbitrators, they should act as a judge in the allocation of marks, and alter marks where necessary. Most UK higher education institutions only allow external examiners to change the marks of an entire cohort, rather than individual marks. However, in exceptional cases, for example with small subject areas or specialisms, where the process of moderating or double marking may be difficult to achieve, they may act as an additional marker, depending on the regulations of the institution.

The role of external examiners as 'consultants' to their subject areas or departments is open to more debate across the sector. Quite commonly, the external examiner is encouraged to comment upon the content and development of a subject or programme; act as a commentator on, and assist with the setting of, examination papers and final assignments; and act as a 'critical friend' to the programme or subject. However, the extent to which a 'critical friend' can also be an 'arbitrator of standards' is somewhat questionable, and many institutions prefer to utilise retired externals in this kind of role.

The majority of HE institutions require the external examiner to submit a written report, and payment of fees is normally dependent upon receipt of this report. These reports are a crucial element in the UK higher education quality assurance system. It is the mechanism by which HE institutions have their academic standards confirmed as appropriate. The external examiners' reports are usually discussed by department, school or faculty committees before being considered at an institutional level. The majority of HE institutions will undertake some form of analysis to identify themes, usually areas for improvement across the institution, and practice for dissemination across the institution.

A question, however, remains as to the true efficacy of this process. It is relatively common for external examiner reports to be fairly limited in their responses to the questions posed. It is equally common for institutions to be demonstrably inadequate in ensuring that all externals receive what they believe to be an 'adequate' response to their report. This is, to some extent, hardly surprising. A reasonably sized institution may have anything up to 300 externals to communicate with each year. Unless processes are absolutely clear-cut and relatively mechanical, loops can fail to be closed quite easily. Thus, while maintaining the aura of respectability and assurance, the process is only as good as those who enact it.

The majority of institutions have criteria for the appointment of external examiners, including having a qualification at least equivalent to that which is being examined and that:

- they are familiar with the subject or programme;
- they have an understanding of how the subject or programme may develop in the future;
- they have appropriate experience of HE, providing an assurance that their judgement in the matter of academic standards is secure;

- they enjoy a professional standing that enables them to provide sound guidance on current and future developments to inform development of the programme or subject;
- they usually have experience of acting as an external examiner elsewhere.

Some institutions limit the number of external examinerships that an individual may hold. Reciprocal arrangements are usually limited (and a time limit set on the period after which a former member of staff may be appointed), to avoid any potential conflicts of interest. Institutions generally set maximum terms of office, usually for four or five years, and seldom allow re-appointment without a period of 'absence'.

How Do We Support External Examiners?

Newly appointed examiners should be suitably prepared to fulfil the requirements of their role. Many institutions, in the light of the UK QAA's *Code of Practice for the Assurance of Academic Quality and Standards in Higher Education* (Quality Assurance Agency, 2004: Section 4, 'External examining'), have elected to offer briefing or induction events. Institutions usually provide examiners with the information needed to undertake the role, including the dates of the meetings they are required to attend. Many institutions have handbooks for external examiners, which include information about their role. Examiners are also provided with subject-specific information, such as the student handbook, programme specification and the most recent external examiner's report, to provide context for their role.

Newly inducted examiners who have not had the opportunity to undertake external examining on a previous occasion are often supported by a mentor, either the outgoing examiner or an existing examiner in a cognate subject. Often there are two or more examiners for a subject, and the newly appointed examiner may be supported by a team approach.

Many institutions adopt a tiered approach to the examination board system, by which lower-level examination boards focus on student performance in individual modules, or units, of an award, and higher-level boards concentrate on progression and award. In such a system, external examiners may have very different experiences, lower-level examiners concentrating on individual achievement at module level and being involved in the scrutiny of student work, with higher-level examiners ensuring the fair application of process across a range of awards. In such cases, externals need to have a clear understanding of their role, and induction is highly desirable. Many institutions have developed these processes into conferences at which externals are able not only to discuss institutional processes, but also to engage with wider debate on the landscape of quality and standards in HE.

What Does the QAA Expect UK Universities to Do?

The QAA indicates an expectation that examiners will comment upon whether or not academic standards set for an institution's awards are appropriate, as suggested by the calibrator or regulator role described above. Examiners should also confirm that processes should be fair, rigorous and ensure equity of treatment, as described in the moderator role above. Examiners should confirm the standard of student achievement as being comparable with that in other, similar institutions, as earlier described in the discussion of the adjudicator or arbitrator role. Finally, in their role as consultants, examiners should identify areas of good practice to the institution.

The QAA states that institutions should provide external examiners with clear information about their roles and responsibilities. Detailed guidance allows institutions to adhere to a number of the precepts outlined within the relevant QAA Code of Practice.

The precepts also detail what might be expected following receipt of the examiner's report by the institution. Institutions tackle this in a number of different ways, for example by devising an action plan to respond to points, or by addressing points raised within the annual monitoring process.

The QAA attempts to strengthen the external examining process by stating that good practice would include opportunities for induction and/or training to be made available by the institution for its examiners. Sadly, institutions normally expect any external examining to be undertaken in the academic's own time. It is not usually a part of the job description for a lecturer. The work is perhaps squeezed in between other demands on a lecturer's time.

Where Do Students Fit In?

Some institutions allow for formal or informal opportunities for examiners to meet students, which can be an opportunity for them really to come to grips with what happens on a course.

There is ongoing debate within the sector around the sharing of external examiners' reports with students, following the review of Teaching Quality Information (TQI) by the Quality Assurance Framework Review Group (QAFRG), convened by the Higher Education Funding Council for England (HEFCE) and chaired by Dame Sandra Burslem (Higher Education Funding Council, 2006). This review led to the removal of external examiners' summaries from the TQI (now Unistats) website.

Many institutions consider that because a student invariably sits upon the committee at which such reports are considered, this is sufficient, and the TQI Review Group agreed. However, other institutions have made or are considering making reports available on internal websites or virtual learning environments.

How Do We Ensure Equity of Treatment for Students?

One way of ensuring equity of treatment is to allow examiners only to adjust the marks of entire cohorts rather than of individual students, or bands of marks, for example adjusting the marks of all students achieving a First.

Studies show that there are gender gaps in male and female achievement, although it is often unclear as to the cause. For example, the following quotation is from Yoon (2008):

> 'At Oxford, overall, men obtain a higher proportion of firsts than women', Dr Mellanby continued. 'Part of this difference is due to the fact that there are more men reading subjects that award a higher percentage of firsts (e.g. Chemistry).
>
> 'We do not have an answer as to why the gap exists in some subjects and not in others. It is frequently proposed that the reason that the gender gap is seen in subjects where presenting an argument is important is that men are more likely to produce a confident, "punchy" style of argument and that this appeals to examiners', she said.
>
> 'There is however no real evidence (from examination scripts) that this is true. One thing we have shown is that there is no difference in the attitude of male and female examiners to the criteria for awarding first class marks'.

Hall (1998) states that:

> Women are outperforming men in education yet again, a new study by academics at the University of Sussex reveals. Delving into the lesser-studied area of gender-related performance in higher education, the research has reached a number of surprising conclusions. By the time they sit their second year exams, it reveals a discrepancy of nearly 10% in the average scores achieved by women and those achieved by certain categories of men . . . though women get many more 2:1 degrees than men, men still get more firsts.

A study by the Department for Education and Skills (now the Department for Innovation, Universities and Skills) (Equality Challenge Unit and the Higher Education Academy, 2008) shows that there is also a difference in attainment between ethnic minority students and white students, with 3 per cent of black Caribbean students, 4 per cent of black African and 5 per cent of Bangladeshi and Pakistani students expected to get a First, compared with 13 per cent of white Irish and 16 per cent of other white students.

The University of Northampton (Crofts, 2007) found that both age and disability can also impact upon attainment, with mature students more likely to gain a good degree, and students with a declared disability more likely to fare less well than their counterparts with no declared disability.

Institutions should make sure that their race and gender equality policies ensure that assessment is fair and appropriate, and impact assessments should be undertaken. Data collected should allow institutions to consider the impact of gender, ethnicity, age and disability on degree attainment, and this should be monitored. The external examiners can support this activity when they are asked to consider examinations or other assessments. Examiners are also asked to comment on curriculum design, such as changes to modules. Degree attainment variation may be addressed through ensuring that curriculum design is accessible to all.

Fees
There is considerable variety in the calculation of fees for external examining, ranging from the very simplistic – a set annual fee – through to the highly complex, calculated on the number of full-time equivalent students and/or the number of modules. In the United Kingdom, universities tend not to recognise external examining commitments as a formal part of a job description. Therefore, the work tends to end up being undertaken in the individual's own time, and it could be argued that the remuneration is not sufficient to recognise this. However, Hannan and Silver (2006) note that there are benefits other than financial that act as an incentive for individuals to undertake the role of external examiner, such as the exchange of ideas and increased competence on the part of the person acting as examiner.

Does the System Work?
In the United Kingdom, the QAA certainly seems to think so. The report *Outcomes from Institutional Audit Reports: External Examiners and Their Reports* (2005) states that '[e]vidence from the audits undertaken suggest that institutions and discipline areas are engaging productively with their

external examiners in maintaining the academic standards of awards and in assisting with the enhancement of the quality of provision'.

There has been a tacit acknowledgement that the system works best when not subject to a high level of public scrutiny. There was considerable debate from 2003 onwards regarding the publication of external examiners' reports on the TQI website. This has since been withdrawn, with the information that had been published regarded as being of no use to potential or existing students (or to other stakeholders, such as parents).

Stensaker *et al.* (2008) note that '[t]he intention is good, but does not work in practice'. They argue that external examiners are not interested or qualified in quality assurance or enhancement, and care only for their own field of study, rather than the programme of study. This is a particular difficulty for modular schemes, where students build their own programme of study as they progress through HE, rather than being recruited to a particular programme. The element of student choice and flexibility is positive but it can make it difficult for institutions to assess the quality of the programme undertaken as a whole, rather than discrete elements, such as the field or modules.

Why Would Anyone Want to be an External Examiner?

External examiners put forward a variety of reasons for wishing to undertake this type of work, including opportunities to remain current with a field of study and its developments. It allows people an opportunity to expand their breadth of knowledge through examining subjects that are not within their immediate or usual remit. It provides an opportunity to shape the subject being taught and to acquire knowledge of practice elsewhere which can be used to inform the examiner's own teaching in his or her own institution. It also provides an opportunity for wider professional development.

Where Else Does the United Kingdom Use 'Externality' in Higher Education?

The QAA is perhaps as obvious as the external examining system as a source of external scrutiny. The QAA was established in 1997, and is independent of government. Its responsibility is to safeguard standards and encourage improvement in quality in HE. This is done through reviewing or auditing standards and quality and through providing national reference points framed in the Academic Infrastructure (see Chapter 13). Institutional audit is the mechanism by which universities are audited in regard to standards and quality. Institutional audit utilises a team of auditors comprising senior staff from institutions, and an auditor is not permitted to audit his or her own institution. Institutional audit is dependent on the production of a briefing document prepared by the institution on its internal quality management processes, and this forms the basis for inquiry by the team of auditors. Auditors spend several days at the institution in question, meeting with staff and students to scrutinise how quality management processes work in practice. The visit culminates in a report on standards and quality at the institution that has been audited. The process is managed by the QAA.

Institutions have gone some way towards replicating this procedure within their own internal mechanisms for quality assurance. Academics from other institutions are invariably used in course design, monitoring and review. External advisers from other institutions, from professional, statutory and regulatory bodies, or from industry are used in course design processes. A notable example is the foundation degree, which by its very nature – combining the academic with the vocational – almost requires the establishment of an industry forum to inform course design in order that it should be appropriate and current, and, crucially, relevant to the employment sector.

Higher education institutions also have to deal with bodies like the Sector Skills Councils, of which there are currently 25, allying themselves with particular areas of industry, such as Skills for Health. These, to a greater or lesser extent, have fallen foul of the HE sector. Many have taken it upon themselves to develop accreditation schemes – usually for foundation degrees – which simply add to the quality assurance burden that institutions bear. The Quality Assurance Framework Review Group (QAFRG) has recently developed some recommendations as a result of its last phase, considering collaborative provision, in 2008, and recommends that Sector Skills Councils simply inform development of the curriculum, rather than offer accreditation opportunities that do not align with other requirements placed upon institutions.

Institutions in the United Kingdom may also work closely with the Higher Education Academy and its network of 24 UK-wide subject centres. A crude delineation often made (perhaps unfairly) is that the QAA is responsible for quality assurance and the Higher Education Academy for quality enhancement. In response to this, the Higher Education Funding Council (HEFCE) is encouraging the QAA and the Academy to work jointly on projects. The success (or otherwise) of this is yet to be seen. Some subject centres have developed registers of individuals prepared to act as external examiners.

Institutions also work closely with professional, statutory and regulatory bodies (PSRBs) and employers directly. Many institutions have something equating to a business support unit and utilise opportunities for knowledge creation and transfer. Many institutions have PSRB accreditation for courses – such as the British Psychological Society recognition for psychology courses. One of the QAA's successes was successfully contracting with the General Osteopathic Council for the Council to conduct its review activity for the QAA, thus ensuring some coherence with the Higher Education Regulation Review Group (HERRG) concordat on reducing bureaucracy and burden in quality assurance.

Institutions are, of course, subject to the every whim of government: in the United Kingdom there have been the Dearing Report (National Committee of Inquiry into Higher Education, 1997), the Leitch review of skills (Department for Innovation, Universities and Skills, 2007) and various Acts of Parliament, which have all had an impact upon institutions, as has the introduction of top-up fees.

And what of students? There has been a continued effort, dating back at least to 2001, to make students more central to quality assurance processes. Students now frequently sit on institutional committees, such as academic standards committees, learning and teaching committees, senates or academic boards.

The QAA has piloted a scheme for the inclusion of a student auditor on its audit teams. This has emanated from the Bologna Process (the creation of a European higher education area). This is still under discussion with the sector and has led to institutions in the United Kingdom also using student reviewers on internal review panels, for example.

Bath Spa University has a Student Representatives Committee, with membership comprising students from each of its seven schools plus its partner further education colleges and private providers. This committee is chaired by the president of the Students' Union, and secretarial support is provided by the university. Students are paid for their attendance at the three termly meetings. Issues important to the students and to the university are discussed, such as employability. This committee also investigates ways in which the input of students can be integrated further into quality assurance processes.

London South Bank University (LSBU) has a Student Affairs Committee as a statutory subcommittee of the board of governors (of which the president of the Students' Union is an ex officio member). This committee is chaired by a pro-vice-chancellor and includes external governors, Student Union representatives and key 'student-facing' support department representatives. LSBU is also in the process of developing a staff role within the Students' Union which focuses on student engagement and representation.

What Next?

One cannot help but wonder whether parents will be next! Olabisi Onabanjo University in Nigeria is already working in partnership with parents on the issue of campus security. There would seem to be a general consensus that externality, whatever its form, is a good thing for assuring and enhancing quality and standards in HE.

Systems are changing to adapt to new challenges and opportunities. So, what does the future hold? We may find that the United Kingdom follows in Denmark's steps and adopts a national body of trained and accredited external examiners, who are not appointed by institutions themselves but are independent of institutions and are perhaps managed by QAA, for example.

On the other hand, the United Kingdom may decide that it is simply impossible to assure comparability of standards for an increasingly diverse and ever-growing sector. The external examining system may be abandoned completely, replaced by self-regulation, with checks made by the QAA.

Alternatively, a European system may be created from the European Higher Education Area. Discussions are already taking place about the inclusion of a European reviewer or auditor on panels assessing standards and quality and institutions. A pan-European system would encourage mobility, one of the action lines identified within the Bologna Process.

However the process develops, it is likely to remain at the core of an increasingly political debate focused upon accountability within HE. In 2001, when there was a move by the QAA away from universal external subject review towards institutional audit, part of the argument rested upon the solidity of the assurance of standards offered by the external examiner system. Since then, there have been expressions, from both sides of the political spectrum, that the 'quality touch' has become, perhaps, too light – the QAA being referred to within a recent Parliamentary Select Committee as 'just a toothless dog' (Phil Willis, chair of the Innovation, Universities, Science and Skills Committee, 17 July 2008).

Whatever the political context of the next decade, there is little hope that the funding of HE will do anything other than decrease, in real terms. Alongside this budgetary squeeze is a clearly expressed wish, from the Higher Education Funding Council, for universities to 'specialise' – the research-led universities (those that emphasise research as their primary focus) separating themselves from the research-informed (those that emphasise teaching informed by research as their primary focus), increasing the disparity that currently exists between such institutions.

Within this context the pressure will continue for a more intrusive and 'inspectorial' approach to external audit – with a clearly expressed view (within the Innovation, Universities, Science and Skills Committee) that the QAA is too close to the institutions it audits. This view may well extend to the external examiner system, which is prone to accusations of 'cosiness'. Such a tendency will serve to push the United Kingdom further and further towards the rest of Europe, and may even challenge the institutional autonomy that derives from degree-awarding powers. Whatever the end result, there is little doubt that the process will be tested and, if found to be unfit for purpose, placed under increasing pressure.

References

BBC News (2007) "Ethnic minority degrees 'mystery'". Online, available at: http://news.bbc.co.uk/go/pr/fr/-/1/hi/education/6301699.stm.

Crofts, P. (2007) 'A statistical overview of "good" degrees awarded 2004–07 and recommendations for future action' (University of Northampton). Online, available at: www2.northampton.ac.uk/portal/page/portal/AEP/Document%20Store/EandDRP/19.ReportGoodDegrees20074-08(word443kb).doc#Disability.

Department for Innovation, Universities and Skills (2007) *World Class Skills* (the Leitch Report). Online, available at: www.dius.gov.uk/publications/leitch.html.

Equality Challenge Unit and the Higher Education Academy (2008) *Ethnicity, Gender and Degree Attainment Project*, York: Higher Education Academy.

Hall, S. (1998) 'The hidden factor fuelling female success'. Online, available at: www.sussex.ac.uk/press_office/media/media37.html.

Hannan, A. and Silver, H. (2006) 'On being an external examiner', *Studies in Higher Education*, 31 (1): 57–69.

Harvey, L. (2004) 'Analytic quality glossary'. Online, available at: www.qualityresearchinternational.com/glossary.

Higher Education Funding Council for England (2006) 'Review of the quality assurance framework: phase two outcomes' (2006/45). Online, available at: www.hefce.ac.uk/pubs/hefce/2006/06_45/06_45.doc.

Massey University (2008) 'Glossary of terms'. Online, available at: http://calendar.massey.ac.nz/information/glossary.htm#e.

National Committee of Inquiry into Higher Education (1997) *Higher Education in the Learning Society* (the Dearing Report), London: The Stationery Office. Online, available at: https://bei.leeds.ac.uk/Partners/NCIHE//.

Northern Illinois University (2008) 'Assessment term glossary'. Online, available at: www.niu.edu/assessment/resources/assessment_glossary.htm.

Quality Assurance Agency for Higher Education (2004) *Code of Practice for the Assurance of Academic Quality and Standards in Higher Education*, Gloucester: QAA.

Quality Assurance Agency for Higher Education (2005) *Outcomes from Institutional Audit Reports: External Examiners and Their Reports*, Gloucester: QAA.

Stensaker, B., Brandt, E. and Solum, N. H. (2008) 'Changing systems of external examination', *Quality Assurance in Education*, 16 (3): 211–23.

University of Birmingham (2008) 'External examiners'. Online, available at: www.as.bham.ac.uk/work/teach/quality/external.

University of Malta (2008) 'University assessment regulations'. Online, available at: http://www.um.edu.mt/registrar/regulations/general/assessment_regulations.

Walker, R. (1997) 'Glossary of Cambridge jargon'. Online, available at: www.queens.cam.ac.uk/queens/misc/jargon/cujargon-e.html.

Yoon, S. (2008) 'Finals "gender gap" leaves dons in the dark'. Online, available at: www.cherwell.org/content.php?id=7523.

CHAPTER 12

Launching the New University Presence

The Case of University Campus Suffolk

PETER FUNNELL
University Campus Suffolk

and **TONY RICH**
University of Essex

Introduction

Across the globe the search for accessible higher education (HE) is accelerating. This in part reflects the perceived value of a university to a local and national economy, and more intangible benefits centred on community engagement and cultural development. This chapter explores the opportunities and challenges associated with the establishment of a new university presence, University Campus Suffolk (UCS), in a UK context. While the case study is time- and place-specific, it also raises generic issues that may inform thinking about the establishment of new and different forms of HE. As such, it offers for consideration a model of practice designed to address the 'new university challenge' of promoting access to HE, unlocking the potential of specific locations, driving economic development and supporting individual achievement.

The county of Suffolk is located in the East of England and has borders with Norfolk, Cambridgeshire and Essex, with the North Sea lying to the east. The county is low-lying, with much of its 3,800 square kilometre land mass taken by arable farming and areas of outstanding natural beauty. The population of some 700,000 is primarily located in and around the urban centres of Ipswich (the county town), Bury St Edmunds and Lowestoft. Alongside agriculture and food processing, Suffolk has significant economic activity in the energy, shipping and logistics, financial services, and information and communications sectors, the latter including the global research centre of the telecommunications company BT at Adastral Park, Martlesham, some 12 kilometres from Ipswich.

Until 2007, Suffolk had no local university presence. As early as 1995 a Touche Ross report, *A University for Suffolk: Testing the Vision*, suggested that

> [a] new University for Suffolk can enrich the life of the County . . . by providing an entirely new model of community based higher education . . . [meeting] emerging demand for locally provided, flexible relevant lifetime learning. Beyond this, it can support the economic development of the whole region by stimulating jobs, investment and innovation and information flows. Above all, it promises to be an internationally visible flagship for Suffolk, and a real focus for community pride.
>
> (1995: 1)

The report went on to suggest that the creation of a university presence, based initially on the HE provision offered by Suffolk College, an Ipswich-based 'mixed economy' further and education college, would generate economic benefits equivalent to £50 million at 1995–6 prices. This report was the first tangible outcome of a Suffolk-based business and community-led campaign seeking to establish a university presence in the county. This proposed new HE presence would address the perceived consequences of the absence of a university. In turn, this absence was articulated in terms of the costs associated with the net migration of talented young people from the county to pursue HE, the limited availability of HE opportunities for the resident population, and the limited inward investment and externalities associated with university activity and a large student population. The campaign was led by the Project for a University for Suffolk Company, a charitable company with a board constituted of senior business and community leaders working alongside existing HE providers. Key voices in the development of the case for a university presence in Suffolk were senior leaders at BT. Indeed, the influence of BT led early thinking towards the extensive application of emerging forms of information and communications technologies and approaches that today would be associated with e-learning and the application of a virtual learning environment (VLE). In 1995, in the Suffolk context these became linked to a concept of a 'Televersity'. This was subsequently implemented in pilot form by a commercial offshoot of the Project for a University for Suffolk Company, the Televersity for Suffolk Company Limited, having secured European Social Fund moneys matched by the Suffolk Training Enterprise Council, BT and others to create and evaluate an interactive web platform, essentially an early form of VLE, designed to support distributed learning in rural communities.

This emerging vision of a 'University for Suffolk' received considerable community support based on an economic rationale typically presented in terms of intangible loss associated with the absence of a resident university. In testing this vision and the application of distributed learning using new technologies, Touche Ross concluded that

> [t]he vision is for a community televersity model which would reach its students across the County, through a network of local learning centres linked to a University centre . . . [in implementing the model] full use will be made of new teaching and learning methods, delivered over advanced communication technologies to provide highly flexible, student centred patterns of study. . . . Overall . . . the vision for a new, community University for Suffolk emerges as exciting, innovative and realistic.
>
> (1995: 2)

It would be another 12 years before the vision of a university presence in Suffolk would be realised. A detailed review of the history associated with this timescale goes beyond the scope of this chapter, but it is worth recalling that Suffolk College worked imaginatively with its validating partner, the Norwich-based University of East Anglia (UEA), to expand HE leading to the award of the 'university college' title following a robust process of institutional accreditation, only to have it snatched away by changes to primary legislation (the Teaching and Higher Education Act 1998, c.25) unrelated to the Suffolk context (National Committee of Inquiry into Higher Education, 1997). Post-1998, government tightened up the provisions for achieving both university and degree-awarding status such that it became increasingly difficult for a 'mixed economy college' to develop independent and innovative forms of HE.

Nonetheless, during the period prior to the creation of University Campus Suffolk (UCS) in August 2007, most higher education in Suffolk was offered by Suffolk College through a successful accreditation arrangement with the UEA. Smaller and more focused elements of higher education provision were also offered by the other further education (FE) colleges in the county, most typically under a franchise arrangement with the Cambridge- and Chelmsford-based Anglia Polytechnic (now Ruskin) University and through the UK Open University. By the early years of the new century it was clear to the Corporation and senior managers of Suffolk College that the challenges of managing the learning experiences of some 2,500 full-time equivalent (FTE) higher education students alongside those of further and adult education learners, including several hundred aged 14–15, was stretching the capacity of staff and capital infrastructure to the limit. Indeed, by 2006–7 Suffolk College was the second largest provider of HE outside the university sector. Despite being directly funded for its HE provision by the Higher Education Funding Council for England (HEFCE), Suffolk College was unable to access capital and other funding streams routinely available to universities. The value of a clear split of activity and mission between higher and further education was becoming increasingly apparent both to maintain existing activity levels and to address the ambitions and expectations of the community.

In this context, during the period 2002–5 a number of studies were commissioned which articulated the value of an expanded and co-ordinated university presence in the county developed alongside an expanded further education offer. More specifically, they concluded that:

- the HE participation rate by residents of Suffolk is below the national average;
- the East of England suffers from lower levels of applications to university than the national average, and this situation is worse in rural areas;
- students from the East of England are more likely to study outside the region than students from other regions;
- the East of England suffers from a 'brain drain', particularly into London, with students either not returning after study, or choosing to work outside the region;
- attainment in Suffolk schools, at university entrance level, is below the national average;
- raising aspirations for education beyond compulsory school leaving age, across the county, is an important element of increasing participation in HE;
- educational provision attractive to potential students in Suffolk was not accessible to them in a way that it was elsewhere;
- the success of Suffolk College's engagement in HE offered a base from which to build;
- a new form of joint venture between two prominent universities, the UEA and Essex, would provide an attractive model of governance for the development of a university presence in Suffolk;
- aspirations for the new university presence should be high and a maturity target of 7,400 FTE students should be set.

Based on this work and significant internal activity, a planning group was established by the vice-chancellors of the two universities and the principal of Suffolk College to drive forward the initiative. Subsequent work by the consultancy firm BiGGAR Economics (2005) concluded that the establishment of a university presence in Suffolk would generate significant regional benefits and be consistent with, and supportive of, the Regional Development Agency's regional economic strategy. It would address issues of widening participation and access to learning, and as such contribute to meeting the UK government's 50 per cent target for 18- to 30-year-old participation in HE, while making a meaningful contribution to regional economic development.

Recognising these potential benefits, the Regional Development Agency, the East of England Development Agency (EEDA) and the Association of Universities in the East of England proposed an increase of 39,000 HE places in the region to the Higher Education Funding Council for England. The creation of University Campus Suffolk was recognised as a key component of this expansion programme. It would also have an important role as a catalyst for attracting inward investment leading to the creation of high-skilled jobs, which would in turn retain and attract qualified young people to the region.

The University Campus Suffolk Model

The establishment of a university presence in Suffolk can, in part, be identified as a response to regional demands, themselves a reflection of national policy objectives. The design of the specific UCS model as the way of expanding provision can also be seen to be a response to imperatives at a more local level. For the Suffolk community, local policy and planning have consistently identified additional value in the creation of a resident university that exceeds that which would be created by increasing the number of students taught through a mosaic of further education colleges or through other forms of hybrid arrangements.

The model chosen for the development of University Campus Suffolk is bold and comprehensive, and unique among English institutions. Formally, UCS is a wholly owned subsidiary company of the Universities of East Anglia and Essex, and is a company limited by guarantee. The company is controlled by the two universities, which have a majority on the board. Other board members include the UCS chief executive, two representatives of the Suffolk community (currently the chief executives of Ipswich Borough Council and Suffolk County Council) and two FE college principals. It is critical to the success of UCS that the two universities continue to share the same vision for its future and that they garner sufficient support for that vision from the local stakeholders. However, with local government reorganisation anticipated in 2010, the potential for unconstructive tensions remains.

At its creation, continuing students on HE courses at each of the further education colleges in Suffolk, and at Great Yarmouth College in Norfolk, became students of University Campus Suffolk. In addition to a new intake of students who applied directly to UCS, they became the first students of the new institution. The creation of UCS was also part of a restructuring and repositioning of the post-compulsory education system in the Ipswich area. After the formation of UCS, Suffolk College ceased to exist and its further education activities were reformed under a reconstructed and rebranded Suffolk New College. Together these two institutions are part of a significant physical and economic regeneration development of Ipswich and constitute the Ipswich 'Education Quarter'.

The UCS model includes both a central facility (the Hub) within the Ipswich Education Quarter and a network of key centres of learning across Suffolk and Great Yarmouth. The Hub houses both the central corporate roles of UCS – including the Chief Executive's Office, Finance, Human Resources and Estates – and academic delivery through two faculties: Arts, Business and Social Sciences; and Health, Wellbeing and Science. UCS provision builds on, and integrates with, the academic excellence of the UEA and Essex, and has been designed to offer new opportunities and support individual achievement while contributing to the economic and cultural development of Suffolk and the wider eastern region.

The UCS strategic plan for 2007–8 to 2011–12 foresees the volume, breadth and depth of HE expanding rapidly and significantly over an extended period, and the quality of the learners' experience being enhanced through the implementation of new approaches to student support, quality assurance and enhancement and capital investment. Student support is co-ordinated across the Hub and other key learning centres, with a focus on employability. Quality assurance and enhancement and other regulatory systems have been aligned with those of the UEA and Essex through co-ordinated planning, validation and assurance arrangements designed to build on best practice, address the differences of approach of the two universities and demonstrate robust, confident and coherent practice to external agencies. Capital investment has focused on the development of new teaching accommodation in Ipswich, with resources also supporting specific developments across the learning network. Student residential accommodation is being developed to UCS requirements by private-sector agencies.

These actions seek to support the doubling of student numbers from 3,400 FTE in 2007–8 to 7,000 FTE by 2015–16. At the time of writing, UCS had operated as a single institution for one recruitment round. However, the indications are that despite not having dedicated facilities, residential accommodation or a well-established market position at this stage of its development, it offers an attractive destination for those progressing to HE, especially those based in Suffolk and the sub-region. Compared with a national growth in 2007 of 5.8 per cent overall, UCS grew its undergraduate population by 8 per cent. This provided an early but nonetheless positive sign that the planning targets outlined above are achievable. Further growth is premised on a combination of addressing, through local provision, the current under-participation in HE in the East of England and attracting prospective home, EU and international students to Suffolk as a preferred location.

For the 2009–10 intake, academic subject areas include postgraduate opportunities in management, tourism and design; professional quali-fications in nursing, midwifery, radiography and social work; new provision in the creative industries, financial services and early years; established provision in biological sciences, the fine and applied arts, education, performance and history; and contemporary study in computer games technologies and the social sciences. These are complemented by innovative programmes of study that support independent and negotiated learning and continuing professional development. This choice of curriculum reflects the legacy of previous development of HE in Suffolk, the areas of expertise of staff who transferred to UCS from Suffolk College and investment in new curriculum areas. Combined, they constitute an offer that seeks to be relevant, explicitly demand-led and accessible.

UCS courses lead to joint awards of both the UEA and Essex, with ultimate academic authority for the quality of the degree provision resting with the Senates of the two universities. In practice, this is handled through a Joint Academic Committee with joint chairs drawn from the UEA and Essex, and representation from the universities and the UCS Hub and learn-ing network.

As part of its core mission, UCS is also developing new commercially funded applied research, knowledge exchange, consultancy and professional development services, and creating new arts and cultural opportunities. Indeed, employer engagement is seen as a key element of the co-ordinated enterprise agenda, and one closely aligned with the HEFCE notion of business and community engagement. The direction of travel for this expan-sion is known, and detailed business and curriculum planning is now in place to drive the collective aspirations of UCS and its founding universities. Initial grant funding from the HEFCE will be supplemented by income-generating activities to 'kick-start' this activity.

The first new university building on the Ipswich waterfront opened for the 2008–9 academic year with significant funding support from the HEFCE, the EEDA and local authorities. A second phase of the development, including significant student accommodation and student union facilities, is scheduled for 2010–11. This will again be largely dependent on grant funding plus borrowing, but expansion thereafter will be largely driven from surpluses on recurrent activity. The challenge will not simply be to grow UCS, but to ensure that its provision remains relevant, that there is a robust infrastructure in place to support students and that there are appropriate employment and other opportunities available at the end of a period of study. These will require strong and sustained levels of business and community engagement and collective community leadership. With these in place, the enormous value associated with the location of a university in a community can be realised.

Exploring the Model: A Theoretical Perspective

The creation of UCS represents a major element of the reshaping of the higher education landscape in the East of England. At the same time as the creation of UCS, the HEFCE enabled a more rational set of alliances between local FE and HE institutions, so facilitating link-ups between the UEA and City College Norwich and the University of Essex and Colchester Institute. The UEA and Essex thereby operate at the heart of a network of FE–HE partnerships stretching from the north Norfolk coast to the Thames. In addition, this realignment brought two potentially competitor HE institutions, the UEA and Essex, together to participate in a bold and imaginative joint venture with very considerable potential.

Nonetheless, the UCS model is contrary to the trend within UK tertiary education for institutions increasingly to seek to combine the delivery of both further and higher education. Elsewhere, there is expansion, particularly of higher education within the further education sector, fuelled to some extent by the introduction of foundation degrees. For example, the University of Teesside has supported the co-location of HE centres with FE colleges in Darlington, Hartlepool and Middlesbrough, with a similar model emerging in Burnley supported by the University of Central Lancashire, while in Cornwall a multi-partner approach has established the Combined Universities for Cornwall to broaden and widen access to higher education within established institutional governance structures. The prospect of some FE colleges being granted awarding powers for foundation degrees (under the Further Education and Training Act 2007) is likely to increase the growth of sub-degree and undergraduate HE provided within the further education sector and to add further complexity to the pattern of delivery of higher education in the future.

The contextual specifics of UCS help to explain why the development of HE in Suffolk is following a different pattern from developments elsewhere. However, building on the work of Thomas and Funnell (2007), and employing perspectives developed by Borys and Jemison (1989) for use in understanding joint ventures in the business world, a theoretical analysis can be adopted to help tease out some of the key features of the UCS venture and further explain some of the causes and challenges of this approach.

Four major areas of challenge can be identified in the establishment and successful implementation of joint ventures:

- value creation;
- joint venture purpose;
- boundary definition;
- joint venture stability.

Borys and Jemison suggest that value creation is the primary motivating force behind the establishment of joint ventures. They claim that parent organisations come together to form a joint venture when they identify that doing so will create value that each partner could not achieve separately. In the case of UCS, both the UEA and Essex identified potential added value and risk reduction in a collaborative approach. While each of the parent institutions is seeking to expand within a competitive environment, additional constraints in this case – what might be called 'regional imperatives' – supported a joint venture approach.

The creation of a joint venture between two independent and competing institutions has the potential to create conflicts of interest and make keeping an appropriate balance of practice between the two challenging. The venture's purpose serves to legitimise the actions of each of the separate institutions and acts as an incentive for those therein to maintain commitment to the venture and to seek solutions to challenges as they occur. In the case of UCS, the stated purpose – to deliver high-quality higher education across Suffolk and beyond – legitimises the actions of each of the participating universities. It is this institutionalised and shared commitment that enables leaders at these institutions to legitimise their actions to stakeholders and the wider communities of interest.

The creation of a new joint venture between two separate institutions requires a number of boundaries to be defined or redefined. Not least among these is the boundary between the parent institutions and the joint venture itself. In the case of UCS this task is made more complex by formal and legal requirements associated with governance, financial probity and academic quality requirements operating in the higher education sector. Discussion earlier in the chapter outlines how complex governance, management and quality assurance arrangements have been developed to address these challenges between UCS and the universities. Such arrangements have also been crafted between UCS and its network of partner colleges and between

UCS, the universities and major funders, including the HEFCE and the National Health Service. Indeed, unlike Suffolk College, UCS is not directly funded by the HEFCE; rather, its income from this source comes through the UEA on behalf of the two parent universities, given the specific legal status of UCS. Such income is, however, explicitly directed to UCS and is not subject to a 'top slice' or handling fee. This situation is different in respect to a major contract to deliver nursing and other allied health professional courses where the contract is directly with UCS, and resultant income is paid directly to UCS. In both these areas the boundaries are clearly defined and codified, and each institution understands its role, obligations and limits.

In other areas the boundaries are less clearly defined, creating management challenges for UCS. One example of this, the curriculum offer at UCS, is in part determined by the management teams across Suffolk and Great Yarmouth; however, final planning approval is required from the parent universities to address concerns regarding unhelpful competition. Where the proposed offer at UCS can be seen as competition by either or both of the parent institutions, multi-agency mechanisms to address potential tensions have been introduced to facilitate resolution and ensure a clear and common understanding of the purpose of the venture and its boundaries. Key to this is the role of the Joint Academic Committee, referred to earlier, and the work of the Partnership Offices of the two universities, which, alongside emerging academic planning structures, support and encourage dialogue and the resolution of disputes.

The fourth challenge for joint ventures concerns their long-term stability and sustainability. There exists an inherent instability where competing organisations come together to create a joint venture of the complexity of UCS. This may result from differences in expectations, institutional values or commitment. In the case of UCS the stability of the institution, and of the partnership between the two parent universities, is supported in part through the influence and active support of extra-hybrid organisations such as HEFCE and EEDA.

Conclusion

UCS is a bold and imaginative experiment. It appears to run with the *Zeitgeist* in that UCS is featured in the Department for Innovation, Universities and Skills' *A New 'University Challenge'* (March 2008), in which the Secretary of State declared:

> The importance of universities and other higher education providers to the national economy is becoming increasingly well recognised. A local, high quality campus can open up the chance of

higher education to young people and adults who might otherwise never think of getting a degree. Higher education now provides the skills and knowledge transfer that enables local businesses to grow and attract new investment to the area. Over and above their contribution to economic regeneration and development, universities and other higher education providers are seen as making a real difference to the cultural life of our towns and cities.

So it is not surprising that increasing numbers of towns and cities are seeking to offer higher education.

With its launch in 2007, UCS has begun the process of addressing its primary economic rationale while contributing to wider community development and cohesion. It has done so with a clear commitment to regional regeneration, widening participation, promoting excellence, and providing a creative and effective contribution to realising the aspirations for a high value-added knowledge economy. But critical issues of stability and future role and position remain. As was noted earlier, Borys and Jemison (1989) point to the inherent instability of such joint ventures, and the dynamic nature of UK higher education will inevitably test the current UCS model of practice in future years. Different models of practice exist both in the United Kingdom and internationally, and, while detailed consideration of these lies outside the scope of this chapter, it is reasonable to assume that the model of an independent university in and for Suffolk, the original aim of the community drive in the county, will re-emerge. Whether this is either politically desirable or economically viable now or in the future is questionable. Clearly, other imaginative models informed by international practice may emerge (see, for example, Newby, 1999; Douglass, 2003), one of which could place UEA and Essex at the research heart of a collection of partner agencies delivering high-quality provision specialised by location and academic excellence across the eastern segment of the East of England. Such developments, as with the establishment of UCS itself, will be context-specific. Indeed, it is this theme of context specificity that emerges strongly from this chapter. The development of this new university presence, its unique governance and management structures, and its complex relationships with stakeholders have been a consequence of a dynamic interaction between policy, strategic intent and serendipity, and it has benefited from the opportunity to align a range of disparate institutional and policy aims, supported and driven by a vocal and robust community commitment. This is a key learning outcome of the UCS experience: that initiatives of this kind are less a function of rational planning and rather more a consequence of opportunities being identified and grasped. In such circumstances the resultant organisational culture also needs to be entrepreneurial and supportive of sensitive risk-taking and transparent communications. Above all, it must be driven by an overarching vision and argument. In the UCS case this can be simply presented. It is that there is fundamental value to be realised in establishing a university presence in Suffolk, a value that transcends the operational difficulties in achieving, maintaining and nurturing it.

Further Reading

Quality Assurance Agency, http://www.qaa.ac.uk (accessed 14 March 2008).
University Campus Suffolk, http://www.ucs.ac.uk (accessed 14 March 2008).
University of East Anglia, http://www.uea.ac.uk (accessed 14 March 2008).
University of Essex, http://www.essex.ac.uk (accessed 14 March 2008).

References

BiGGAR Economics (2005) *Business Plan for University Campus Suffolk*, Roslin: BiGGAR Economics.
Borys, B. and Jemison, D. B. (1989) 'Hybrid arrangements as strategic alliances: theoretical issues in organizational combinations', *Academy of Management Review*, 14 (2): 234–49.
Department for Innovation, Universities and Skills (2008) *A New 'University Challenge': unlocking Britain's talent*, London: DIUS.
Douglass, J. A. (2003) 'Is California's higher education system a model for UK HE?', *Perspectives*, 7 (2): 41–7.
National Committee of Inquiry into Higher Education (1997) *Higher Education in the Learning Society*, London: NCIHE. Online, available at: https://bei.leeds.ac.uk/Partners/NCIHE//.
Newby, H. (1999) 'Higher education in the twenty-first century: some possible futures', *Perspectives*, 3 (4): 106–13.
Thomas, W. and Funnell, P. (2007) 'Regional imperatives: remodelling the relationship between two competitor universities', paper presented at the Annual Conference of the Society for Research in Higher Education, 11–13 December, Brighton.
Touche Ross Consultants (1995) *A University for Suffolk: Testing the Vision*, London: Touche Ross.

CHAPTER 13

Assuring the Quality of Educational Provision in Universities

JOHN DISHMAN

Leeds Metropolitan University

Universities as institutions have a responsibility to ensure that students who choose to study with them can achieve a recognised and accredited award that is meaningful to the outside world. In a globally competitive university market, potential students can choose to study almost anywhere they wish, so long as they can afford to pay the relevant fees. It is therefore extremely important for national systems of higher education to inspire confidence that the quality of provision in universities is high. This chapter will explore how this process is undertaken, focusing principally on the United Kingdom but with short case studies for comparison outlining the approaches in three other nations: Denmark, the Republic of Ireland and the United States of America.

The Quality Assurance Landscape for Higher Education in the United Kingdom

Institutional audit is the means by which universities in England and Northern Ireland are reviewed in order to ensure that they are providing higher education awards and qualifications of an appropriate standard, and are exercising their legal powers to award degrees in a proper manner. Universities in the United Kingdom are constitutionally autonomous organisations, and as independent corporations they exercise their legal powers to develop and award academic qualifications. Their degree-awarding powers are both unlimited and irrevocable. However, since universities rely to a very large extent on public funds for both teaching and research, they are accountable for the quality and standards of their educational provision to the appropriate funding council. In England this is the Higher Education Funding Council for England (HEFCE). Other parts of the United Kingdom are covered by the Higher Education Funding Council for Wales (HEFCW), the Scottish Funding Council (SFC) and the Department for Education in Northern Ireland. Each of these funding councils has a legal responsibility for ensuring the quality of the education it funds.

Quality assurance and enhancement processes in the United Kingdom have had a number of iterations over the past two decades, including a very thorough and rigorous process of subject review between 1993 and 2001 (Quality Assurance Agency, 2003), which has now been replaced with a lighter-touch approach, on which this chapter concentrates. In England the HEFCE has devised a framework for securing the quality of teaching and the standards of awards: the Quality Assurance Framework (QAF) was brought into operation in 2002–3 and it consists of:

- institutional audit (and where there is substantial collaborative provision, a collaborative provision audit);
- publication of teaching quality information (TQI), which includes the results of the National Student Survey (NSS) and the Destinations of Leavers from Higher Education survey.

The HEFCE does not carry out the audits itself but contracts with a separate organisation, the Quality Assurance Agency for Higher Education (QAA), to carry them out on its behalf. In England and Northern Ireland the audit is known as an institutional audit. The QAA carries out a similar role in Scotland, the 'enhancement-led institutional review', and in Wales, the 'institutional review'.

The QAA was established in 1997 to provide an integrated quality assurance service for UK higher education. It is an independent body funded by subscriptions from universities and colleges of higher education, by contracts with the funding councils and by a number of professional bodies. It describes its mission as 'to safeguard the public interest in sound standards of higher education (HE) qualifications and to inform and encourage continuous improvement in the management of the quality of HE' (Quality Assurance Agency, 2006). To that end, it sees its role as ensuring quality through providing threshold standards for university awards, both identifying and promulgating good practice, strengthening institutional self-regulation and helping to provide a valid basis for the reputation of higher education in the United Kingdom.

The QAA carries out its quality assurance responsibilities in two main ways. First, it has developed the 'Academic Infrastructure'. This is a set of standards and reference points that universities and colleges with degree-awarding powers use to develop awards and manage the quality of their provision. The Academic Infrastructure (Figure 13.1) was developed in conjunction with the HE sector, and underpins the QAA's quality assurance activities. It comprises:

- Two frameworks for HE qualifications (one for England, Northern Ireland and Wales and one for Scotland). These are intended to promote a clearer understanding of the achievements and attributes represented by the main qualification titles, for example Bachelor's or Master's degrees.
- Subject benchmark statements, which set out expectations about the standards of degrees in a range of subject areas.
- Programme specifications, which are the sets of information each institution provides about its programmes.
- The Code of Practice for the assurance of academic quality and standards in HE, which is a guideline for good practice relating to the management of academic standards and quality.

Second, it uses the Academic Infrastructure as the basis for audits and reviews of both academic standards and the academic quality of learning provision at the institutional level.

'Academic standards' refer to the level of achievement that a student has to reach to gain a particular award (e.g. Bachelor's or Master's degree). They should be at a similar level in all HE institutions in the United Kingdom. Since the QAA provides a national service, it is in a position to compare academic standards across all UK institutions, so that a degree in one university has broadly similar expectations of student achievement to a degree in any other.

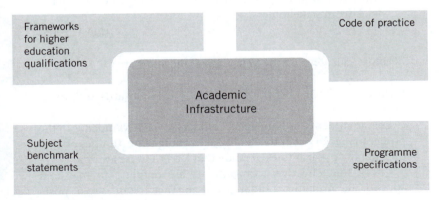

Frameworks for higher education qualifications

Code of practice

Academic Infrastructure

Subject benchmark statements

Programme specifications

Figure 13.1 The Academic Infrastructure.

'Academic quality' refers to the learning opportunities that are provided to students to enable them to achieve their qualifications. These include teaching, assessment, facilities, learning support and the learning environment.

Institutional Audit

The institutional audit, which currently takes place on a six-yearly cycle, uses a peer review process, drawing upon the experience and expertise of academic staff in the HE sector or from industry and the professions. It is 'evidence based' in that it draws conclusions about quality that are under-pinned by evidence provided by the institution. A key aspect of the audit process is that it focuses on students and their learning experience.

Aims and Objectives of the Institutional Audit

The QAA describes the aims of the audit as being to meet the public interest in knowing that universities and colleges in England and Northern Ireland have:

(a) Effective means of ensuring that the awards and qualifications in HE are of an academic standard at least consistent with those in the Framework for higher education qualifications in England, Wales and Northern Ireland (FHEQ) and are, where relevant, exercising their powers as degree-awarding bodies in a proper manner.

(b) Effective means of providing learning opportunities of a quality that enables students, whether on taught or research programmes, to achieve those HE awards and qualifications.

(c) Effective means of enhancing the quality of their educational provision, particularly by building upon information gained through monitoring, internal and external reviews and feed-back from stakeholders.

(QAA, 2006)

Furthermore, it states that the objectives of the audit are to:

Ensure that the academic standards of UK HE awards and quali-fications are maintained and securely managed.

Enable students and other stakeholders to have confidence in the proper management of the quality of learning opportunities offered through the programmes of study that lead to those awards.

Check that effective arrangements are in place to maintain appropriate academic standards and enhance the quality of post-graduate research programmes.

Contribute, in conjunction with other mechanisms and agencies in HE, to the promotion and enhancement of quality in teaching, learning and assessment.

Ensure that students, employers and others can have ready access to easily understood, reliable and meaningful public information about the extent to which the HEIs in England and Northern Ireland are individually offering programmes of study, awards and qualifications that meet national expectations in respect of academic standards and quality of provision.

Ensure that, if the management of academic standards or of the quality of provision is found to be weak or seriously deficient, the process forms a basis for ensuring rapid action to improve it.

Provide a means of securing accountability for the use of public funds received by HEIs.

(Quality Assurance Agency, 2006)

Focus of the Audit

At an institutional level, the audit examines four key areas:

- *The effectiveness of the institution's internal quality assurance systems*: the audit will examine the extent to which the Academic Infrastructure (and the European standards and guidelines for quality assurance in higher education) are being used to underpin the institution's own quality assurance processes. In particular, it will look at the mechanisms for review of its education provision and standards, and at how effective the organisation is in implementing improvement.
- *The effectiveness of the arrangements for maintaining appropriate academic standards* and enhancing the quality of postgraduate research programmes.
- *The effectiveness of the institution's approach to quality enhancement*: the extent to which it uses the outcomes of the internal quality assurance processes, external reviews, and feedback from students, graduates and employers in order to develop and implement institutional approaches to enhancing the quality of its provision.
- *The accuracy and completeness of the information* that an institution publishes about the academic standards of its awards and the quality of its educational provision.

Institutional Audit and the Academic Framework

QAA audit teams use the Academic Infrastructure as a source of reference points as they review the way in which an institution secures the quality of its academic standards and manages the quality of its learning provision. However, rather than regarding it as a rule book, institutions should use the Academic Infrastructure to inform their practice of quality management.

In addition to the Academic Infrastructure, institutions also have to demonstrate that they have taken account of the European Standards and Guidelines for quality assurance in higher education (ESG; see European Association for Quality Assurance in Higher Education 2005), particularly in the context of the Bologna Process (for constructing an European higher education area).

It is useful to examine how the audit team uses each of the four parts of the Academic Infrastructure.

The Framework for Higher Education Qualifications. The audit teams examine how the institution ensures that there is an alignment between the academic standards of their awards and those in the levels described by the FHEQ.

Code of Practice. The QAA published the *Code of Practice for the Assurance of Academic Quality and Standards in Higher Education* in response to the Dearing Report (National Committee of Inquiry into Higher Education, 1997a) and its Scottish Committee (the Garrick Report, NCIHE, 1997b). The Code of Practice, is intended to help higher education institutions to meet their responsibilities for the assurance of academic standards and quality by providing a framework within which they can consider the effectiveness of their individual approaches to a range of activities.

The Code of Practice is divided into sections containing the key issues that an institution should consider in the respective areas of activity. The precepts encapsulate the matters that an institution could reasonably be expected to address through its own quality assurance arrangements. The guidance that accompanies each precept suggests possible ways by which those expectations might be met and demonstrated.

During the audit, institutions will not be asked about their adherence to the Code of Practice on a precept-by-precept basis. They will be expected to explain how they have addressed the intentions of the precepts, including any resulting changes to their practices and any areas of difficulty that they have experienced.

Subject benchmark statements. The subject benchmark statements set out expectations about standards of degrees in a range of subject areas and were achieved by negotiation with the relevant subject communities. They describe what gives a discipline its coherence and identity, and define what can be expected of a graduate in terms of the abilities and skills needed to develop understanding or competence in the subject. The audit team looks to see how the institution has taken the subject benchmark statements into account and how it manages the use of subject benchmarks.

Programme specifications. A programme specification is a concise description of the intended learning outcomes from a higher education programme, and how these outcomes can be achieved and demonstrated. For the purpose of audit, they are the definitive publicly available information on the aims, learning outcomes and expected learner achievements of programmes of study. The audit team wishes to be assured of their accuracy, their uses and their usefulness to students and staff of the institution.

Enhancement

Quality enhancement is defined by the QAA (2006) as 'the process of taking deliberate steps at institutional level to improve the quality of learning opportunities'. Audit teams comment specifically on the approach taken in the institution to developing and implementing institutional strategies for enhancing the quality of educational provision. Enhancement is concerned with systematic institutional-level planning to bring about steady, reliable and demonstrable improvements in the quality of learning opportunities. It should be a strategic development process operating institution-wide and not merely a collection of isolated examples of good practice or innovation.

Enhancement applies only to the quality of learning programmes, since learning is a process and its quality can be enhanced. Academic standards are a defined level of achievement and cannot be enhanced.

The audit teams examine the institutional approach used to enhance the quality of both its taught and its research programmes. They seek to see the extent to which enhancement is institution-wide, how embedded the enhancement strategy is, the impact it is making and whether improvements have taken root and are themselves being enhanced.

Quality enhancement, which had not previously been prominent in the institutional audit process until this current round, is perhaps the most significant area that UK institutions should focus on. Successive iterations of the audit methodology have moved from ensuring that standards are met and processes followed to examining the way in which the institution sets about continuously improving the quality of the student experience. Increasingly, universities will need to identify an organisational approach to quality enhancement that is intrinsically linked to the cycle of quality assurance. They need opportunities to identify areas that are in need of improvement from internal monitoring processes and teaching quality information (TQI), acting on this information to introduce sustainable improvements. They also need to engage in more developmental activities, identifying and sharing good practice within and outside their own institution to introduce systemic improvement.

Audit teams will look for how the staff in the organisation utilise its enhancement processes to improve student learning. It is important that they understand how quality enhancement fits into the university's quality assurance strategy. It is important, too, that universities do not limit their quality enhancement activities to isolated projects that are self-contained and neither last beyond the life of the project nor are applied university-wide.

> At Leeds Met a number of quality enhancement audits have been undertaken over the last three years, using an approach developed by Brown and Holmes at the University of Northumbria (2000). A short-term working party is established to review a theme identified by the Pro-Vice-Chancellor for Assessment, Learning and Teaching: themes have included formative assessment, international students and student retention. Looking initially at the documentation the university provides (including course handbooks, the prospectus, academic papers, and so on), the team then interviews staff, students, senior managers and other stakeholders in sample schools or faculties to evaluate the extent to which the university is fulfilling its promises. The most important aspect of the quality enhancement audit teams' work is the compilation of a series of 'reasons to be cheerful' when good practice is identified and 'plans for action' where gaps are found. The resulting report is then presented to the Academic Committee, which ensures that the quality loop is closed by disseminating the positive learning from the experience and following up indicated action required.

Gathering the Evidence

The audit team has access to a variety of information sources both before the audit itself takes place and during the actual visit.

- *The Institutional Briefing Paper.* This is a paper prepared by the institution that is being audited. It should set out how the institution ensures the academic standards of its awards and the quality of its educational provision. It should also contain the institution's judgement on the effectiveness of its approach. Since the review is evidence based, the Institutional Briefing Paper should contain references to evidence that supports the judgements made.

- *Key documents.* These include such documents as the strategic plan, corporate plan, quality manual, etc. These documents, unlike the Institutional Briefing Paper, are not manufactured for the purpose of the audit. They exist as part of the way an institution communicates within itself and the outside world. They should naturally reflect the institution's approach to securing academic standards and providing a quality learning experience.
- *Reports and information not prepared by the institution* – for example, reports that can be accessed directly by the QAA about the institution, such as those written by the QAA or other relevant bodies, such as professional, statutory and regulatory bodies, within six years of the date of the audit.
- *Teaching quality information,* which is prepared by HEFCE and is available on the Unistats website (www.unistats.com). It contains information gathered about the institution from three main sources: the National Student Survey (NSS), which contains feedback from final-year undergraduates about the quality of their courses; the Destination of Leavers of Higher Education (DLHE) data, which provide information about the destinations of leavers, job categories and job types; and statistics from the Higher Education Statistics Agency.
- *A summary paper* about the institution prepared for the audit team by the QAA.
- *A student briefing paper.* Students of the institution are invited to prepare a written submission. The QAA advises them to consider four questions: How accurate is the information that the institution publishes? Do they know what is expected of them? What is the student experience as a learner like? Are students able to voice their views to the institution?

During the audit, the audit teams use 'audit trails' to gather information and evidence in an organised and systematic way. They are used to focus in on a particular institutional approach, policy or procedure and to test its effectiveness. The teams will use 'sampling trails' to follow the implementation and outcomes of institutional policies and procedures down to programme level and back, or across the organisation to see how a policy or procedure operates in different contexts.

There are normally two sampling audit trails. They focus on the institution's internal periodic review procedures and their outcomes, and the choice of these will be discussed with the institution. Sampling in this way means that the audit team need only use the documentation normally prepared by the institution for its own review processes; this should reveal how the institution carries out its published policies and procedures in practice and how opportunities for enhancement are used, and enable the team to identify how accurately the institution reflects the data captured in periodic review, external examiners' reports and the National Student Survey in published TQI. The audit team also meets students and staff involved in outcomes of institutional policies and procedures to determine their effectiveness in practice.

The Audit Visit

Normally, institutional audits are carried out over the course of a week; however, institutions will prepare for their audit week well in advance. This preparation should not involve the development of new, special or different quality processes or procedures arranged in response to the imminence of audit. Changes and developments in quality assurance, control and enhancement need to be rooted in the normal cycle of institutional development. Those that are devised to impress the QAA audit team usually have the opposite effect.

Institutions will often brief their staff prior to the audit about what they may be asked by the audit team. It can be useful to remind staff about the quality assurance processes, since not everyone uses the terminology and techniques every day. However, institutions that are attempting to 'manage the message' that staff give the audit team may find it difficult to sustain the attempt across a week of interviews. The audit team is looking for a consistent approach to the management of quality across the institution. Are the university's regulations being universally applied? Have local practices been developed which are inconsistent with those being used elsewhere? Are the quality control principles, benchmarks, external examiners' reports, etc. being used appropriately across the organisation, assuring the standards of the awards and providing the best learning opportunities for students?

Outcomes, Judgements and Comments

The audit results in a report that is published on the QAA's website. In the report, as well as providing summaries of the main findings, the audit team reports on its judgements. It makes judgements on:

- The confidence that can be reasonably placed in the soundness of the institution's present and likely future management of the academic standards of the awards. The judgement is being made not about the academic standards themselves, but on how the institution ensures that its academic standards are secured by the work of both internal and external examiners, judged against the reference points in the Academic Infrastructure.

- The confidence that can reasonably be placed in the soundness of the institution's present and likely future management of the quality of the learning opportunities for students. Again, it is not the quality of the learning opportunities as such that is being judged, but how effectively the institution manages the learning opportunities such that they are of a level of quality appropriate to the guidance in the Academic Infrastructure.

Outcomes of the Audit Visit

If the audit team finds that the institution is managing the security of its academic standards effectively and looks set to continue doing so, it will express its 'confidence'. Equally, it will express its confidence where it finds that an institution is managing the quality of the student learning opportunities soundly and effectively and it appears that this will continue.

If the audit team has substantial doubts about either the management of the security of academic standards or the management of the quality of the learning opportunities, it may express 'limited confidence'. This indicates a positive outcome but that improvements need to be made. If the audit team believes there are serious concerns about the current management of the security of academic standards and/or the quality of provision and/or the future of either or both, it may judge there to be 'no confidence'. This indicates substantial evidence of serious and fundamental weaknesses.

In addition, the report will specifically comment on:

- the institution's arrangements for maintaining appropriate academic standards and the quality of provision of postgraduate programmes;
- the institution's approach to developing and implementing institutional strategies for enhancing the quality of its educational provision in both taught and research programmes;
- the reliance that can be placed on the accuracy and completeness of the information that the institution publishes about the quality of its educational provision and the standards of its awards.

The audit reports can include recommendations for further consideration by the institution. There are three levels of recommendation:

- *essential*: matters that require immediate and urgent action as they are putting academic quality and/or academic standards at risk;
- *advisable*: matters that have the potential to put academic quality and/or academic standards at risk;
- *desirable*: matters that have the potential to improve the quality of the learning provision and/or further secure academic standards.

Collaborative Provision

If there is collaborative provision involved with other universities or colleges in the United Kingdom or internationally, this will be specifically referred to, although institutions that maintain substantial quantities of collaborative provision are normally subject to separate audit arrangements.

Postgraduate Research Programmes

Audit teams specifically have to comment on the institutional arrangements for securing standards and the quality of educational provision in relation to postgraduate research degree programmes. These should be in alignment with the guidance in the Code of Practice.

How the United Kingdom's Approach Compares to Some Other Countries' Approaches

The QAA's approach balances the need for public accountability with respect for the autonomy of universities as degree-awarding institutions. Since its inception the model for external quality assurance has moved from 'inspecting and policing' quality to 'audit and enhancement'. The emphasis has changed, reflecting increasing levels of trust. It is useful to compare the UK model with comparators internationally.

Institutional Review of Higher Education Institutions in the Republic of Ireland

The Irish higher education system comprises two main sectors: the 7 universities and the 13 institutes of technology (plus the Dublin Institute of Technology, which is recognised separately under state legislation and awards its own qualifications). National legislation provides for cyclical reviews of the effectiveness of quality assurance procedures of institutions within both sectors, but distinct legislation applies to each, reflecting their differing history and origins.

The traditional autonomy of the universities was in large part preserved under the Universities Act 1997, with the provision that the governing authority of each university should periodically review the effectiveness of its own quality assurance procedures. This responsibility has now been voluntarily delegated by each university to the Irish Universities Quality Board (IUQB) in relation to the protocols and the selection of agencies to conduct the reviews. The Act does, however, specify that the Irish Higher Education Authority may review and report on the quality assurance procedures developed by the

---

universities, and that the Authority be consulted by the universities in their review of the effectiveness of their quality assurance procedures.

The first formal review of quality assurance procedures and their effectiveness in the seven Irish universities began in January 2004 and was completed in February 2005. The review was jointly commissioned by the Irish Higher Education Authority and the IUQB and carried out by the European University Association (EUA).

The Qualifications (Education and Training) Act 1999 provides that the Higher Education and Training Awards Council for Ireland shall periodically review the effectiveness of the quality assurance procedures that it has established for the institutes of technology (other than the Dublin Institute of Technology), including those with delegated authority to make awards, and for other providers of education and training programmes whose programmes have been validated by the Council.

While the universities and institutes of technology operate under different quality assurance regimes, external quality reviews undertaken in both sectors draw on existing international models of good practice, being based on reflective self-assessment validated by external peer review and leading to quality improvement planning. The systems in both sectors are informed by the *Standards and Guidelines for Quality Assurance in the European Higher Education Area* (European Association for Quality Assurance in Higher Education, 2005), adopted by the ministers responsible for higher education in the Bologna signatory states in 2005.

Further simplification and rationalisation of the structures of external quality management of Irish institutions was raised by the expert group commissioned jointly by the IUQB and the Irish Higher Education Authority to review the performance of the IUQB in carrying out its functions and in its execution of HEA-funded projects. The panel also examined the IUQB's coherence with European standards for external quality assurance agencies. The report of the expert review recommended that

> a continued effort should be made by IUQB and other organ-
> isations to ensure synergy and co-operation between the
> activities and programmes of the various bodies and structures.
> Where opportunity for greater integration or alignment exists
> these prospects should be investigated.
>
> (Higher Education Authority, 2008)

continued

The Irish government brought forward the 2009 budget announcement to October 2008 in response to the economic crisis. This budget included a major rationalisation of state agencies and quangos, including a provision that

> [t]he National Qualifications Authority of Ireland, HETAC and FETAC will be amalgamated. The new organisation will also take responsibility for the external quality assurance review of the universities – a function currently performed by the Irish Universities Quality Board and the Higher Education Authority. In seeking to ensure a coherent approach to qualifications and quality assurance, there will also be discussions with the National University of Ireland around the possibility of including some of the related functions of the NUI in the new organisation.
>
> (Irish Republic Department of Finance, 2008)

No further directives have yet been publicly issued from government on this matter at the time of writing.

Neil Quinlan
Waterford Institute of Technology, Republic of Ireland

Institutional Review in the United States of America

There are essentially three main external mandates related to student learning in US higher education. First, most states require and monitor assessment of some undergraduate learning constructs. Generally the constructs relate to general education, or that aspect of education that underlies all major programmes. For instance, in the state of Virginia each two- and four-year institution is required to report 'value added' (typically defined as longitudinal change) learning in written communication, oral communication, critical thinking, quantitative reasoning, and scientific reasoning. Some states link moneys, often called 'performance funding', to assessment results. Also, some states utilise 'high-stakes' tests to monitor student progression.

Second, each college or university must pass accreditation reviews in order for its students to receive federal financial aid (see www. ed. gov/admins/finaid/accred/index.html for further details). These reviews cover all institutional aspects; however, in recent years it is the student assessment of learning component that has received much attention. Each external team of peers usually contains an assessment specialist, and many institutions are found wanting in their assessment programmes. It is now common for campuses to have an assessment director who co-ordinates assessment activities.

Third, the federal government has been more vocal in its concerns about institutional quality, particularly as it relates to student learning. Through federal student financial aid and research programmes, almost as much money comes to institutions of higher education as through state aid. Therefore, some officials in the federal government believe it has a stake in educational outcomes. Other officials see higher education as a national investment, while other people see a need to ensure that the 'consumer' receives information about quality. Monitoring of the accreditation organisations falls to the federal government.

Dary Erwin
College of Integrated Science and Technology,
James Madison University, Virginia, USA

The Process of External Quality Inspection in Danish Universities

In Denmark, public higher education institutions are publicly financed and consequently they have for many years followed the national legislation concerning, for example, degree structures, teacher qualifications and examinations, including a system of external examiners.

Since the middle of the 1980s, quality assurance has had a consistent place in Danish educational policy. The concept of quality has been accompanied by the growth and spreading of quality assessment activities throughout the educational system. This happened first and most visibly in higher education, where an independent national agency, the Centre for Quality Development and Assessment, was established in 1992 on the initiative of the Minister of Education. The mission of the Centre was to undertake recurrent quality assessment of all higher education programmes. The institutions were obliged to submit their activities for evaluation. The authority to request evaluations was given to the Ministry and to the advisory councils that exist in different areas of education. The councils pursued a policy

continued

that all study programmes in long-cycle higher education should be evaluated at regular five-year intervals. In 1999, after having completed most of the first cycle of evaluation, the Danish Centre for Quality Development and Assessment was transformed into the Danish Evaluation Institute (EVA), with a broader mission to undertake quality assessment and development in all areas of the Danish educational system.

However, during recent years, quality assurance and accreditation has come much more in focus, especially due to:

- the Bologna Process;
- legislation from 2002 concerning transparency and openness concerning education;
- the Organisation for Economic Co-operation and Development (OECD) evaluation of Danish universities in 2004;
- new educational legislation concerning university education in 2004;
- recommendations from the Globalisation Council in 2006.

The Danish Act on the accreditation of higher education programmes was passed by Parliament in March 2007. The Act established an accreditation council composed of a limited number of experts on higher education and institutional provision for preparing the accreditation decisions. ACE-Denmark was established for the accreditation of university programmes.

The Act specified that all Danish higher education programmes, both existing programmes and new ones, are to be accredited over a relatively short span of years. The criteria for accreditation have been specified in a government order. There are ten criteria, each of them including several sub-aspects:

1 the societal need for the study programme;
2 the labour market prospects of graduates;
3 the research base for the programme;
4 the presence of active researchers in teaching;
5 the quality and strength of the research environment behind the programme;
6 educational structure;
7 the design of teaching and the skills of teachers;

8 internal quality assurance in the programme;
9 the professional and academic profile of the programme;
10 the learning goals and realised learning outcomes of the programme.

Procedures according to the new external demands have now been decided and developed at the universities. Information about education and study programmes, results of students' evaluations and accreditation processes is now published on university websites.

Lone Krogh
Aalborg University, Denmark

Conclusions

In a number of countries worldwide in the past 20 years there has been a focus on ensuring the nation's confidence in the quality of its higher education systems. While each system differs in its approach, there are considerable similarities between them, brought about no doubt at least in part by the existence of international conferences on higher education quality at which divergent approaches are discussed at length. While countries tend to begin with a model of quality assurance, in time many move towards an enhancement approach, which seems most likely to have long-term benefits. Yet despite such consonance of approaches, it is unlikely that there will ever be a single, worldwide approach to quality assurance and highly undesirable that there should be one.

References

Brown, S. and Holmes, A. (eds) (2000) *Internal Audit in Higher Education*, London: Kogan Page.

European Association for Quality Assurance in Higher Education (ENQA) (2005) *Standards and Guidelines for Quality Assurance in the European Higher Education Area*. Helsinki: ENQA.

Higher Education Authority (2008) *Review of the Performance by the Irish Universities Quality Board of Its Functions by the Higher Education Authority. Report of the Expert Group*, Dublin: Higher Education Authority.

Irish Republic Department of Finance (2008) 'Budget 2009 – Annex D – Rationalisation of State Agencies' (14 October). Online, available at: www.budget.gov.ie/2009/downloads/AnnexDRationalisationOfStateAgencies.pdf (accessed 5 December 2008).

National Committee of Inquiry into Higher Education (1997a) *Higher Education in the Learning Society* (the Dearing Report), London: The Stationery Office. Online, available at: https://bei.leeds.ac.uk/Partners/NCIHE// (accessed December 2008).

National Committee of Inquiry into Higher Education (1997b) *Higher Education in the Learning Society: Report of the Scottish Committee* (the Garrick Report). Online, available at: https://student.bton.ac.uk/citrix/SCAACD/Scottish.htm.

Quality Assurance Agency (2003) 'Learning from subject review'. Online, available at: www.qaa.ac.uk/reviews/subjectReview/learningfromSubjectReview/subjectreview.asp (accessed December 2008).

Quality Assurance Agency (2006) *Handbook for Institutional Audit: England and Northern Ireland.* Mansfield: QAA.

PART **IV**

Maximising Student and Staff Engagement

CHAPTER 14

Getting the Most from Staff

Using Talents to the Full

STEWART HARPER, SARAH GRAY, SUE NORTH
and **SALLY BROWN** with **KATHY ASHTON**

Leeds Metropolitan University

Introduction

Universities depend on the knowledge, skills and talent of their workforce – academic, business support and learning support – to deliver a distinctive and attractive range of academic courses in an increasingly competitive market, as well as in striving towards goals of greater inclusivity and fulfilling missions of social engagement. Employers have long talked about 'the war for talent' and the importance of recruiting, engaging, motivating and developing high-quality staff. This issue is particularly relevant and challenging for organisations such as universities that rely on their 'knowledge workers' for their competitive advantage. As a result, many higher education institutions have put the greater part of their investment into the recruitment and development of their academic staff.

Leeds Metropolitan University (Leeds Met) is one of the largest universities in the United Kingdom, with more than 30,000 students and 3,000 staff. The workforce includes roles from cleaning and hospitality staff to professorial and senior management roles. It is a student-centred university focusing its resources on delivering a high-quality student experience. Recognising that all of its employees play a critical role in creating a positive learning environment and striving to overcome organisational obstacles to progression, the university invests in a range of innovative learning and development opportunities for staff at all levels, which we will outline in this chapter.

Leeds Met's Vision and Character statement (which in many universities, together with the corporate plan, would be called a mission statement) puts 'using all our talents to the full' at the heart of its commitment to engaging, motivating, and developing staff (Leeds Metropolitan University, 2006). In Matthew 25:14–30, the New Testament describes a man entrusting stewardship of his fortune in the form of coins ('talents') to three servants in variable sums 'each according to his own ability'. Two of the servants made the most of the money and increased it, but the most timorous instead buried it and therefore returned only the capital. The master praised the first two 'good and faithful servants' but chastised the third for wasting the opportunity. The implication is that individuals need to make the best of the chances given to them, using imagination and creativity to maximise their potential rather than 'hiding their light under a bushel'.

As organisations that promote lifelong learning, universities have sub-stantial responsibilities to be genuine learning organisations. Since we are significant suppliers of continuing professional development (CPD) to other organisations, we need to demonstrate that we invest in helping our own staff learn and grow. A considerable majority of higher education (HE) insti-tutions spend more than 50 per cent of their total income on staffing, and yet frequently we are wasteful in how we use our staff, allowing colleagues long in post to become stale and unproductive, and failing to stimulate new staff to look for opportunities to develop in post. This is good neither for the organisation nor for the individual.

Helping Staff Use Their Talents to the Full Throughout the Year

To enable staff to fulfil their potential, a university needs to offer diverse development activities. Leeds Met has developed a suite of opportunities that run throughout the academic year to help us get the best from our staff. At the commencement of the academic year we organise a two-week-long Staff Development Festival in which all staff are expected to participate. This is followed by a window of opportunity to apply for our internal second-ment scheme, 'Using Talents to the Full', and then throughout the year we offer staff CPD workshops and events. We are also keen to 'grow' our own outstanding employees, so we recruit graduate trainees to work as interns across the university immediately after their graduation in July. We also offer staff the opportunity to participate in and lead local, national and inter-national volunteering projects (see also Chapter 15), which aim to expand staff horizons, develop their skills beyond the remit of their current roles and enable them to make a contribution to the wider community.

The benefits for Leeds Met as an employer are that we have more highly motivated staff, who have more fulfilling jobs and who recognise us as employers who value personal growth and development that is not narrowly constrained to job-related training. Staff who do their jobs reasonably well on a day-to-day basis but do not engage with the range of development opportunities on offer or engage in enrichment of their own learning are not quite 'thrown into outer darkness', as the biblical parable concludes, but are less likely to achieve career progression within the university.

Outlined next are some of the strategies and initiatives that Leeds Met has put in place to underpin that ethos and ensure that staff have the attitudes, character and talents necessary to make a difference. The university's inclusive approach to developing a high-performing workforce is based, in addition to the areas outlined above, on a number of core features:

- A clear framework of behaviours and skills has been introduced which helps managers and staff understand what the university expects of a professional and committed workforce. The Leeds Met ACTs (Attitude, Character and Talents) framework (Leeds Metropolitan University, 2007) is directly linked to the university's Vision and Character statement (Leeds Metropolitan University, 2006) and was developed through extensive consultation with staff. It sets out clearly what kinds of behaviours and attributes we expect from staff and provides the basis for the university's performance management and development planning processes. A single Performance and Development Review scheme has been established for all staff, which defines performance as a combination of objectives and behaviours. This process informs the award of individual and team contribution rewards to recognise and reinforce high performance.
- An extensive year-round programme of staff development activities and workshops ranging from online materials, mentoring and coaching initiatives to team-building and management development for staff who want to make a contribution and develop their skills in new and challenging ways.

The Staff Development Festival

Since 2005, Leeds Met has held a Staff Development Festival before the beginning of the academic year. We know of no other university that mounts an event on such a large scale, with such ambitious scope and such a celebratory atmosphere as this fortnight-long event in which all staff can engage. The fortnight includes away-days for each of our six faculties, where the dean can bring together the whole faculty staff for a day of training, review, planning and enjoyment. Our Registrar and Secretary's Office (RSO) similarly organises a (not-away) day for the administrative staff in university-wide departments. We also have one- or two-day conferences on assessment, learning and teaching, and research, and for support staff from all faculties as well as from the university-wide support departments.

Alongside these core days we have drop-in staff development sessions and events for staff across the university, plus themed day conferences (on, for example, Refugees and Asylum Seekers, Childhood, and Northern Studies), plus IT training and events foregrounding equality and diversity issues.

Wrapped around the staff development there is a full programme of leisure and personal development options, including, for example, sporting activities (both participative and for spectators), attendance at musical or dramatic events, and community-based events. There is a festival launch and finale which contain celebratory and performance events.

Unique, we think, to this university is the expectation that all staff of all categories participate, and this is reinforced by the requirement that express permission be sought from the vice-chancellor for any leave to be taken during this period. A normal expectation for academic staff members would be therefore that they attend at least their own faculty day and the research and/or the assessment, learning and teaching conferences alongside their admissions duties and preparation of teaching materials during this time. An administrator would attend their faculty day and the support staff conference, with personal development options, and would be encouraged to attend at least another day's worth of staff development. Attendance at other events is a matter of personal choice through negotiation with line managers.

In 2007 and 2008 more than 800 events were organised throughout the festival and we estimate that more than 90 per cent of our staff participate in the event as a whole.

There is enormous benefit in having an occasion each year in which the whole staff of a very large university spend significant time together. Conversations held, for example, between a cleaner and a senior administrator while hill-walking together emphasise the cohesion of a very diverse community and our commitment to valuing the contribution of all. Instead of having lots of expensive and ill-attended events throughout the year, our money is spent instead on activities that are highly cost-effective. For example, our equality and diversity strategy commits us to training all staff in inclusivity issues, but this is often difficult to achieve with, for example, cleaning staff, who attend only in the early mornings. In 2007 we held a morning performance of a specially commissioned play, with subsequent discussion that addressed issues in an enjoyable way for large numbers of staff.

The Staff Development Festival helps us achieve other aims too: we wanted to hold focus groups to discover what barriers prevent disabled people from applying to be staff or students at Leeds Met, so in 2007 we held a well-attended community garden party to which we invited all the local organisations for disabled people and asked our questions over a well-stocked tea table before offering them the chance to attend a brass concert by our university partners the Black Dyke Band. The resultant report and action plan have helped us be more inclusive in our practices. In 2008 this event was broadened to become a Community Festival, encompassing diverse groups from the community and enabling us to explore wider diversity issues.

Over the four years during which the festival has been held, attitudes to it have changed from some initial reluctance to almost complete recognition of the value of the event.

Case Study 1:
Staff Development Festival Fortnight

Louise Lytlle is a cleaning supervisor who was excited by the opportunity to try out scuba diving during the festival in the on-site university swimming pool. Sessions were led by one of our lecturing staff, who enlisted his colleagues from the local British Sub-Aqua Club (BSAC) scuba diving club to enable around 50 staff to try out a new sport. Afterwards, Louise said:

> This was well outside my comfort zone as I don't like my head under the water, so doing that was a great challenge to me and it helped me overcome one of my great fears. It made me realise if you want to do something different and challenging there are people who will support you and be there for you, encouraging you all the way. I would have never even thought about doing it if it had not been for the Staff Development Festival. I learned never to be scared to try something new; it's amazing what you can learn about yourself and others, so my advice to others is to try something that they would never have dreamed of doing. Not only were the instructors on these courses good but the other staff who attended them encouraged each other and gave you support when you needed it. That's what is important: we are all in the same team and we should all be there for each other. I had a great time and can't wait for the next festival in September to see what great courses they have got and to challenge myself to try something else new.

The 'Using Talents to the Full' Secondment Scheme

Following the 2005 festival, the first 'Using Talents to the Full' opportunity was launched by the vice-chancellor. Recognising that individuals sometimes became stale in roles that failed to stretch them, he invited staff to identify potential secondment opportunities for themselves that would enable them to develop their skills, talents and careers further in different roles and areas of the university. It provided staff with a unique opportunity to take the initiative in trying out new roles and making a contribution to the university in perhaps unexpected ways.

The secondment process operates as follows:

- Applicants are given the opportunity to undertake a self-identified role or project that provides scope for personal and professional development.
- The team setting up the secondment arrangement, chaired by a pro-vice-chancellor and including other cross-institutional representative staff, ensures that the secondment delivers organisational as well as individual benefits.
- The secondment is undertaken on the individual's current grade: the scheme is not a direct route to promotion or salary progression.
- The 'receiving' department does not meet salary costs (these are met by the department where the secondee is normally based). In the past, we have always tried to ensure that no department is overstretched.

The scheme has expanded significantly since the first year of operation, when three secondments were organised. In 2007–8, 38 applicants came forward with a diverse range of proposals, as a result of which 25 secondments were arranged, and in 2008–9 similar numbers are being considered. The growing number of staff participating in the scheme is not only evidence of staff awareness of and engagement with the development opportunities available, but also testament to the support and commitment of senior managers, who have demonstrated flexibility in releasing and supporting applicants.

Case Study 2:
'Using Talents to the Full': Learning Officer to Business Developer
Geoff Gifford worked for five years as Principal Learning Officer for Special Skills and Projects in our technology faculty, Innovation North.

This was an IT-centric role, which had some management and project management elements in it. He says:

> After changes in my personal life I realised I hadn't moved on and it came as shock that I lacked experience in my career direction of choice. I am also studying my MBA alongside my post, which gave me glimpses of where I saw my future, but I lacked an essential element of day-to-day experience. Under the 'Using Talents to the Full' scheme I now have a business development remit within the Northern Technology Institute (NTI), working closely with its head to foster innovation within the community and link our technology and businesses faculties, acting as an ambassador for Leeds Metropolitan University. We engage the wider business community at all levels from pre-incubation to partnerships with multinational companies like Apple and Zend. What I really love about the NTI is that we always start off by saying 'yes'. For me personally this has been a phenomenal, life-changing experience. My confidence has been boosted exponentially, and I am now able to clearly visualise my future. My motivation is also off the charts and I love what I do on a daily basis. The big learning points for me relate to the importance of access to people with whom business relationships can be forged.
>
> This process is like staff development on steroids. I now know that the lack of confidence can be more asphyxiating to your career than any other factor. I feel my focus and enthusiasm is rubbing off on my immediate environment. If anyone ever finds themselves – as I was – in a career cul-de-sac, this [Using Talents to the Full] programme with its 'no limits' mindset is possibly the best thing I have ever come across. My advice to someone contemplating such an opportunity would be to be prepared to work hard and to be open-minded about your placement opportunities.

The impact of taking part in the scheme on participants has been profound, as can be seen from the case studies. A significant number of 'Talents to the Full' participants have benefited from the secondment process by securing permanent roles in their seconded area and have been able to achieve a change in career direction that might not have been accessible to them via other routes.

Participants in the scheme to date have indicated that they have benefited from the experience in the following ways:

> My personal/professional gains are in gaining new perspectives and working with new colleagues.
>
> It has been both a refreshing and liberating experience.
>
> I saw 'Talents to the Full' as an exciting opportunity to learn new skills, meet new people and to use my experience to be part of a project which involved all staff throughout the university.
>
> During my secondment I worked both horizontally and vertically in the university, and beyond, on a range of projects. This was great, and really improved my confidence in terms of working with senior staff.
>
> It was good to feel I was making changes and taking responsibility for the type of work area I really wanted to explore.
>
> I have presented at two international conferences and have two book publishing projects under way. The research focus has encouraged collaboration with colleagues elsewhere in the university.

Case Study 3:
'Using Talents to the Full': Student Services Manager to Equality and Diversity Officer

Ian Clarke was Student Services Manager at Harrogate College, then part of Leeds Met. He felt that he needed a change and a new challenge. He comments:

> I applied for a secondment, and an opportunity came up in the Equality and Diversity team. This was originally a six-month secondment but it later became the permanent post I am in today. I immediately bounced back and felt refreshed by new challenges and a new environment.

Ian felt able to put his skills to use devising and leading a range of staff development activities and workshops at various staff development events.

> My management and interpersonal skills were also fully utilised and appropriately 'stretched' when I was asked to take on the co-ordination of the university's mediation service. My

---

background in disability support was also called upon when I was asked to lead a small working group to draft a staff disability policy.

I feel appreciated and comfortable with the challenges of equality and diversity and I feel that the secondment has mutually benefited me and the university.

As the scheme progresses and the number of past and current participants increases, the university will benefit from a growing number of individuals who are more fully engaged and motivated and who have gained a breadth of experience from undertaking different roles across the institution.

Case Study 4:
'Using Talents to the Full': Cleaner to IT Worker

Shamsurizam Norsham comments:

I joined Leeds Met as a part-time cleaner in 2004 and also run an IT and web solutions business. I graduated from Loughborough University in Electrical and Electronics Engineering with a strong desire to develop an IT-based career. As part of the 'Using Talents to the Full' scheme I was given opportunities to work in areas which better utilised my IT skills. Initially I worked as a media loans assistant, which involved front desk customer support, assisting students and staff with enquiries, dealing with audio-visual equipment loans and providing technical assistance for equipment in teaching areas. Working within the team really helped to improve my confidence. Also, as English is my second language, dealing with customers every day both face to face and on the telephone has really improved my communication skills.

Although this time was extremely beneficial, I felt that my programming and web development skills still weren't being fully utilised. After discussing this with my manager, he agreed to transfer me to work alongside programmer analysts. I have seven years' experience of website and system programming, and I hope to utilise and develop these skills within this new team. I'm really looking forward to this new experience. It will be challenging but

continued

I love a challenge. I feel that the scheme is a great opportunity for staff looking to enhance their careers, develop their skills and gain experience in areas in which they enjoy working, allowing them to demonstrate capability in the workplace, rather than just in an application form. Also, the university benefits, as staff members' talents are fully utilised and developed, leading to a better-skilled and, ultimately, more satisfied staff.

Volunteering at Home and Internationally

Many university staff take part in a whole range of volunteering activities in their local communities, and Leeds Met has always been keen to encourage its staff to do so. As a university with a strong international ethos, Leeds Met has placed significant emphasis on enabling as many students as possible to take part in volunteering projects both in the United Kingdom and overseas. However, the opportunity to take part in international volunteering experiences has increasingly been extended to staff. There are a number of reasons for this approach:

- It offers personal development of a quality and extent that truly take staff beyond boundaries, encouraging them to use all their talents to the full.
- It provides members of staff with opportunities to work alongside students on real challenges away from familiar surroundings.
- It provides members of staff with the chance to experience the university's international strategy and vision to develop 'worldwide horizons' in a very practical sense.
- Having the opportunity to lead and/or participate in international volunteering projects provides the scope for staff in 'non-management' roles to develop leadership and project management skills away from the workplace which enhance their performance and confidence at work.
- The opportunity to do something personally and socially rewarding often enhances the level of commitment that staff have towards the university.

The university matches staff contributions for each day of annual leave taken for volunteering with a pro rata day's work. Staff volunteers are recruited to diverse projects and need to demonstrate in advance what they want to achieve and learn through the experience. Once they have been selected, often as a project leader to work with students, they are required to recruit the team members who will participate on the expedition and to ensure that some team-building activities take place before the group sets off. While they are abroad, the team leader needs to demonstrate flexibility, problem-solving skills and leadership skills. Many of the projects involve long-term partnerships, so there need to be clear objectives and expectations of what the team will achieve during their visit. In particular, the project leader needs to represent the university, develop relationships and ensure that the expedition achieves the goals that have been agreed with the partner organisation.

Staff who have participated in these experiences to date tell us they have been really energised by them, as demonstrated in the next case study. They are keen to put their confidence and skills into practice by engaging in local community projects, seeking secondment opportunities and delivering workshops at the Staff Development Festival.

Case Study 5:
Overseas Volunteering
Gill Porter says:

As a Study Abroad Officer I prepare and send students on international exchange to some fantastic destinations. In January 2008 I had the opportunity to travel abroad myself through Leeds Met's International Volunteering programme. A group of us travelled to Ahmednagar in India to live and work with disadvantaged children and young adults. It was an incredible experience. I taught computing and arts and crafts, although I originally thought I was going to be teaching English! It was a steep learning curve but I loved being away from my comfort zone and rising to the challenge of doing something different. I went with a totally open mind, wanting to contribute just a little something of myself. I came away feeling that not only had the children learned a little from us, but we had learned so much from them. The co-ordinators of these projects are awe-inspiring: committed, dedicated and beyond generous. On my return, I have a different focus and am deeply committed to fund-raising for these life-enhancing projects. I am also starting to volunteer with the Leeds Asylum Seekers Support Network.

Continuing Professional Development Throughout the Year

Almost every higher education institution offers a programme of workshops, learning lunches and day events designed to help staff develop personal competencies, skills and capabilities. Many people regard CPD as a painful and boring process associated with the compilation of action plans to satisfy the requirements of professional bodies or to achieve recognised status. Few embrace it as an opportunity to set exciting and dynamic personal learning and development goals. At Leeds Met we see CPD not as a means to an end, but as an ongoing process designed to assist the individual in identifying desired outcomes, for example promotion to a management position, the acquisition of skills or the changing of professional direction by undertaking a programme of academic and professional study. Our annual CPD programme is announced during the Staff Development Festival, so that staff development is seen as a process that continues throughout the year, with activities and enthusiasm triggered during the festival at the beginning of the academic year.

Continuing professional development is not a luxury option; it is the process by which individuals, teams and organisations gain competitive advantage and achieve world-class status. Megginson and Whittaker (2007) define CPD as

> [a] process by which individuals take control of their own learning and development, by engaging in an on-going process of reflection and action. This process is empowering and exciting and can stimulate people to achieve their aspirations and move towards their dreams.

Covey (2004) argues that one should begin with the end in mind and discover how to set goals to inspire ourselves. The individual goals that we want to achieve may or may not align with those of our employer. At Leeds Met there are expectations at different levels set out in our Attitude, Character and Talents approach (Leeds Metropolitan University, 2007), and annual Personal Development Reviews are designed to enable an analysis of the skills required for other job roles and discussions to help match them with an individual's self-identified development areas. Other approaches include asking others for feedback on performance, for example through psychometric, 360-degree feedback or Occupational Competency Personality tests and competencies, or by working with a coach or mentor who will assist in setting goals.

Making Appraisal Work Well

A performance development review or appraisal is an opportunity to communicate in a two-way dialogue directly with one's manager to set work objectives for a specific time period, usually 12 months, to be reviewed throughout the course of the year. The review or appraisal is an opportunity to ask for support in terms of resources and learning and development from the manager. Learning and development are not restricted to simply attending training courses: they can involve a wide range of on-the-job and off-the-job activities, as Table 14.1 shows.

TABLE 14.1 Learning and Development Opportunities

Off-the-job	On-the-job
Training workshops Lectures/seminars Programmes of study leading to formal qualifications Role plays Simulation/in-tray exercises Visits and tours Conferences Online learning packages Distance/open learning courses Team-building away-days Volunteering activities	'Sitting with Nellie', i.e. learning from an experienced colleague Observation/imitation Job instruction National Vocational Qualifications Mentoring Coaching Job rotation Temporary promotion 'Assistant to' positions Committee/project work Apprenticeships Shadowing someone in a different role Secondment
Advantages:	*Advantages:*
Allow experimentation without risk Away from interruptions and demands of workplace Allow for own pace of study Suit theoretical and reflective learners Skills development (but these are quickly lost if not transferred to the workplace)	Relevant to job skills 'Fit' with job context Relatively low cost Establish work relationships Suit activist and pragmatic learners Assist in understanding culture of organisation
Disadvantages:	*Disadvantages:*
High cost, high financial investment	Pressure of real work content Depend on training skills of managers/supervisors

Personal Training and Development

During annual review or appraisal, an individual can formulate an agreed personal training and development plan, which might look like the example shown in Table 14.2.

TABLE 14.2 Example of a Personal Training and Development Plan

Activity	Where	Why	When	Resources required	Progress to be reviewed
Qualification: Neurolinguistic Practitioner course	External training provider	To improve influencing skills	One full week attendance on course in June and self-study	£2,000 Time to attend Travelling costs	With manager in next review
Coaching	Internal coach from training and development department	To improve confidence in giving presentations, and participating in meetings with senior staff	Six sessions to be agreed and held throughout the academic year	Internal coach and time	Self-reflective learning log and with manager in next review

Achieving a 'Just Do' Attitude

From time to time, an individual might encounter a situation where their manager is not open to learning and development, owing to the manager's restrictive views or because resources are scarce. Frustrations can build and CPD can function as an escape valve for ambition and desire to succeed. In this instance one can develop a personal plan of action involving a wide range of activities such as those suggested in Table 14.3, opposite.

Mentoring and Coaching

A proven method of support to gain an edge in developing your career along the right track is to get a mentor. The word 'mentor' originates from Greek mythology; Odysseus set out to war and left his son, Telemachus, in the care of his friend Mentor, who undertook to tell him all he knew. A mentor therefore can be a trusted friend, a sounding board and someone to explore ideas with. At Leeds Met there are a number of formal and informal mentoring schemes. For example, new deans are mentored by a pro-vice-chancellor, and new teaching staff work closely with established teacher fellows, who are staff promoted on the grounds of their excellent teaching with an advocacy and support role within their faculties for innovative assessment, learning and teaching.

In recent years at Leeds Met, since we became the National Centre for Coaching Excellence in 2008, there has been a strong focus on coaching across the university in diverse contexts. Coaching can be a powerful opportunity for exploration and development of potential, and the coach

TABLE 14.3 'Just Do' Supplementary Activities

Activity	Purpose
Apply for other jobs or register with recruitment agencies and collect information on, for example, job descriptions and specifications of jobs you aspire to	To audit your skills and experience to inform a personal action plan of what you need to do to get out of a dead end situation
Networking	Professional bodies hold networking events which are useful for building knowledge and getting to know other employers
External courses leading to professional and academic courses	To gain qualifications to enhance career development, for example degree, postgraduate Master's, management diplomas
Mentoring	Find an external mentor; this can sometimes be achieved through professional bodies or through your networking contacts
Volunteering opportunities and pro bono work	Working for charitable organisations and community groups to gain valuable experience

serves to assist the coachee in identifying what their potential can be. Whitmore (2002) critiques common review and appraisal systems:

> Unless the manager or coach believes that people possess more capability then they are currently expressing, he will not be able to help them express it. He must think of people in terms of their potential, not their performance. The majority of appraisal systems are seriously flawed for this reason. People are put in performance boxes from which it is hard for them to escape, either in their own eyes or their manager's.

Coaching can be a tool to help individuals to break out of habits and patterns that are not working well. Where there is no formal coaching system within a university, there are a growing number of options of how to gain an understanding of experience of coaching, and these are listed in Table 14.4 on p. 240.

What is a 'Coaching Culture'?

Clutterbuck and Megginson (2005) describe a coaching culture as being one in which '[c]oaching is the predominant style of managing and working together, and where a commitment to grow the organisation is

TABLE 14.4 Self-Help Options to Gain Coaching Skills

Read a good text, for example *The Coaching Manual* by Julie Starr (2003)

Attend an internal or external training workshop to acquire basic coaching skills

Join a coaching network, for example one organised by the Association of Coaching, and work towards an accredited qualification

Find two colleagues with whom you can form a coaching triad – a coach, a coachee and an observer – and then rotate

Self-coach – use a reflective technique to set goals, ask important questions and explore options using creative techniques, for example mind mapping or Edward de Bono's 'creative ideas' (2007)

embedded in a parallel commitment to grow the people of the organisation'. Typically, an organisation where a coaching culture exists is one where coaching is linked into organisational strategic objectives, not seen as a stand-alone panacea for all development needs. The Chartered Institute of Personnel and Development's 2007 learning and development survey confirmed that 71 per cent of organisations now use coaching as a learning and development tool. However, results from the survey indicated wide variations in practice to develop a coaching culture, with clear objectives in relation to coaching being rare at senior management level. An organisation's definition of coaching must be congruent with the existing culture and language of that organisation. Passmore (2006) defines the difference between coaching and mentoring as follows:

> A mentor has experience in a particular field and imparts specific knowledge, acting as adviser, counsellor, guide, tutor, or teacher. In contrast, the coach's role is not to advise but to assist coachees in uncovering their own knowledge and skills and to facilitate coachees in becoming their own advisers.

Organisations that have introduced coaching have noted some of the following benefits:

* more effective leadership;
* reduced sickness absence;
* increased productivity;
* improved outcomes;
* a workforce better equipped to manage change;
* greater job satisfaction;
* a more motivated workforce.

Self-Reflection

Leeds Met encourages continuous reflection among its staff, not least through our daily online reflections (blogs). For those whose preferred learning style is self-reflection, keeping a learning diary or log can provide a tool that helps to convert experience into abstract thinking on how to improve performance in the future, for example by using the following checklist.

Checklist for Writing a Learning Log

- Select an experience that was important to you. Why was it important?
- Write a brief account of what happened – no evaluation, just description.
- How did you react? What were your feelings? What were the reactions and feelings of others?
- Analyse the situation – what sense can you make of it?
- Identify your learning points from the experience. What did you learn about yourself? What did you learn about others?
- What have you concluded from your analysis, about your own way of behaving and working and about others?
- In the light of your conclusions, what will you do differently next time?
- Finally, how and when will you get or make an opportunity to put this changed behaviour or way of working into action?

The Graduate Trainee Scheme

One way to recruit outstanding staff is to grow your own talent. Leeds Met's graduate trainee scheme was launched in 2006, a ground-breaking and innovative development, and one of very few in UK higher education to directly recruit its own students on their graduation specifically to enrich engagement. In the first year the university recruited two graduate trainees, who were joined by another ten graduates in 2007. Fourteen graduates were offered places on the two-year scheme from July 2008.

The scheme to date has only been open to Leeds Met graduates and aims to give them the best possible range of opportunities to develop an administrative or management career in the HE sector. Graduates normally undertake six placements, each of about four months, during their two years on the scheme, undertaking these placements across different parts of the university to gain a good general experience across the corporate functions

(Finance, HR, Registry, Communications, Marketing, Estates and IT) and faculty management. The range of placements is designed to provide varied experience and, as far as possible, to support the development and career aspirations of the trainees, although this can be altered by mutual agreement to give maximum flexibility.

In many cases, graduates have had opportunities that would have been unavailable to them on other schemes, or if they had gone straight into external employment. One student, for example, has spent a placement with Leeds Carnegie, a professional rugby union club that is supported by the university (see Case Study 6), and another has represented the university overseas with international partners in Mumbai.

Case Study 6:
Graduate Trainee

Emma Beith joined the graduate trainee scheme in July 2007 after graduating with a BA (Hons) in Sport and Recreational Development from Leeds Met and then spending two years as president of the Athletic Union. She says:

> Leeds Met's graduate trainee scheme gave me an opportunity to use my interest in sport and develop my skills in marketing and events. For the past six months I have worked with the Director of the Headingley Carnegie Stadium Partnership as Leeds Carnegie Rugby Union returned to the Guinness Premiership – Rugby Union's elite competition. I've been responsible for organising match-day entertainment and helping to create a match-day experience that attracts families, Leeds Met staff and students to come and support the team.
>
> Working in partnership with a professional sports club and a university is not an experience that comes along every day, but I've tried to make the most of it. The university has made a big investment in these placements: the 12 trainees have been given staff development and HR input that someone of my age just graduated wouldn't normally get.
>
> I suppose from the university's point of view they've been able to keep a dozen students with different experiences who want to put something back in. There are obvious benefits in capital- ising on this experience. Staff can benefit from what we can offer, and we benefit from their experiences – so it is definitely a partnership.

Key to the success of the scheme is senior management support and a comprehensive development programme. Students collectively meet the vice-chancellor weekly to discuss current strategic issues and to hear first-hand how the university is implementing its Vision and Character statement (Leeds Metropolitan University, 2006). In addition, all graduate trainees are allocated a senior mentor with whom they meet regularly. The trainees participate in an in-house management development programme for aspiring managers and are supported to complete a further professional qualification. In addition, one senior colleague has taken overall responsibility for the scheme and meets all the trainees individually and collectively on a regular basis. This package of ongoing CPD and support allows the trainees to enquire and take risks, but retain the knowledge that they will be supported in their activities.

When graduate trainees are on placements, line managers are expected to involve them in regular team meetings and other activities: they are very much 'part of the team'. For example, managers are strongly encouraged to accommodate the trainees within open-plan offices to allow them to engage more closely with colleagues. There are obvious benefits for staff, and for the university, in that the scheme allows a close interaction with recent keen, outstanding and talented graduates. As these graduates then have knowledge of more than one area of the university's core business, the scheme also helps improve links between faculties and the corporate services.

Outside their formal placement opportunities and normal line management, the trainees are expected to engage within the university's spirit of festivals and partnerships. For example, the trainees are all involved with the Staff Development Festival, Freshers' Festival and Graduation Festival. Many of them will travel with the student recruitment team when major events take place across the United Kingdom and Ireland. All of this is designed to give the trainees an even closer understanding of the workings of a major university and the interrelationships between its various parts.

Staff too benefit from what such recent graduates can bring to the team: they may gain a better understanding of the student voice from people very close to their own student experiences, and gain refreshing inputs into their own activities. At an organisational level the trainees provide the university with a potential talent pool that will enable Leeds Met to grow future managers and help some of its talented graduates have a wider impact across the HE sector.

Graduate trainees are fully accountable for what they do: they have as high expectations placed upon them as any other member of staff, and are expected to embrace the university's vision in the way they conduct themselves. In exchange, though, they are presented with opportunities that they would struggle to find elsewhere and as a result are likely to benefit hugely from the experience.

Learning from Experience

Our experiences at Leeds Met over the five years or so in which this development work has been undertaken have led to significant reflection and learning. We are aiming to continuously improve how we get the most from our staff by creating and making best use of diverse opportunities. The key learning points have been as follows:

- Experimental approaches can be risky, but this does not mean that they are not worth trying. We have encountered resistance to some of our approaches, for example the restriction of vacation-taking during our Staff Development Festival, but over the years this has diminished as staff have come to understand its value and purposes.
- It helps greatly if communication channels about what we are trying to do and how it fits in to our overall Vision and Character statement are clear, and if there are opportunities for staff to input ideas and interrogate the rationale underlying programmes.
- Senior management commitment and involvement are essential if these university-wide initiatives are to be successful. For example, the university's 'Using Talents to the Full' secondment programme would not have got off the ground if deans and senior managers had failed to co-operate with the principle of supporting the salary costs of members of their teams while they work elsewhere.
- It can be difficult to fully evaluate the impact of these types of initiatives, but it is important to demonstrate how they are contributing to the performance of the university if they are to be sustainable.
- It is crucial to continue working with staff to follow through on some of the experiences in order to embed the learning. So, for example, we often ask staff subsequently to deliver workshops at the Staff Development Festival to share what they have gained with others, or ask individuals to produce 'reflections', which are posted on our website for other colleagues to read.
- It is very rare to get these initiatives 100 per cent right first time, and many of the programmes that we have outlined in this chapter have evolved in response to feedback from participants and a commitment to continuous improvement.
- The impact of these programmes is greatly enhanced because of the clear links that they have to the university's behavioural framework (ACTs) and Vision and Character statement. Through the university's Performance and Development Review Scheme, staff are expected to link their development plans back to the ACTs

framework; therefore, the development needs they identify and the learning they experience through the Festival, volunteering or secondments should always align with the university's goals and expectations.

Conclusions

We find it noteworthy that a growing number of staff, when applying for new opportunities for self-development, make specific reference to other experiences and opportunities that they have been given access to through the Staff Development Festival, ongoing CPD sessions, UK volunteering opportunities, the graduate trainee scheme and more long-term staff development, including achieving MBA qualifications, or through involvement in the university's overseas volunteering projects. This demonstrates that staff are engaging fully with our diverse range of development opportunities and gaining the motivation or confidence to challenge themselves professionally in new roles as well. The combination of the Staff Development Festival with year-round development activities, overseas and community projects, the Teacher Fellow network and the 'Using Talents to the Full' secondment programme is delivering a varied range of opportunities designed to promote and stimulate the personal and professional growth of staff across the university.

Leeds Met is not unique in recognising the value of developing its staff. The cost of recruiting and training staff is such that retaining good staff is economically sensible as well as operationally necessary. The retention of good staff, in an increasingly competitive global market, can only become more important. Richard Scase (2007) put this quite succinctly when he argued, 'Today, if you want to recruit and retain the best Western talent you need to be creative, finding ways to offer psychological as well as material well-being'.

The opportunities for development (in its widest sense) form part of a 'psychological contract' that staff are buying into. Staff clearly look for 'meaning' in their work, rather than simply financial reward. Leeds Met's approach has been a straightforward one:

- Define an overall vision and character for the university.
- Set clear expectations of the attitude, character and talents expected of staff and design processes to assess these.
- Put in place development options for all staff – both to 'do things better' and to 'do better things'.
- Set an expectation that staff should always be 'raising the bar' to self-improve.

Around this is a culture of ongoing refreshment and development. Within one of the major spaces in the Headingley Campus, our newly refurbished Gandhi Hall, hangs the following saying from Mahatma Gandhi: 'As human beings, our greatness lies not so much in being able to remake the world . . . as in being able to remake ourselves'. This is, surely, the purpose of staff development: to allow individuals and staff to continually refresh and renew themselves. Leeds Met's approach to 'using all our talents to the full' shows we are striving to do so.

Useful Websites

Association of University Administrators, www.aua.ac.uk
Institute of Administrative Management, www.instam.org
Institute of Chartered Secretaries and Administrators, www.icsa.org.uk
Chartered Institute of Personnel and Development, www.cipd.co.uk
Association for Coaching, www.associationforcoaching.com
The Coaching and Mentoring Network, www.coachingnetwork.org.uk

References

Chartered Institute of Personnel and Development (2007) *Learning and Development*. Survey Report. London: CIPD.
Clutterbuck, D. and Megginson, D. (2005) *Making Coaching Work: Creating a Coaching Culture*, London: CIPD.
Covey, S. R. (2004) *The 7 Habits of Highly Effective People: Powerful Lessons in Personal Change*, 2nd edn, London: Simon & Schuster UK.
de Bono, E. (2007) *How to Have Creative Ideas*, London: Vermilion.
Leeds Metropolitan University (2006) 'Vision and character'. Online, available at: www.leedsmet.ac.uk/the_news/docs/visionandcharacter08.pdf.
Leeds Metropolitan University (2007) 'Attitude, character and talents'. Online, available at: www.leedsmet.ac.uk/metoffice/hr/index_acts.htm.
Megginson, D. and Whitaker, V. (2007) *Continuing Professional Development*, 2nd edn, London: CIPD.
Passmore, J. (2006) *Excellence in Coaching: The Industry Guide*, London: Kogan Page.
Scase, R. (2007) *Global Remix: The Fight for Competitive Advantage*, London: Kogan Page.
Starr, J. (2003) *The Coaching Manual: The Definitive Guide to the Process, Principles and Skills of Personal Coaching*, London: Pearson Education.
Whitmore, J. (2002) *Coaching for Performance: Growing People, Performance and Purpose*, 3rd edn, London: Nicholas Brealey Publishing.

Thanks to Kathy Ashton, Leeds Met, for contributions to this chapter on coaching.

CHAPTER 15

University–Community Engagement

Analysing an Emerging Field

MAX FARRAR
Leeds Metropolitan University

with **RICHARD TAYLOR**
University of Cambridge

This chapter presents a discussion of various approaches to university–community engagement in the United Kingdom and offers a new approach to defining this work as a value-driven, mutually beneficial process of respectful negotiation and practice with partners outside the university. We suggest that volunteering by staff and students is central to this practice, while the historic role of universities in providing opportunities for adult education and lifelong learning is noted as the pioneer of university–community engagement. The chapter concludes with a discussion of some of the data on volunteering and the problems of evaluating the field of university–community engagement. The following linked chapter provides examples from Leeds Metropolitan University (Leeds Met) of diverse forms of community engagement in practice.

What is Meant by University–Community Engagement?

There are several historical roots for what is now known as 'university–community engagement' which need to be considered in the search for a viable definition of this emerging field of higher education activity in the United Kingdom. Apart from Watson's important book *Managing Civic and Community Engagement* (2007), this is a relatively new area for academic scholarship, in the United Kingdom at least.

The first strand of activity feeding into university–community engagement today was known as 'extra-mural education' (so called because courses were taught 'beyond the walls' of the institution) and is now more frequently referred to as 'adult education' or 'lifelong learning'. Adult education, as a distinctive practice, has been marginalised by the trend over the past 15 years or so to include adults, often as part-time students, in the more flexible, modularised programmes of study in UK universities. Instead, some universities have developed this field under the heading of 'lifelong learning' and/or the development of 'access' programmes for educationally disadvantaged adults; and/or the development of 'knowledge transfer' programmes.

Models of Adult Education in British Universities

Universities have a long history of engagement with their local communities. In the modern industrial and post-industrial context, most universities had their origins in the perceived need of a local community, usually the local establishment, for a university presence. Most of the 'civic' universities in the United Kingdom were created around the turn of the twentieth century. Leeds, for example, was originally founded on the local industrialists' concerns with educating the workers in the textiles, engineering and mining industries – and to this day these subject areas are a central part of the University of Leeds and its culture. It is also worth noting that at Leeds, as at other civic universities, a large majority of students were locally, not nationally, recruited until well after the end of the Second World War (Gosden, 1983).

Many of these civic universities, and later others too, such as Hull and Leicester, had large and centrally important extra-mural departments whose primary concern was adult education provision in their local and regional communities, often in partnership with the Workers' Educational Association (WEA), through the Joint Tutorial Classes Committee. Cambridge and Oxford had been the first universities, in 1873 and 1878 respectively, to establish programmes of extra-mural lectures, an early form of what we would now call 'outreach'. This was organised on a national scale across England, particularly in the industrial north and the Midlands, and, of course, predates the foundation of virtually all other English universities. So, these traditions of community engagement are deeply rooted historically and culturally in the British higher education system; and community engagement has remained, albeit in different forms, a major aspect of the UK higher education (HE) system (Watson, 2007).

The existence and continuing importance of this tradition are therefore not in dispute. However, the nature, purpose and ideological position of such work *are* contentious. At the risk of being overly schematic, we argue that there are now at least three different perspectives, or ideologies, in operation:

- the 'high culture', liberal elite model;
- the knowledge transfer, business model;
- the radical social purpose, social inclusion model.

The pioneers of extra-mural work in the late nineteenth and early twentieth centuries certainly fell predominantly under the high culture, liberal elite perspective. Influenced by the neo-Hegelian idealism of T. H. Green (Mander and Dimova-Cookson, 2006) and others, and by a strand of high Anglican Christian evangelism, the extra-mural lecturers and, indeed, the founder of the Workers' Educational Association, Albert Mansbridge, believed in knowledge for its own sake as an a priori good. Further, they believed passionately that the intellectual riches of the university should not be restricted to a tiny elite, but as far as possible communicated to the wider society. In that sense, the inspiration was *democratic* and in keeping with the changing social and political structure and culture. It was also, of course, elitist; the concept was very much one of transmitting a given, unquestionable body of accumulated wisdom and aesthetic and scientific excellence to the uninitiated. Moreover, some analysts (notably Roger Fieldhouse, 1996) have argued that both the university extra-mural movement and the WEA were in reality agencies of social incorporation and thus of social control. With a newly enfranchised mass working class, it was important for the established order to ensure that accepted wisdom, or bourgeois ideology, was instilled into opinion leaders in the working class, and the spectre of socialism and revolution countered through education.

This strand of liberal, elite education persisted throughout the twentieth century, though more often finding its expression in middle-class programmes than reaching out to what we would now call the educationally disadvantaged (though there were exceptions, as discussed later in the chapter).

From the 1940s onwards, the second perspective, the knowledge transfer business model, has become increasingly dominant. There has been a growing realisation by government, and certain sections of the employing class, that education and training at a high level are essential for economic competitiveness. The application and realisation of the rich intellectual 'knowledge banks' contained in universities – especially in the applied sciences, medicine and some of the applied social studies areas – were of particular importance. As universities expanded from the 1960s, and particularly from the 1980s, so the demands of government for more *utilitarian* approaches by universities became more strident. This climate was of course exacerbated by Thatcherite, and later New Labour, general ideological stances (Taylor, 2009; Coffield, 1999); J. F. Lyotard, one of the intellectual founders of post-modernist thought, put this presciently some time ago:

> The question (overt or covert) now asked by the professionalist student, the State or institutions of higher education is no longer 'Is it true?' but 'What use is it?' In the context of the mercantililization of knowledge, more often than not this question is equivalent to 'Is it saleable?' And, in the context of power-growth, 'Is it efficient?'
>
> (1984: 51)

'Knowledge transfer' and the growing importance for government and employers of the so-called knowledge society have given this area of development increasing prominence in the university system.

Throughout its history, however, university adult education has always had a third – and vociferous and significant – strand of opinion that has been linked to socialist and other progressive ideological stances. 'Knowledge is power' has been a strong motivating force for those who have believed that only through educational access and enlightenment could a genuine democracy be created. From the time of the working-class 'moral force' Chartist movement, education in general, and adult education in particular, has been seen as the key catalyst for social change and emancipation.

What were effectively compensatory, albeit large-scale, programmes of workers' education were an important part of the provision of post-compulsory education and training from the 1920s onwards in many late capitalist societies. From the 1970s these have been complemented by community education, women's educational initiatives and more general access development. There is now a recognition that in our persistently unequal society there are complexes of disadvantage going beyond the traditional, male, manual working class: disadvantaged women, ethnic minority communities, disabled people, tenants and the unwaged are among them.

It is important, though, to emphasise that universities are inherently elitist institutions and that such egalitarian impulses have remained relatively marginal. Interaction with 'the community' has been seen by those in authority in universities very largely as a combination of the transmission of the liberal high culture of the academy, and the 'knowledge transfer', continuing professional development (CPD) and self-funding or surplus-generating work, undertaken in liaison with the large corporations and institutions of the capitalist system. It hardly needs adding that since the eras of Prime Ministers Margaret Thatcher and Tony Blair, it is the latter perspective, with its neo-liberal overtones, that has become even more dominant.

Volunteering as a More Recent University–Community Engagement Activity

It is tempting to see adult education, lifelong learning, knowledge transfer and access programmes as segueing into the emergence of 'community engagement' centres in the universities, but this chapter aims to reveal the differences of emphasis among these projects, stemming from differing ideologies of education. It also aims to mark out 'volunteering' as a central more recent feature of community engagement work for universities.

'Volunteering' is one discrete element in 'community engagement' which is not adequately described within access programmes, lifelong learning or knowledge transfer. The promotion of volunteering by staff and students has been central to universities' focus of community engagement over the past few years, and considerable resources have been deployed in the development of volunteering in British universities. The Higher Education Funding Council (HEFCE) provided £27 million from the Active Community Fund (ACF), with the goal of creating 14,000 new opportunities for volunteers by 2004 (Fitzgerald and Peterman, 2004).

Propelled into action by the offer of relatively large sums of money, almost all UK universities now have volunteering programmes for their staff and students, and thus the ideas of 'active communities' (the title of the HEFCE programme, reflecting wider government projects to inspire 'active citizens') and volunteering have been linked. The emergence of the national youth volunteering agency 'V' in 2006, with a budget of £100 million (Miliband, 2007), based on the Russell Commission's report *A National Framework for Volunteering and Engagement* (2005), is further indication of governmental support for volunteering as a vehicle for community engagement. V defines volunteering as 'spending time, unpaid (bar necessary expenses) doing a form of activity which benefits others in the community, society or the environment' (V website, 2008). But it would be wrong to make 'community engagement' synonymous with, and reduced to, volunteering. The fact that the Active Community Fund was wound up in 2006 and the relevant HEFCE programme at the time of writing is now called 'Business and Community', recalling its Higher Education Reach-Out to Business and the Community programme of 1999, indicates that, for HEFCE at least, the stress is on linking 'community' with 'business', another reduction that rings alarm bells with those of us who aim for a much broader remit for community engagement.

Defining University–Community Engagement

Given their scholarly remit, we might expect universities themselves to spell out what they mean when they use the term 'community engagement'.

Fitzgerald and Peterman (2004) interviewed five elite Russell Group universities with long-standing community engagement programmes, one of which defined its overall aim as 'to empower local communities'. Their actual programmes included sports coaching, community counselling, a legal advice centre and the provision of volunteers for local organisations, but no clear definition of community engagement emerged. When Universities UK issued its short leaflet *Universities: Engaging with Local Communities* in January 2006, it felt no need to define 'community engagement', stating simply that '[o]ne of the core aims of UK higher education has been to meet the needs of the wider community'. 'Wider community' here appears to be a synonym for 'society at large', and 'engagement' seems to be providing services to society, listed as follows (ibid.):

1 knock-on economic effects (e.g. 89 'knock-on' jobs created for every 100 university jobs);
2 providing skilled graduates;
3 knowledge transfer;
4 spin-out companies (151 created in 2003);
5 providing professionals in health, law, teaching, architecture and engineering;
6 student purchasing supporting local businesses;
7 accommodation strategies which contribute to urban regeneration;
8 university museums, galleries, theatres;
9 lifelong learning;
10 sporting facilities (open to the public in England and Wales for 71 per cent of the time and 91 per cent of the time in Scotland);
11 student volunteering;
12 tackling anti-social behaviour by students;
13 producing students who are tolerant and active citizens.

It is significant that seven of these are economic objectives, and this reflects a distinct ideological strand in the current government's thinking on the kinds of engagement to which universities should contribute to promote economic growth. In fact, the 'Active Community Fund' has since 2006 been tapered off and until 2009 was integrated into the Higher Education Innovation Fund (HEIF). After 2009, no money will be allocated by government to this strand of higher education's work. Despite its statement that universities should make 'a significant and measurable contribution to economic development *and the strength of communities*' (our emphasis), the outcomes that seem to mainly interest government are economic ones (Watson, 2007: 49–52).

Professor Sir David Watson, who was instrumental in the extensive community engagement programmes at Brighton University (Watson, 2007), provides a stimulating review of various definitions of civic and community engagement developed over the past few years. In his view, civic engagement should be much more than knowledge transfer: it implies 'a dialogue across the boundary between the University and its community which is open-ended, fluid and experimental' (Watson, 2007). This emphasis on process is picked up in the definition provided by the Association of Commonwealth Universities in 2002, which went on to spell out the fields in which this engagement should take place:

> Engagement implies strenuous, thoughtful, argumentative interaction with the non-university world in at least four spheres: setting universities' aims, purposes and priorities; relating teaching and learning to the wider world; the back-and-forth dialogue between researchers and practitioners; and taking on wider responsibilities as neighbours and citizens.
>
> (Watson, 2007: 3)

This approach implicitly sets economic objectives in their proper place as one aspect of teaching and research that is relevant 'to the wider world'. It is again clear that 'community' stands for 'society', and only the last of these spheres implies any specific activities by staff or students outside their normal university responsibilities. However, much more specific, outward-facing requirements have been set elsewhere. Watson summarises the declaration at a Tufts University conference whose 'Talloires Declaration, 2005' is worth careful study. It enjoined universities to work actively on 'civic engagement and social responsibility programmes'; to 'embed public responsibility through personal example'; to encourage and reward 'social service' by staff and students; to foster community partnerships that 'enhance economic opportunity, empower individuals and groups, increase mutual understanding' and make education and research more relevant; to demonstrate universities' 'contribution to social advancement and well-being'; and to help schools with 'education for active citizenship' programmes (Watson, 2007: 4–5). The preamble stated, 'We pledge to promote shared and universal human values, and the engagement by our institutions within our communities and with our global neighbors' (Talloires Declaration, 2005).

While we endorse these commitments, several practical and theoretical issues need to be debated if they are successfully to be put into practice. Leaving aside the thorny problem of whether or not there *are* universal human values, the problem of what is meant by 'community' has to be addressed.

Greg Miller, the deputy head of Access and Community Engagement at the University of Leeds, explained how his unit's thinking about these matters has developed over the past few years. He described 'community engagement' in these terms in a personal communication of 2008:

> Our early engagement was about seeking to improve relationships with the local communities through self-directed interventions that we believed would improve perception and ameliorate problems associated with large student populations. This approach however has evolved considerably into a genuine two-way dialogue with the local community to identify opportunities for collaboration and partnership for mutual benefit.

In this approach, community engagement is a process of dialogue for the benefit of both the local community and the university. However, Miller is aware that the term 'community' requires unpicking:

> We hold reservations about self proclaimed community groups in that they tend to be single issue groups brought together through adversity. Whilst we value and work with many of these groups and recognise they are community led – they, in the main, do not have broad representation either of students or the more disadvantaged members of their communities.
>
> (ibid.)

Community Action at Leeds Metropolitan University (CALM) picks up the 'empowerment' point mentioned above, but emphasises empowering students, rather than residents, stating, 'The aim is to enable and empower student volunteers to manage, deliver and participate in voluntary community action projects, in response to local needs' (LMUSU website, 2008). But CALM emphasises that its social action is rooted in the requirements of local organisations and would no doubt endorse the idea of 'community empowerment'.

Research at Leeds Met (Farrar, 2002) deconstructs the notion of community, arguing that it carries both realist and idealist connotations. In the realist tradition, community is measured geographically (what are its boundaries?), emotionally (how extensive and deep are the bonds between people?) and in terms of its values and goals (how widely are these shared among people in this so-called community?). Miller (2008), like many others in universities who are engaging with communities, is well aware that, in every neighbourhood, claims to represent 'the community' have to be interrogated, since even if the neighbourhood can be clearly demarcated, it is very rare that shared goals and deep emotional bonds proliferate across the entire neighbourhood. The idealist approach on the other hand suggests that community is not a measurable entity but an ideal, a longed-for state in which there are deep emotional bonds and shared values and goals among definable groups of people. When the 'community' flag is being waved, it is usually to call people into line behind this ideal.

In the inner-city, multicultural-area research undertaken here in Leeds, it was evident that radical social movements were the bearers of this yearning for the ideal community, but in other neighbourhoods it might be religious groups or political parties of both left and right. Whether we take a realist or an idealist approach to defining 'community', the notion of *engaging* with 'the community' is, therefore, fraught with difficulty. In the realist approach, universities must recognise multiple 'communities' in any one neighbourhood, and their engagement with one 'community' might provoke cantankerous debate with another 'community'. Thinking of 'community' as an ideal, even utopian, state might well help when universities set out their visions, and might make universities heighten their respect for the often inchoate strivings of local organisations, but this approach requires much additional discussion when devising practical engagement strategies.

Given both the complexity of the meaning of terms like 'engagement' and 'community' and the inherently political nature of the activity, universities need to think hard about their definitions of community engagement. We suggest that 'community' is such a multifaceted concept that universities use it simply as a portmanteau term for all those groups whom we seek to serve other than our own staff and students. While in our view 'empowerment' is a laudable aim, it is only one among many important goals, and the focus of our definition should be on process and values, rather than particular outcomes. Our proposed definition is therefore as follows:

> University–community engagement is a process in which universities identify and nurture partner groups and organisations among all the constituencies they seek to serve (in their locality, nationally and abroad). In a process of dialogue with partners, universities initiate activities in line with their core values, and respond appropriately to initiatives arising from those constituencies. Engagement with these various partner 'communities' is based on clear understanding of each party's values and goals, and engagement activity results in mutual benefit and enrichment for both partners. The principles which underlie these engagements are mutual respect, reciprocity, transparency, and equality of status.

The particular goals set out in the Talloires Declaration 2005, described on p. 253, would normally be an excellent guide to community engagement activities, but universities will need to set their own priorities. Broadly speaking, engagement activity should normally develop citizenship skills among the university members and the partners. The emphasis on equal status in this definition would work against the elitist model of education.

Thus, for example, we would argue that we should redefine what the government calls 'knowledge transfer' as 'knowledge exchange'. Access/widening participation and lifelong learning agendas will require specific types of partnerships (in the former, crucially, with schools serving disadvantaged neighbourhoods; in the latter with a wide range of organisations, including trade unions, professional associations, civic societies, businesses, etc.). Knowledge exchange should be seen as a form of university–community engagement that serves not-for-profit voluntary organisations and social enterprises as well as commerce. Clearly, the 'volunteering' aspect of community engagement is a distinct stream of activity, which might be defined as an effort by universities to develop ethical global citizens who engage altruistically and supportively with not-for-profit organisations and marginalised groups. Here, again, an anti-elitist ethos that prioritises work with excluded populations across the globe is advocated. Common principles, set out above and further elucidated in the following section, should underpin universities' approach when engaging in all these types of work.

Values, Ethics, Ethos: Volunteering and More

The partnerships established at Leeds Met (some of which are described in the following chapter) are highly diverse in their nature, with different parts of the university focusing on different types of organisation. They are being developed in line with the ethos of community engagement expressed by the Board of Governors and implemented by the university's senior management, as set out in the Leeds Met Vision and Character statement, for example:

- 'putting students at the centre of our way of doing things . . . increasingly going beyond boundaries throughout the student experience' (para. 1);
- 'a university of festivals and partnerships . . . which values pioneering relationships with [organisations in] . . . wider community life' (para. 2);
- 'the Leeds Met rose [part of our logo] [will be] widely known as a symbol of engaging and stretching students and communities' (para. 4);

- 'a university of reflections where the curriculum and the wider university is refreshed by running streams of insights, expertise & creativity' (para. 6);
- 'using all our talents to the full . . . encouraging students to deepen participation by valuing extra-curricular activities, such as volunteering, and ensuring that this approach embraces diverse communities' (para. 7);
- 'a university with world-class horizons where an international, multi-cultural ethos is pervasive throughout our scholarship, curriculum, volunteering and community engagement at home and overseas' (para. 9).

(Leeds Metropolitan University, 2006)

In refining the values that underpin its community engagement work, the Community Partnerships and Volunteering (CPV) team has set out 'four Rs' as principles to guide its work: Respect, Reciprocity, Renewal and Reflection. We insist that our volunteers offer proper respect to the organisations and the organisations' clients that they are engaging with, irrespective of their class, gender, ethnicity, sexuality, ability or religion, and we expect the same of our partner organisations. We believe that the relationships set up must be reciprocal: all parties must benefit mutually from the partnership. The overall purpose of the volunteering is to refresh and reinvigorate the organisation's work and, wherever possible, to contribute to the renewal of the wider neighbourhood, as well as renewing the volunteers' zest for life and for learning. Finally, we ask for continuous reflection, particularly from the volunteers, but also from the partner organisations, about the meaning, purpose and effect of the work undertaken. As a university dedicated to reflection, we have a specific section of our website dedicated to Community Reflections (www.leedsmet.ac.uk/cpv/index_communityreflections.htm).

Reflections from Student Volunteers

Being a volunteer with the 'University' of the Fourth Age is a fantastic experience. You gain an enormous sense of well-being for making a positive difference within the community. Donating just two hours of your time per week makes an invaluable contribution to the life of someone in care. Building a relationship with a care home resident over the weeks is a special experience. It is rewarding to work or build on a specific interest, encourage them to develop new skills with you or just to sit, have a cup of tea and chat!

continued

Volunteering with u4a also enables you to develop new skills that other opportunities might not. For me, learning how to interact with and provide support for people who suffer with the early stages of dementia was a very important skill to develop. It also looks fantastic to employers, demonstrating that you have gone that extra mile to make yourself stand out. The skills that you will hone, as well as how much you can help others, are fantastic. I would flag it up as a brilliant opportunity and it does not matter how much experience you have already, it is lots of fun and hugely rewarding.

Laura Johnson
Volunteer Learning Mentor, 'University' of the Fourth Age

A community of beaming smiles, the waving of hands and the vague sound of surprise. This is our first visit on the municipality bus to a township in Durban. Stepping out of the bus, bare feet gather and people of all ages congregate. The coaches, who seem no older than 16, arrive with other young people, all of whom have brought enthusiasm, respect and laughter. We begin our drills, arms waving, hands moving, our eyes meeting theirs in our best attempt to utilise non-verbal communication along with our English words. We try to overcome the language barrier and a sea of nodding heads shows that an understanding is being reached.

The young people carry out the drills incredibly well and we all feel united as a community, by achievement. With time, passing drills turn to set plays and small games develop into full-court netball games. The ability of the children is astounding. Despite many having no shoes and facilities consisting of a court dug out of dried mud, wooden posts and just a single netball, they thrive. Everyone's here because they want to be, and this is shown by their positive attitude and continuous effort in all we do.

Sarah Bancroft, South Africa volunteer, 2008
Second-year Physical Activity, Exercise and Health student

The Community Partnerships and Volunteering team at Leeds Met was until recently mainly dedicated to providing opportunities for staff who want to volunteer, and to supporting the work of community partners who need volunteers. Initially the team advertised itself as the 'first stop' for not-for-profit organisations that wanted help from the university, and at the time of writing there are 59 community organisations whose appeals for volunteers have been advertised via a regular email bulletin to all staff, as well as on our website. Staff were provided with sufficient information to decide whether they wanted to offer their services; the CPV team put them in touch with the organisation of their choice and provided any support needed. The team also provided volunteers for activities brokered by Leeds Cares (part of Business in the Community (BiTC, 2009)) and organised tailor-made volunteering 'action days' for groups of university staff.

Second, the team recruited and supported staff and student mentors in one high school and three primary schools, and supplied volunteers for a reading support scheme (run by the voluntary-sector organisation Learning Partnerships) in several other schools. It also ran a scheme for mentoring refugees into employment (where a refugee with high qualifications was matched with a member of staff with similar qualifications). Some changes to these arrangements have subsequently been made.

Third, CPV runs the university's international volunteering projects for staff and students. Leeds Met puts large sums of money into supporting this activity, as one of several strands of its comprehensive Internationalisation Strategy (2009). In 2007–8 the university sent 143 volunteers to 12 countries. Half of the total cost of each activity (which ranges from about £500 to £1,000) is paid for by the university. Staff members are allowed half the volunteering time as work time, and the team leader, a member of staff, is considered to be in working time for the whole trip. The individual volunteer is expected to provide the rest of the costs, usually by fund-raising activities. Volunteers report life-changing experiences, and the partner organisations tell us that our staff and students have made a huge difference to their projects, their staff and their clients.

Other community partnership activities supported by CPV normally do not involve volunteers. Its cultural and campaigning partnership work ranges from simple practical activity such as supplying surplus computers to not-for-profit organisations in the region and abroad, to collecting food and clothes for destitute refugees and asylum seekers. Other activities include small research and consultancy projects for partner organisations, celebratory festivals with educational input (e.g. our Leeds Met Celtic festival around St Patrick's Day), events during Black History Month, and activities in support of National Refugee Week and the campaigning charity Together for Peace.

The CPV team also promotes 'community-based learning', where students carry out an agreed programme of work with a community organisation as an assessed part of their coursework. Increasing numbers of courses are integrating this type of learning into their modules, akin to the more familiar 'industrial placements'. The team offers sessions to students setting out the university's 'engagement' ethos and the national context in which the government seeks active citizens and community cohesion, and it supports staff in brokering individual learning agreements with community organisations. While this is directed learning, assessed in the normal way within a module, rather than volunteering, it often results in students staying on as volunteers with the organisation that sponsored their studies.

If students want their volunteering to be accredited, they are able to access the Leeds Met Global Citizen Award, which provides bronze, silver and gold awards depending on the amount of time and the quality of work they have put in. (They can become 'Global Citizens' by volunteering with multi-ethnic groups in the United Kingdom, as well as by volunteering abroad.)

To promote these opportunities to volunteer and to explain their link to the university's Vision and Character and Human Resources policies, the team gives frequent talks to staff (in particular during the annual Staff Development Festival, described in Chapter 14). Volunteering at Leeds Met is valued in and of itself, but it is also integrated into the university's Performance Development Review (PDR) and its Attributes, Character and Talents (ACTs) programme. Each staff member completes a form that explains how volunteering will develop their skills and how it integrates with their personal development plan, a process informed by reference to the ACTs documentation. The volunteering pro-forma provides the basis for a discussion with the volunteer's manager, and if the activity is approved, achievements are examined and recorded in the volunteer's PDR.

This process clearly signals the university's intent to increase the number of its staff who volunteer, and provides a clear framework for acknowledging and potentially rewarding staff who engage with communities in this way.

The funding for this team comes from the residual allocation from HEFCE's Active Community Fund, but this is currently lower than the costs of running the programme, hence the university subsidises this work from its own resources as an indication of its commitment to this area of activity. The team's income is sometimes supplemented by small externally funded projects.

Evaluating Continuing Education

It is perhaps surprising how little academic evaluation there is of university–community engagement programmes in general, or university volunteering in particular. Earlier forms of engagement, such as the university extension programmes, which later became known as lifelong learning programmes, have been subject to extensive review. The Labour government's record in this field has been strongly criticised by us in relation to the way that that the drive for skills (or its 'human capital perspectives') have dominated government policy, overriding wider aims for education:

> This perspective omits any recognition that there is a need to enable more and different learners to have access to a liberal and critical education; nor does it allow any collective or community notion of education – it assumes an entirely individualistic (and 'marketised') frame of reference.
>
> (Taylor, 2009)

For much of its existence, university adult and continuing education in the United Kingdom operated with earmarked funding direct from the Department of Education and Science (DES), rather than being dependent upon the mainstream University Grants Committee (now the Higher Education Funding Council for England) regime, and thus the views of university vice-chancellors and administrators. This was underwritten by a rigorous but generally benign 'quality assurance' programme run by Her Majesty's Inspectorate. University departments of adult and continuing education thus operated with what seems now an enviable degree of freedom and 'self-policing': there was no 'audit culture' in those days. Since the 1970s, however, the screws have tightened inexorably. There have been a succession of changes in the funding regime – *always* negative in their effects on the departments and their adult learners, in our view – culminating in the (much-criticised) 'ELQ' (equivalent or lower qualifications) policy introduced by the Labour government in 2007, which removed funding from students who had previously studied at this level.

The reasons underlying this rather depressing trajectory are a matter of debate. As noted, the prevailing 'audit culture' has certainly been one factor – exacerbated, we suggest, by a series of bureaucratic complexities inherent in such provision. For example, most adult education programmes are 'open entry', rather than being subject to the normal admissions criteria; provision is often innovative and not tied into the university's 'mainstream' teaching activities; such departments are inherently multidisciplinary, thus making them irrelevant for the Research Assessment Exercise; and so on.

The prospects for such departments in our increasingly monochrome HE world are not good. While the ELQ policy has hit hard the specialist institutions – notably the Open University and Birkbeck, London – it has also threatened the very existence of departments of adult and continuing education outside Oxford and Cambridge (and even here, radical restructuring and reconfiguration is already well under way).

On the other hand, adult educators and, even more importantly, adult *learners* are committed, resourceful and ingenious in their strategies for circumventing the negative bureaucratic regimes of government and its funding agencies. University adult and continuing education has survived, and to an extent prospered, in generally negative contexts for many years now. There are, therefore, grounds for optimism: such work *will* survive.

Evaluating Volunteering in Universities

Our argument in the earlier part of this chapter that the government has a virtually exclusive emphasis upon the individual rather than the collective is crucial, and this criticism can also be applied to its emphasis on volunteering, in the sense that individuals are exhorted to volunteer both as personal acts of altruism and as a means of improving their personal chances in the labour market. But it is important to note the counter-perspectives that circulate in volunteering. Most student union-based volunteering shares the collectivist ideology of Leeds Met's Community Action volunteering, where there is a strong emphasis on students working together as a group in support of the aims of already-constituted social action groups in their localities.

Similarly, we have demonstrated earlier in this chapter that at least one university has stated that the aim of its community engagement strategy is to 'empower local communities'. In our efforts to motivate staff and students to volunteer and/or undertake community-based learning, Community Partnerships and Volunteering at Leeds Met always draws attention to the 'civic responsibility' and 'citizenship' dimensions of national policy. This allows us to place volunteering in its societal context. For example, to bring about civil renewal, David Blunkett, while Home Secretary, argued that society needed 'active citizens', 'strengthened communities' and 'partnerships in meeting public needs' (2004: 6). This approach was reiterated by government minister Hazel Blears (2008). These goals would fit quite comfortably with those set out in the Talloires Declaration (2005), except where the UK government's stress on the economic dimensions of 'strengthening communities' outweighs the social, cultural, political and spiritual dimensions.

If volunteers are a crucial element in universities' community engagement strategies, and if the stakes are as high as the government appears to be setting them, then it is incumbent on universities to evaluate their progress in reaching their own goals, and/or the government's. Angela Ellis (2002: 27), reviewing the research up to 2002, said that the anecdotal evidence of the benefits of volunteering was unsatisfactory. There is now a huge amount of research on volunteering in general (and some relating to young people), but very little on volunteering in universities (Institute for Volunteering Research, 2008). Open University students are reported to have gained much personal satisfaction from volunteering – to have made new friends and developed new skills, which were considered particularly helpful in considering what jobs to apply for. On the other hand, about 40 per cent of the volunteers reported feeling undervalued and having acute pressure on their time (Open University and Institute for Volunteering Research, 2006).

At Leeds Met we are heavily reliant on the self-evaluations that Ellis refers to, and while we emphasise that our Community Reflections and the weblogs that accompany our international volunteering should include negative as well as positive features in the volunteers' experiences, they largely seem to be positive evaluations. (This may, of course, represent the true picture, but we cannot prove it.)

The obvious reason for this failure to evaluate rigorously is that most universities are so busy actually doing the engagement work, and on such limited budgets, that research is considered a luxury. A more interesting reason might be that it would be very hard to do this properly. Measuring the impact of community engagement by universities is complex both conceptually (what exactly would be measured and by what criteria?) and methodologically. At least a ten-year longitudinal study would be needed, and such studies are very hard to fund and to manage. One spin-off from a thorough research programme would be that we would obtain much greater clarity on what universities mean by their community engagement strategies, and thus perhaps move towards some consensus in definition on what are the most effective programmes.

Systematic evidence of positive effects will become crucial if government shifts its focus away from civic engagement, and thus the already limited funding from HEFCE disappears, or if individual vice-chancellors decide that this is no longer a priority for their universities. It would make sense for universities to anticipate these worst-case scenarios and to take active steps to seek alternative resources. Some universities have proved highly effective in obtaining community project funding from central and regional government agencies. At Leeds Met we are utilising the talents of our Events Management staff and students to undertake large and small fund-raising activities, and our Alumni Office is seeking support from graduates for our various volunteering programmes.

Finally, another problem we face is moving outside the charmed circle of the already altruistic among our staff and students. The Home Office Citizenship survey found that 67 per cent of its sample volunteered informally and 39 per cent of people volunteered formally (through groups, clubs or organisations) at least once in the past 12 months (Blunkett, 2004: 8). Furthermore, 57 per cent of young people aged 16–24 had volunteered in a 2007 survey undertaken by the Institute for Volunteering Research, and

34 per cent of Open University students were reported as having volunteered (Open University, 2006).

At Leeds Met we have nothing like this percentage of our staff or students engaged in formally organised volunteering. We estimate that about 1 per cent of our full-time student population are volunteering; and although we have no formal data, we estimate that about 6 per cent of our staff are volunteering. (We are beginning to track this activity more systematically.) The ACTs and PDR programme outlined earlier may increase the percentage of staff who volunteer, but it is undeniable that staff are under great pressure to deliver on their contracted work, and the university does subscribe to the view that staff should have a healthy work–life balance. It is hard to see how the proportion of students will increase unless the resources for promoting and supporting this work are greatly improved. Our community-based learning strategy is designed to involve larger numbers of students who make a contribution to community life. While this must always be distinguished from volunteering, it does allow for more formal emphasis (via lectures and assessment) to be placed on the citizenship and neighbour-hood renewal aspects of community engagement work, and it does provide a means of developing our Vision and Character among those who have not brought with them to university the ethos of civic responsibility we are trying to promote. It might also help us overcome the anomaly that the vast majority of active staff volunteers come from the support services; relatively few are academics. Community-based learning requires academic super-vision and may therefore be a means of encouraging them to engage more often with communities.

Conclusion

In this chapter we have offered a definition of university–community engagement which builds on that presented by Watson (2007) by empha-sising the values and ethics that should underlie engagement activities, and seeing engagement as a process, rather than a set of one-off projects, while recommending the types of activities suggested by the Talloires Declaration (2005) without attempting to prescribe exactly what universities should do. Our approach, which outlines the competing models or ideologies operating in universities' engagement activities, is, we argue, anti-elitist and socially progressive. Although it needs further refinement and enhancement, we propose it as an ongoing model for our continuing engagement in this field.

References

BiTC (2009) 'Business in the community'. Online, available at: www.bitc.org.uk (accessed 12 January 2009).

Blears, H. (2008) 'Blears commits to a thriving community sector', Department for Communities and Local Government. Online, available at: www.communities.gov.uk/news/corporate/886884 (accessed 12 January 2009).

Blunkett, D. (2004) 'Active citizens, strong communities: progressing civil renewal'. Pamphlet lodged on the Communities and Local Government website: www.communities.gov.uk/publications/communities/activecitizensstrong (accessed 20 April 2008).

Coffield, F. (1999) 'Breaking the consensus: lifelong learning as social control', Inaugural Lecture, Department of Education, University of Newcastle.

Ellis, A. (2002) *University Based Volunteering: A Review of Current Literature*, London: Institute for Volunteering Research.

Farrar, M. (2002) *The Struggle for 'Community' in a British Multi-ethnic Inner City Area: Paradise in the Making*, Lampeter: Edwin Mellen Press.

Fieldhouse, R. (1996) *A History of Modern Adult Education in Britain*, Leicester: NIACE.

Fitzgerald, K. and Peterman, W. (2004) 'UK research universities and community engagement: developing a practical framework for community partnerships', paper presented at City Futures Conference, University of Illinois–Chicago, July 2004. Online, available at: www.uic.edu/cuppa/cityfutures/papers/webpapers/cityfuturespapers/session2_1/2_1UKresearch.pdf (accessed 14 March 2008).

Gosden, P. (1983) *The Education System since 1944*, Oxford: Martin Robertson.

Institute for Volunteering Research (2008) *Young People Help Out*. Online, available at: www.ivr.org.uk/NR/rdonlyres/35546F68-CD79-4E0C-AD9A-3E08AFD5B9D6/0/young_people.pdf (accessed 30 August 2008).

Internationalisation Strategy at Leeds Met (2009). Online, available at: www.leedsmet.ac.uk/metoffice/Revised_Internationalisation_Strategy_2008_-_2012.pdf (accessed 12 January 2009).

Leeds Metropolitan University (2006) *Vision and Character*. Available at: http://www.leedsmet.ac.uk/the_news/docs/visionandcharacter08.pdf (accessed 27 August 2008).

LMUSU website (2008). Online, available at: www.lmusu.org.uk/DisplayPage.aspx?GroupId=37564&id=6441 (accessed 14 March 2008).

Lyotard, J. F. (1984) *The Postmodern Condition: A Report on Knowledge*, Manchester: Manchester University Press.

Mander, J. and Dimova-Cookson, M. (2006) *T. H. Green: Ethics, Metaphysics and Political Philosophy*, Oxford: Oxford University Press.

Miliband, E. (2007) Cabinet Office Parliamentary Secretary's reply, House of Commons, 31 January, Hansard. Online, available at: www.publications.parliament.uk/pa/cm200607/cmhansrd/cm070131/debtext/70131-0001.htm (accessed 14 March 2008).

Open University and Institute for Volunteering Research (2006) *Active Learning: Understanding Volunteering among Open University Students*, London: Open University.

Russell Commission (2005) *A National Framework for Volunteering and Engagement*. Online, available at: http://archive.cabinetoffice.gov.uk/russellcommission/report/index.html (accessed 14 March 2008).

Talloires Declaration (2005). Online, available at: www.tufts.edu/talloiresnetwork/?pid=17&c=7 (accessed 27 August 2008).

Taylor, R. (2009) 'New Labour's lifelong learning policy: an Orwellian critique', *Power and Education*, 1 (1).

Universities UK (2006) *Universities: Engaging with Local Communities*, London: UUK.

V website (2008). Online, available at: www.wearev.com/index.php?option=com_content&task=view&id=123&Itemid=1 (accessed 14 March 2008).

Watson, D. (2007) *Managing Civic and Community Engagement*, Maidenhead: Open University Press.

CHAPTER 16

Practical Examples of University–Community Engagement

Some Case Studies from Leeds Met

SALLY BROWN, DAVID WARD, CHRIS BAILEY, PETE RODGERS,

TINA CONKAR, MICHAEL GRAY, BRIGID McCLURE,

INDER HUNJAN and JILL ADAM

Leeds Metropolitan University

Introduction

In the previous chapter, Max Farrar and Richard Taylor explored the theoretical perspectives underpinning community engagement activities by universities, looking particularly at volunteering as a significant locus for community engagement. Leeds Met's statement of Vision and Character explicitly lays out our commitment to 'creating a culture of celebration which values pioneering relationships with other world-class regional organisations across education, the arts, sport, business and wider community life throughout the North of these islands' (Leeds Metropolitan University, 2006). In this chapter we provide some examples from Leeds Met of diverse forms of community engagement in practice in sporting, cultural, educational and social contexts.

Leeds Met is arguably unique in the range and scope of its partnerships with a whole range of communities. Each of these partnerships is characterised by a number of common factors:

- Believing organisations are judged by the company they keep, we choose to partner world-class organisations and communities that share with us values including the redressing of social disadvantage, and helping individuals to maximise personal capabilities and 'use their talents to the full'.

- All our partnerships are designed to add value to each party. We may engage in full partnerships, promotions or sponsorships, but in each case the arrangement is never merely a financial transaction.
- As an organisation striving to be a world-class regional university with worldwide horizons, our partnerships may be local, regional or international, but all are selected to enhance opportunities for our students, our staff and our partners.
- Not all partners are equal in a partnership: in some of our partnerships Leeds Met is the lead partner, in others we recognise that we are subsidiary partners where we have most to learn, and elsewhere the partnership is evenly balanced.
- All our partnerships should be sustainable; we are an organisation that prides itself on being 'in for the long run'. At the same time, it is recognised that partnerships can have a fixed duration.

This chapter will explore some of our partnerships, demonstrating how our approach is brought to life in diverse, imaginative, innovatory and sometimes surprising ways.

University–Community Work in Bradford

One of our early partnerships changed the way some of the local communities regard universities, and its ground-breaking approach was rewarded in 2006 by a *Times Higher Education* award for 'outstanding contribution to the local community' in recognition of our pioneering partnership with Bradford City Football Club, which helped save the club from collapse. Bradford City FC had been placed in administration, but Leeds Met stepped in to help with community engagement and brought it back from the brink.

David Ward, a principal lecturer from the university, was seconded to manage the project at Bradford City while placement students helped provide facilities for the club and community. A classroom was created to deliver sessions to local children, a Saturday club was formed to provide football coaching, and £100,000 capital was secured, along with £100,000 a year of recurrent funding, to set up the 'Playing for Success' study centre. Many other community events were organised and a charitable company was set up to help secure future funding for community projects.

Case Study 1:
Bradford City Football Club

In late June 2004, Bradford City Football Club was in deep financial trouble and within hours of being closed down. Leeds Met University approached the club's administrators to offer help. The university, which prides itself on its association with sporting success, was offering support to a failing club in another city. What on earth was it doing? It would be false to suggest that the club's eventual survival can be attributed to Leeds Met's intervention, but at a time when the 100-year-old club badly needed friends, the university stepped in when very few others were willing to help. The university used Higher Education Innovation Fund (HEIF) money to place staff and students in the club at a time when the administrators were the only ones allowed to sign cheques and such was the state of the club's finances that they were even refusing to allow non-essential light bulbs to be replaced.

Many football and rugby clubs make a powerful contribution to their communities through a range of education, recreation, health, anti-crime and social cohesion activities. Bradford City FC was too focused on survival to have time for a wide range of community-related initiatives, although great credit should go to the chairman at the time, who personally led the creation of a classroom for visiting school groups. As a seconded university academic I built up a series of partnerships with local schools, youth centres, community groups, a drugs project, the local Youth Offending Team and others. We helped the club engage more with its local Asian community, as well as providing it with staff and student resources to help it through a difficult financial period and to obtain funds to develop an education centre. Leeds Met students, as volunteers and on placements, became actively involved with the community, seeing its problems at first hand and finding and implementing solutions.

Sport became a mediator for community tensions and promoted engagement that brought discipline to unruly behaviour by uniting around saving the club. A major contribution of the university was in providing a staff member with the time, local knowledge and facilitation skills to build bridges between the club and the local organisations, which were all very keen to work with and at the club. The partnership between the club and the university still continues, but the working arrangement is beginning, as the club's financial situation stabilises, to build up the club's internal capacity for sustaining and developing its own community

continued

department. It could be argued that the best evidence of knowledge transfer is when the university is no longer required by the 'transferee'.

David Ward
Principal Lecturer, Sports Partnerships

Leeds Met's Sporting Partnerships' Contributions to the Wider Community

Some of our best-known and most high-profile partnership arrangements are with sporting organisations. Sporting partnerships contribute to the university's wider community engagement in six pioneering ways, through:

- better communication of community engagement to stakeholders;
- raising aspirations to HE through iconic sporting stars;
- helping bring communities together through sport;
- improving lifestyle attitudes in communities through sport;
- engaging the university with international communities through sporting partnerships;
- supporting our sports business partners with skilled staff and student resources.

First, sporting partnerships can help the university reach a wider number of stakeholders than knowledge transfer activities. Knowledge transfer has an important role but tends to be limited to one or two stakeholders, in contrast to the depth and breadth of communications achieved by sporting partnerships.

Case Study 2:
The Rugby League Carnegie Challenge Cup

Apart from raising Leeds Met's profile with national sporting and political bodies, which helped us bid successfully to become the UK Centre for Coaching Excellence and to win the Coaching Environment of the Year award in 2008, the Carnegie Championship schools and colleges league competition enabled us to engage with communities in the north of England and further afield.

In 2008 over 420 schools across the United Kingdom with 25,000 pupils took part in the Carnegie Champion Schools tournament, and

48 colleges with over 800 students took part in the Carnegie Champion Colleges Cup 8. We are able to take the Carnegie Challenge Cup out to new communities each year, promoting the competition and engaging in creative community activities, raising the profile of the university to wider groups of stakeholders, particularly those in the less advantaged communities, where rugby league as a sport usually predominates. This is beyond the boundaries of the approach of most universities, which tend to focus on communicating with one or two specific stakeholders at a time, usually with one specific university project. In many cases, university–community engagement goes largely unrecognised by stakeholders, but the media interest in our sporting partnerships, with dozens of Carnegie or Leeds Met mentions per day in the local or national media, demonstrates the power of sporting partnerships to communicate our engagement activities with stakeholders.

Pete Rodgers
Dean of Sporting Partnerships, Leeds Metropolitan University

Second, raising the aspirations of young people and their families in poorer communities has been a challenge in the higher education (HE) sector for many years. Engaging with this sector of the population is not easy, and parents, other family members, teachers and others in those communities are an important influence on a young person's decision to become the first member of their family to enter HE. The university uses sports stars from its partnerships to influence young people to consider HE. For example, rugby league's Leeds Rhinos first team and England players Kevin Sinfield, Matt Diskin and Jamie Jones-Buchanan are all graduates of Leeds Met, and all are the first members of their families to enter HE. Similarly, Sue Smith, the England and Leeds Carnegie Ladies football player, also represents the university as a 'Carnegie Champion' to talk about how she entered HE and became a star footballer and TV personality. We argue that disadvantaged young people are much more likely to be influenced by these 'champions' when they hear what they gained from higher education than they are by a member of university staff who has never been part of their community.

Third, sporting partnerships can also go beyond the normal processes of community engagement by helping to bring communities together through sport. In Northern Ireland, Gaelic football is traditionally a Catholic sport and rugby union is traditionally played by Protestants. Competitions at both school and adult level are similarly divided. Premier league football in

Northern Ireland is less sectarian, and we saw an opportunity to help unite these two communities by supporting the Carnegie Schools Cup, which involves over 60 schools with equal representation from both communities. Our partnership with Cricket Ireland crosses both the Republic and Northern Ireland, and the Carnegie 9s competition crosses the current rules division between rugby union and rugby league and takes the best parts from the game of both codes into a celebration of rugby as a whole.

Leeds Met's partnership with Bradford City FC, described earlier as Case Study 1, helped the club to survive in one of the most troubled communities in the country. Equally, we have helped Yorkshire cricket to raise its profile and values among the Asian community in Bradford, with a full-time community worker to develop links between the club and the Bradford community. We have worked with Saima Hussain, the first Asian woman to represent Great Britain in rugby league, and Ikram Butt, the first Asian to play for England at rugby league, to engage with the Asian communities to raise the profile of rugby as a sport and promote its values in developing young people and contributing to community cohesion. Sporting partners as organisations or individuals have indeed enabled the university to make a difference in these communities and give something back in areas where our students are recruited.

Fourth, the university has helped improve the lifestyles of the communities it serves through sporting partnerships, particularly in terms of health, exercise and young people's engagement with sport. Improving men's health is challenging, particularly in certain socio-economic groups. Sport offers an opportunity to target large numbers of men with specific preventive health messages. At rugby games at the Headingley Carnegie Stadium, staff from our Health Faculty launched a successful and well-regarded men's health check programme at matches, for example by testing blood pressure, weight and diet, and by providing information on prostate and testicular cancer, among other things.

Similar activity is currently being piloted at Carnegie World Club Challenge events and at the Carnegie Challenge Cup (Rugby League) final at Wembley Stadium. At Oldham RFL matches we piloted a similar men's health awareness programme and we support the club with a breast and testicular cancer awareness scheme. In all our sporting partnerships we encourage girls and boys in school sporting competitions and use major events to provide opportunities for families and communities to enjoy exercise.

In women's sport we have encouraged women's participation in football through our partnership with Leeds United Ladies, now Leeds Carnegie Ladies, and Northern Ireland women's football. In other women's sports we have supported participation in Super League netball, Yorkshire women's cricket, rugby league and rugby union. Thus, the Carnegie brand supports women's engagement with sport as strongly as it does men's sport.

Fifth, engagement with international communities is an important part of the university's contribution to the global village, sharing understanding, knowledge, resources and building mutual respect. We plan to support Kazan in the Republic of Tatarstan to develop the World Student Games in 2013 and the Krasnodar region in Russia to help higher education and further education engage with the 2014 Winter Olympic Games. We have engaged with communities in Abu Dhabi through supporting a cricket tournament with our partner Yorkshire Carnegie Cricket Club in May 2008; with communities in Ethiopia in partnership with the 2008 African Games; with communities in India with our partner British Asian Rugby Association at the Calcutta Cup competition in 2007; and with communities in Ireland and beyond through our partnership with Cricket Ireland and Rugby League Ireland. In Australia we supported the Irish student and men's team in the respective Rugby League World Cups, engaging with the many international communities taking part in the competition. In rugby we have worked with both Fiji and Tonga, supporting them with university resources and engaging students and staff with their culture and customs. Sporting partnerships, because they take place within international competitions, provide excellent alternative vehicles to traditional university methods of engaging with international communities and students.

Sixth, engaging with the business community has always been an important part of university activity and is supported by research and 'third stream' funding as well as providing additional sources of income. Our sporting partners are businesses, and sports business represents a major part of the United Kingdom's economy. We support all our partnerships as part of our 'partnership deal' with staff, student and facility resources that help the organisations and provide development opportunities for our staff and students. Projects range from offering IT support to providing student interns and volunteers from events management, sports science, marketing and hospitality management programmes. In turn, the university is able to engage with the business suppliers and sponsors of our sporting partners, which provides further knowledge transfer opportunities. Sporting partnership terms range from 3 to 15 years and offer opportunities to combine comprehensive university engagement with sports business partners in our community.

Engagement Through Cultural Partnerships

Equally important to the university are our partnerships with cultural organisations, which go well beyond conventional university arrangements with local arts organisations. Describing itself as a 'university of festivals and partnerships', Leeds Met has sought to systematise and develop as a distinctive strength its relationships with cultural organisations. Clearly, not all such relationships, vital as they are, constitute a partnership with the university. A quick trawl, carried out in 2006, of the external contacts used by the Faculty of Arts and Society in its everyday business of delivering teaching, placements, research and live projects, ran without effort to 13 closely typed pages.

Contrary to the stereotype of universities as isolated from their surrounding communities, faculties involved in practice-based disciplines of any kind would find it impossible to function without some engagement with a wide variety of 'communities', defined by issue, practice, geography, outlook, disadvantage, and so on. Leeds Met has sought to distinguish between these mutual working relationships, which can and must thrive without overbearing attempts to manage them centrally on the one hand, and profile-driven sponsorship relationships on the other, to identify relationships that are characterised not just by the recognition of mutual advantage, but by longer-term agreement on the values, vision and character of both organisations. Within that range, the relationship may be that of junior to senior partner on either side, but in all cases depends on mutual respect.

The range of cultural partnerships currently supported by Leeds Met is wide and has originated in many ways, from a sponsorship relationship, from the partner organisation's commissioning activity or from a strong personal contact. It is felt that around a dozen such relationships can provide the desired level of interaction with staff and students. Current partners include the BBC; international award-winning Yorkshire-based brass band Black Dyke Band; Eureka, the Children's Museum; Festival Republic (which organises Latitude and Leeds Music Festivals); the Harrogate International Festivals, including the Crime Writing and Sporting Words Festivals; the International Indian Film Academy, which organises annual 'Bollywood' celebrations annually; Leeds City Museums; Northern Ballet Theatre; and the West Yorkshire Playhouse (see www.leedsmet.ac.uk/partnerships/reflections/index.htm).

The benefits for Leeds Met of these cultural partnerships were accurately summarised by Professor Philip Wilby (2008), referring to Leeds Met's work with the Black Dyke Band in an article in *British Bandsman*:

> Work with young people has led to the creation of the Yorkshire Youth Brass band, interaction with student music-tech specialists has led to them working directly with the band musicians, and staff members have been astounded by some highly-energised presentations on staff away-days.

Professor Nick Childs, band director, speaking to the audience about the work of the Yorkshire Youth Brass Band in York Minster in 2008, commented that members were drawn from 70 communities around the county, many of them offering few opportunities for young people.

If these comments emphasise the 'widening participation' aspect of community engagement, then it is equally important to take account of the content of the experience for students, staff or cultural partners. The conviction that the nature of the work undertaken matters has its roots in the nineteenth-century social reform movement. Just as today we engage our students as community volunteers in a variety of constructive activities to support communities, as described in the previous chapter, so in 1874 the art critic John Ruskin invited a group of his students at Oxford University to rebuild a deeply rutted and near-impassable road between the town and the neighbouring but impoverished villages of North and South Hinksey. This was tough manual labour, but Ruskin associated it directly in the minds of his students with moral improvement (*New York Times*, 1900). That developing the mind and learning through work could be yoked together in this way deeply affected many of the students involved, including Arnold Toynbee, founder of the East End settlements, and Hardwicke Rawnsley, founder of the National Trust.

The value of specific kinds of manual and craft work, celebrated in the Pre-Raphaelite paintings of Ford Madox Brown and others, and championed by Ruskin, was passed on, via William Morris and William Lethaby, so that their legacy is still apparent in much current practice in visual arts higher education (see, for instance, the discussion of the influence of the Arts and Crafts Movement by Tanya Harrod, 1999). It is therefore not surprising to find a propensity in many UK design courses to seek out project briefs that convey social or health benefits to sick or disadvantaged people. Leeds Met's community-based organisations such as Design Leeds, AXIS or the numerous local 'cafés scientifiques' stem from the same engrained ethos as the will to sustain some of the country's earliest-established courses in architecture, planning and playwork.

The challenge for Leeds Met is to finds ways for the university as a whole to engage with partnerships while not overwhelming or distorting the partner's own audience or staff development objectives. Thus, Festival Republic, the force behind some of the United Kingdom's most successful music events, can provide invaluable experiences at the annual Latitude and Leeds Festivals for student volunteer filmmakers, performers and event managers. Northern Ballet Theatre, whose partnership with Leeds Met encompasses construction of a new centre for excellence in dance in the city, where in turn our students will be able to rub shoulders with champions while learning and rehearsing alongside professional dancers, can draw upon business and marketing experts, exercise and nutrition scientists, designers and visual artists. Each of the partners is accepted because, in its reputation or aspiration, it is world-class.

Communicating the achievements of partners through daily 200-word Partnership Reflections on the university's website, and through participation in the Graduation, Staff Development and Freshers' Festivals, described elsewhere in this volume, ensures that awareness of partnerships and the opportunities they afford to staff and students is ubiquitous. Seeing the partnership in action can also transform the self-image, even the self-esteem, of students and staff. A ceremony to award honorary doctorates to major figures of the Indian film world, including the widely venerated star Amitabh Bachchan, resulted from the link to the Indian International Film Awards, held in Yorkshire in 2007 and in Bangkok in 2008, with student volunteers prominent at both. Seeing their heroes on campus meant that many students and staff of South Asian origin reported viewing 'their' university in a new way. A new connection was made between the world of 'work' and personal and social lives. That was also Ruskin's point, typically reinforced by a literal example when he took up a stonemason's chisel and hammer to carve elaborate Gothic arches for the new museum in Oxford. Engagement between academic and other communities through cultural partnership is at its best when setting itself a lofty objective – the realisation of the ideals and values, as much as the fabric, of the university.

Partnerships with Educational Communities

Leeds Met's partnership working with schools and other educational establishments provides excellent examples of the broad range of reciprocal opportunities such connections can bring to the benefit of students, staff and the wider communities of both parties. Leeds Met has a strong tradition of working with schools, across both the primary and secondary sectors, as well as in other educational settings and contexts, including the Regional University Network of further education college partners (RUN), educational trusts and charitable trusts. Our tradition of working with schools is rooted in our heritage in initial teacher training, although the range of students and the foci of engagement with such establishments have evolved significantly since those first days of pupil–teacher practice.

Although Leeds Met's partnership work still includes the placement of student teachers – that is, those wishing to enter the teaching profession and required to obtain the mandatory professional award of Qualified Teacher Status (QTS) – the changing nature of the teaching profession and the multi-agency approach to working in school settings necessitate opportunities for engagement by other students with other professionals, including those associated with social services, play work, primary Health Care Trusts and local businesses.

Some of our school-based partnership activities are linked to government initiatives, including those aimed at increasing collaboration between different institutions and agencies, such as 'The Independent/State School Partnership Scheme', in which Leeds Met is engaged in collaboration with Ryburn Valley High School and Rishworth School, West Yorkshire. This particular scheme aims to 'promote collaborative working by maintained and independent schools in partnership to raise standards in education' (Sharp *et al.*, 2001). The programme brings together students from a local state school and a local independent school to engage with HE activities at the university, demonstrating the breadth of opportunities available in HE and raising the aspirations and expectations of all those involved.

Other activities include those operating within the Aimhigher framework (see Chapter 5). The Leeds Met 'Get Ahead' team is responsible for developing and delivering a comprehensive programme of on- and off-campus activities and events to raise the aspirations of young people from primary through to post-16 education and their families across the north of England. Each year over 15,000 young people and their families participate in Get Ahead initiatives. The programme seeks to raise the motivation, aspiration and attainment of young people through events such as summer schools, revision programmes, campus trails and focus days. A key element of the scheme is the Progression Module, an accredited programme of study helping post-16 students prepare for university. Students are awarded 30 UCAS points on successful completion of the course. The activities covered within the programme explore issues such as finance, accommodation, course options and student life. Student ambassadors from Leeds Met facilitate many of the workshops, providing role models for the participants and giving a true insight into the university experience.

All of our partnership activities with schools are collaboratively determined between Leeds Met and school staff, ensuring that mutual aspirations and benefits are addressed and that they are in line with both the university's statement of Vision and Character (Leeds Metropolitan University, 2006) and the overall mission of the school concerned. Examples of such work currently taking place include:

• The joint writing and delivery of teacher postgraduate professional development programmes (PPD). Some of these are aligned to key priorities of the Training and Development Agency for Schools (TDA), for example provision focused upon 'Managing Challenging Behaviour', written in collaboration with Baliol School, North Yorkshire.

- Staff development programmes embracing provision for teachers in the early stages of career development, to those pursuing the mandatory award for headship delivered on behalf of the National College for School Leadership, through to provision tailored for those already working as established headteachers and school leaders.
- Student placements, including student teacher placements in relation to the achievement of QTS and placements for students from other disciplines, including nutrition and dietetics, performing arts and music technology.
- Curriculum development activities, including the introduction and development of a number of specialised diplomas and the integration of the International Baccalaureate.
- Articulations of progression for post-16 students through the Regional University Network (RUN) and the inclusion of the Progression Module in post-16 curricula.
- Externally funded research-based projects focusing on creative and assistive technologies.
- School governance and trustee work: Leeds Met is a formal partner in a number of educational trusts including the Wakefield ASPIRE Trust and the Education Ossett Community Trust.
- International links with schools and colleges including some based in Ethiopia, Sri Lanka, Tanzania and China.

These examples illustrate the diverse range of opportunities covered in Leeds Met's partnership work with schools and educational partners. While undergraduate student recruitment may be one benefit of such collaborative working, it is certainly not the main or the sole driver. Rather, it is about university–school community engagement and collaboration involving students, staff and the wider local communities of both partners.

Case Study 3:
Partnership with Hollybank Trust

Leeds Met's partnership with the Hollybank Trust epitomises the reconceptualisation of partnership work referred to above and our pioneering approach to developing such opportunities.

The Hollybank Trust is a charity that works with some of society's most vulnerable members: children and adults with complex physical disabilities, which are often coupled with severe learning difficulties. The Hollybank Trust is committed to the care and development of each individual – for life: 'We're not simply a school. But neither are we merely a home – we are a combination of the two, providing a range of excellent services under one roof'.

Since signing a formal memorandum of understanding with the Trust in 2007, our collaborations with Hollybank have flourished. The formalisation of partnership between the two organisations not only reflects the spirit of co-operation and friendship that we share, but, importantly, provides students, staff and wider community members with opportunities to benefit from the sharing of expertise, interests and support. Activities included in our work so far include projects from across the faculties of Leeds Met as well as opportunities for volunteering, research and engagement in various partnership festivals and carnivals. Our joint success in becoming Guinness world record holders for the longest conga on ice is just one example of collaborative success that challenges stereotypes and raises the aspirations and experiences of students, staff and service users from both establishments, while providing distinctive opportunities for learning, friendship and interaction.

The partnership is truly reciprocal and in addition to working with service users, staff and specialist facilities, university students and staff also have access to Hollybank's Disability Awareness training. A range of exciting and innovative project work is also under way; examples include:

- horticulture therapy, in which a group of Leeds Met students have designed an interactive sensory garden for the main Trust site aimed at improving Hollybank students' cognitive, social, psychological and physical development;
- research and development of 'iTracker' software, a technology that uses eye movement to measure profoundly disabled students' understanding and recognition;
- placements for speech and language therapy students;
- guest lectures and masterclasses from the practitioners at Hollybank to a range of Leeds Met students and staff, including teacher training students, music technology students and students studying speech and language therapy;
- sensory art projects, including the development of tactile posters representing Hollybank students' dreams and aspirations.

Jill Adam
Leeds Met

Some Advice on Establishing and Maintaining Community Partnerships

- A clear vision and high-level commitment are essential for good community partnerships.
- When establishing a partnership with an external organisation, it is important to establish from the outset what added value each party can expect to gain, how the partnership will be managed, what (if any) financial arrangements there are and who will lead the partnership on each side.
- A university should not assume that it will always be the senior partner in any working relationship: leadership should stem from the locus of excellence.
- Where multiple partnerships are in operation and many staff are likely to be involved in different aspects, it is useful for one person to be designated the lead for that partnership on behalf of the university, to avoid crossed wires and unproductive overlap.
- Relationship-management databases can be helpful in assisting universities to keep track of multiple partnerships, but ultimately there is no substitute for person-to-person communication.
- A university can undertake a tremendously important brokerage of relationships between partners who might not otherwise be aware of each other's work (for example, in our case, between Leeds Rhinos rugby team and Hollybank Trust).
- While it is always good to have an advance plan for any partnership, some of the most productive aspects of some of our partnerships have been serendipitous, so over-rigidity in planning should be avoided.

Conclusion

Partnership working in diverse contexts and with a range of organisations, all of which share our commitment to excellence, collaboration and social inclusion, is undoubtedly a fast-evolving and dynamic dimension to the work of Leeds Met, and one that we are keen to share. This pioneering approach aligns with our ambitions to go beyond boundaries, working in many cases in areas not traditionally associated with universities. As the partnerships mature, some will inevitably broaden and deepen, while others, having achieved the desired outcomes for all parties, will mutate into different kinds of working relationships or cease altogether, while new partnerships are brokered. In this way the vibrancy, mutual supportiveness and energy of the partnerships will be constantly renewed.

Websites

The Hollybank Trust, www.hollybanktrust.com or www.leedsmet.ac.uk/partnerships/index_A0FD7B4503A04706B600B346A6528265.htm (accessed January 2009)

The Progression Module, www.leedsmet.ac.uk/getahead

References

Aimhigher. Online, available at: www.direct.gov.uk/en/EducationAndLearning/UniversityAndHigherEducation/index.htm (accessed January 2009).

Harrod, T. (1999) *The Crafts in Britain in the Twentieth Century*, London: Yale University Press.

Leeds Metropolitan University (2006) 'Vision and character'. Online, available at: www.leedsmet.ac.uk/the_news/docs/visionandcharacter08.pdf (accessed January 2009).

New York Times (1900) 'Ruskin: the experience of Canon Rawnsley and two "Atlantic" contributors', *New York Times*, 31 March. Online, available at: http://query.nytimes.com/mem/archive-free/pdf?_r=3&res=9E01EEDB1339E733A25752C3A9659C946197D6CF&oref=slogin&oref=slogin (accessed 8 January 2009).

Sharp, P., Higham, J., Yeomans, D. and Mills, D. (2001) 'Working together: the Independent/State School Partnerships Scheme: sustainability of 1998–1999 funded projects'. Online, available at: www.leeds.ac.uk/educol/documents/00002223.htm.

Wilby, P. (2008) 'New universities, new relationships: a shared vision for cultural partnership', *British Bandsman*, no. 5503 (April): 14–15.

CHAPTER 17

Employability

Realising the Potential of a University Education

SIMON BARRIE
University of Sydney

JACQUELINE ANDREWS
Nottingham University Business School

LAURA DEAN
Leeds Metropolitan University

and **INTA HEIMANIS**
University of Sydney

Introduction

Universities worldwide are being subjected to increasingly strident calls to provide employable graduates. Such calls are not new, dating as they do from the early 1960s; however, the increasingly explicit linking of higher education to economic prosperity by many governments, the trend (not least by students themselves) to position students as consumers of higher education, and the rise of vocationally orientated university degrees all lend weight to the demand for employable graduates.

Despite nearly four decades of university and government interest in producing employable graduates, employability itself is not necessarily a well-understood concept, even by its advocates, and is approached in a variety of ways. In both the United Kingdom and Australia, approaches to employability often conflate it with concepts such as career development skills or the outcomes of particular pedagogical and curriculum initiatives such as work-integrated learning or personal development planning. Many of these approaches effectively position employability as something that exists outside of the mainstream curriculum and as being primarily the responsibility of careers services or dedicated professional development subjects. Other understandings of the concept of employability see it as an integral and highly practical dimension of the purpose of higher education and, as such, something that everybody in universities should contribute to fostering.

Employability in its narrower interpretations is often described in terms of a discrete set of non-specialised 'employable skills' that enable a graduate to obtain employment. Such interpretations of employable skills often manifest themselves in university policy as a subset of the higher-level skill sets described as graduate attributes and are seen to be acquired as an addition to the content of the discipline and these higher-order generic attributes. Such a conception of employability is often associated with the use of simple graduate employment statistics as an indicator for quality and the provision of skills training as an addition to the university curriculum.

The more complex understandings of employability position it as more than a set of job-readiness skills. Employability is instead about the skills and attributes, the ways of thinking, which allow a graduate to thrive among the uncertain challenges that typify graduate-level employment. This understanding of employability is in terms of ongoing personal aptitudes, often about creating solutions to unfamiliar challenges, and for learning and developing in a job – and, indeed, the entrepreneurial aptitudes required for developing the job itself. Employability is not seen as another set of skills in addition to the subject content and generic attributes. Instead, it is about how the higher-order generic attributes manifest themselves in the context of employment. The skills and aptitudes themselves are the same as those that will allow graduates to thrive and contribute to society. The world of work is simply one context (albeit a very important one) in which graduates will operate. Also, the world of work is itself changing, with moves away from linear careers towards portfolio working over a lifetime for many. Such a conception of employability obviously requires more than simply a few skills training courses: it requires an approach to learning that focuses more on the development of reflective capabilities and values than on simple behavioural competencies. It also suggests that more is needed as an indicator of quality outcomes than simple measures such as percentages of graduates in work six months after completing their degrees, as these do not capture the quality of the graduates' engagement in that work.

While the more complex articulations of employability have far more in common with contemporary understandings of knowledge and society, they do not of themselves provide the full answer for universities seeking to address the employability agenda in a meaningful way. Perhaps the most interesting of contemporary perspectives on employability combine a view of employment as a key context for expression of generic attributes with innovative pedagogical approaches and educational experiences that are likely to foster such outcomes. These educational experiences are about more than simply providing vocational experience as an addition to the existing curriculum or about offering final-year students a talk from a prospective employer. If this were all that is required to develop employability, there would be no need to change university curricula to foster it, as will be discussed in later sections of this chapter.

Rather than the approach of 'sending the students out there', we argue that these more innovative curricular approaches are equally about bringing the employers (and others) into the university environment – that is, engaging them in planning work experiences and curriculum discussions, bringing them into teaching and research and, perhaps most importantly, into discussions about what constitutes employability itself. All too often, universities engage with employers sporadically as external voices who might be asked to tell the institution what skills they think graduates need to start work. This often leaves employers effectively outside, articulating in a survey the sorts of basic skills lists that are used in job advertisements, but not engaging them in authentic dialogues to co-create an understanding of what is actually needed to succeed in the world of work. Typically, the basic lists generated by 'industry consultation' are not the sorts of graduate aptitudes industry leaders and professional associations articulate in response to a more prolonged and meaningful engagement with universities, and often not the sorts of aptitudes employers actually look for in graduate interviews.

The sorts of educational employability experiences that we will describe later in this chapter are intended to illustrate a range of responses to some of the more complex understandings of employability. In conclusion we will return to the key challenge of developing strategies to achieve institutional change towards employability and, within that, the question of how to 'measure' employability.

Curriculum Development for Employability: Graduate Attributes

As was indicated earlier, fostering employability is closely aligned with universities' efforts to foster graduate attributes. In Australia, this is illustrated in definitions of graduate attributes as:

> [t]he qualities, skills and understandings that a university community agrees its students should develop during their time with the

institution and consequently shape the contribution they are able to make to their profession and society . . . they are qualities that also prepare graduates as agents of social good in an unknown future.

(Bowden *et al.*, 2000)

This definition avoids the separation of the 'graduate-ness' debate from the 'employability' debate, and is an example of an approach that positions employment as a key context for the expression of graduate attributes. Working from such a position, the whole academic community (not just selected members of it) should assume responsibility for curriculum review and development, and creating a university experience in relation to these attributes. The potential advantage of this is that employability, as a dimension of graduate attributes, will be addressed as part of the curriculum and general student experience rather than risking being sidelined as something that can be adequately dealt with through the provision of additional work experience, or skills training by specialist units such as careers, without changing the curriculum itself. This integrated approach does, however, bring with it other challenges, as few Australian or UK universities have thus far managed to successfully integrate graduate attributes in an effective way across the full range of undergraduate disciplinary and vocational curricula.

Case Study 1:
Integrating Graduate Attributes at the University of Sydney

An example of how one Australian university is moving towards achieving this is seen at the University of Sydney. Sydney is unusual among Australian universities in its development of a two-tiered statement of generic attributes. The two tiers are based on the research finding (Barrie, 2006) that there are different types of generic attributes. That is, the outcomes listed as attributes are not all the same sorts of things (consider, for example, the difference between 'skills' and 'capabilities'). More importantly still, research has revealed that different types of attributes are developed through different sorts of educational experiences (Barrie, 2007; Kember *et al.*, 2007). At the top level of Sydney's attributes (Barrie, 2004) are three broad overarching attributes or 'ways of being in the world': global citizenship (an attitude towards the world and one's place in it), scholarship (an attitude towards knowledge) and lifelong learning (an attitude towards oneself as a learner). Such attributes are developed not through explicit instruction in classroom curricula, but rather through engagement with a range of experiences, over time, that challenge existing ways of thinking and support students in constructing new ways of thinking.

The second level of attributes includes more familiar skills which are readily developed through explicit classroom learning experiences. This level of attributes includes discipline-specific abilities related to communication, inquiry, information literacy, personal autonomy and professional understandings. The research indicates that these disciplinary attributes are best developed through the experiences of learning the discipline knowledge rather than separately from it. Both levels of attributes in the policy are supported through the development of foundation-level skills for new university students, although foundation skill strategies alone cannot develop the higher-level attributes.

From the perspective of employability, the challenge for the university is how to provide the employment-related experiences relevant to the development of both levels of attributes. In considering the top-level attributes, global citizenship is an example of an attribute highly prized by employers. It is a way of being in the world that is underpinned by some more specific skills such as 'an awareness of variation in communication contexts and the range of suitable genres to use in professional communication'. These are discipline-specific skills (for example, the genres will be different for a lawyer and a musician) and can be developed through explicit curricula, whether curricula based on industry placements, work-integrated learning or a lecture series. We will first consider strategies related to this level of attribute before turning to the more complex task of improving the broader university experience in order to develop ways of being in the world such as global citizenship.

Each faculty of the University of Sydney has developed its own discipline-based statements of the second level of attributes, and faculties use these to review and develop curricula that focus on the development of such outcomes. The consultation involved in the development of these attributes statements was a vehicle for involving graduates and employers in an ongoing discussion about employability in the context of shaping the university's courses. This dialogue has been most effective and most sustained in the professional faculties, where the statements of graduate attributes have integrated professional competencies and standards. The dialogue is ongoing through work with students, helping them to learn how to articulate the development of these attributes to employers in their CVs. The process of professional accreditation of these faculties has also driven the curriculum review

continued

more rapidly and coherently than the institutional quality assurance processes related to graduate attributes. While curriculum review often initially equates to mapping the claimed development of graduate attributes in curriculum documents, accreditation and quality assurance are now evolving towards assuring the outcomes of learning, where evidence is sought from assessment that students have in fact developed the claimed attributes.

Simon Barrie

This more complex conceptualisation of graduate attributes leads universities inescapably to confront the limitations of current assessment practices. The sorts of outcomes articulated by faculties as graduate attributes typically integrate content with application. The assessment of such applied and integrated outcomes challenges the familiar focus on content inherent in much university assessment and requires the use of more holistic and authentic assessment strategies, for example capstone assessments, viva voces or the sorts of practice-based assessment tasks often used in work-integrated learning. This in turn suggests a role for authentic assessors and application experts (employers, for example) as partners in assessment.

While assessment remains a challenge, most faculties have made more progress on developing innovative curricula and pedagogies that foster the development of such attributes. These pedagogical efforts all share a focus on active and authentic student learning. Often this has involved strategies to make existing teaching more relevant to the real world and to work, for instance using case study-based teaching, sometimes with the cases presented by, or in co-operation with, an industry expert. Often the relevance is further emphasised with the integration (rather than simply the addition) of work placements within taught curricula. Other strategies used at the University of Sydney are perhaps more innovative, focusing for example on developing work-integrated learning experiences for first-year students, wholly work-based learning curricula for postgraduate courses, and mentoring and peer-assisted study schemes where the mentor or peer is from industry rather than another student.

Addressing the challenge of providing students with experiences that challenge and support them in developing ways of thinking that are pluralistic and suited to the complexities and uncertainties which characterise graduate employment is somewhat more difficult. While this might begin in classrooms, it is the nature of students' broader experiences that shapes these attributes over time. A student is more likely to develop the sorts of global perspectives valued by an employer through engaging in a meaningful way with other members of that global society, be they staff, students, workers or employers. Universities can already provide many opportunities for such experiences, for instance access to a culturally diverse student and staff population, access to other university populations, overseas study opportunities, social and political clubs and organisations, international cutting-edge research programmes, community outreach programmes and employer networks. However, what is lacking is a way of encouraging the majority of students to meaningfully engage with such experiences in order to develop valuable attributes. First and foremost, this requires the development of a culture in the university which values time spent on such activities alongside time spent in classrooms. This must be valued by staff as well as students if the institution hopes to create a culture and environment that truly foster the development of these attributes.

The valuing of time spent on such activities can be powerfully shaped by assessment. For students this is likely to be achieved through the next wave of professional development portfolio assessment tools, which will provide a way for students to record (assess) their learning from such experiences. A logical step will be for universities to develop strategies for students to integrate this assessment with teacher- or employer-based assessment from the traditional curriculum. The use of these portfolios will then need to be supported by employers. Interestingly, the assessment driver extends to staff too. In order for staff to spend time engaging with students outside classrooms, fostering student engagement in these 'other' activities (possibly including their own research), as well as supporting student reflection and learning arising from these opportunities, a rethink is required about how universities define, allocate time to, and assess (reward) academic work. This is consistent with many of the current debates about reconceptualising academic practice. However, those debates are far from over, and Australian universities have made little headway thus far in supporting institution-wide staff or student engagement in such activities in the pursuit of the development of such employability attributes.

Accompanying this focus on embedding generic attributes as a core element of the 'Sydney experience', the Careers Centre has been working closely with faculties, using workshops to help students identify the generic graduate attributes that relate to their course of study, how these attributes might be generalised and demonstrated in their wider university and extra-curricular experiences, and how to translate these into the language of 'employability skills' for the purposes of the graduate recruitment process.

Another strategy at the University of Sydney has been the development of an ongoing dialogue with employers. This dialogue encompasses several levels, ranging from a forum for senior staff from the university and industry to exchange views on strategy and policy, to more practical sessions with graduate recruiters to harvest feedback on student performance and to discuss process and employer profile on campus. The Careers Centre is also working closely with the university's Alumni Relations Office to implement an online mentoring project that will facilitate contact between current students looking for advice and information about specific career options and alumni who are willing to contribute their time and expertise within an online environment.

Another element of the approach is a new university-wide programme called SydneyTalent, which provides paid employment to assist students to improve their work readiness and employment prospects while completing their studies. Students are offered internships within the university, which affords them flexibility to manage their study commitments while under-taking meaningful, course-related paid employment. The challenge with this initiative has been to frame it within the institutional graduate attributes statement to ensure that students and the broader university community can clearly see that student time spent in such employment activities directly supports students in developing the university's graduate attributes.

To complement the mentoring received through these internships, a performance measurement framework ensures that each student's key development goals are attained and recorded as the student progresses through the programme on their way to graduation. Participating students also attend skills development courses provided by the Careers Centre and designed to augment the practical workplace skills learned on the job.

Having sketched one example of what we see as an integrated approach, in the next section we will consider four specific strategies employed in the United Kingdom and Australia to foster employability to illustrate elements of this approach in more detail, before returning to the challenge of 'assess-ment' from a quality assurance perspective and suggesting some ways forward for universities seeking to implement employability strategies.

Personal Development Planning

Advocates of embedded employability interventions have often used personal development planning (PDP) as a vehicle, which leads to further confusion but also greater implementation, as the UK Quality Assurance Agency (QAA), the English Funding Council (HEFCE) and employers have acted as drivers for the development of PDP in the curriculum.

The QAA introduced PDP on the recommendations of the 1997 Dearing Report (NCIHE, 1997). QAA guidelines stated that it 'is a structured and supported process undertaken by an individual to reflect upon their own learning, performance and/or achievement and to plan for their personal, educational and career development' (Quality Assurance Agency, 2001b).

PDP is often conflated with both graduate attributes and employability, and all three can be argued to contain common elements, such as global citizenship, work-related learning, entrepreneurial activity, career development learning, skills-building, etc. The original guidance from QAA was that all undergraduate and postgraduate courses should incorporate PDP in their curricula, starting from the 2005–6 academic year. Subsequently the element of compulsion was removed, but not before the concept had begun to gain ground, since many universities recognised the value of the approach in its own right. Consequently, most higher education programmes have integrated some form of PDP or employability into their programmes, although for some this can be somewhat tokenistic, for example using a series of 'tick box' exercises with little meaningful engagement in the process by either the students or the institution.

In 1987 the Enterprise in Higher Education (EHE) initiative was introduced, for which the Training Agency (1990) identified two broad aims (Burniston *et al.*, 2000):

- Every person seeking a higher education qualification should be able to develop competencies and aptitudes relevant to enterprise.
- These competencies and aptitudes should be acquired at least through project-based work designed to be undertaken in a real economic setting, which should be jointly assessed by employers and students in higher education institutions.

Universities were able to bid for funds to help develop initiatives that brought businesses and education closer together to promote knowledge transfer and develop enterprising and entrepreneurial skills in their students. The debate surrounding the purposes of higher education is still continuing: is its role to meet the requirements of the economy, or should it be considered as education for its own sake, for personal growth and the development of the subject? The latter argument has been used against both PDP and employability interventions: they are still contested as appropriate concerns for academic courses, even though most students enter higher education to improve their career prospects (Institute for Employment Research, 2007).

Foundation Degrees

The most recently introduced category of higher education courses in the United Kingdom has been developed in direct response to the needs of the UK economy: two-year, employability-focused foundation degrees were developed to offer a fast-track route to increased employability in particular sectors.

At a national level, foundation degrees (FDs) were seen as a rapid route to increasing the employability of large numbers of students, making them fit for the workplace and emphasising the skills needed to become employed and remain employable in a particular sector. These courses were developed in conjunction with employers, sometimes to very specific requirements. For example, the FD Offender Management caters specifically to the requirements of the prison services. The aim of these programmes was to develop people already working in a particular sector to meet the employer's needs via a process of personal development planning, work-related learning and subject content delivery. The UK Higher Education Statistics Agency reports that foundation degrees have been successful in recruiting students, with the number of applicants and students on these programmes having grown each year since their inception in 2001. However, they can be criticised for focusing on specific employer requirements to the detriment of long-term employability. The emphasis on specific occupational skills, for example, can be at the expense of transferable skills, of more benefit in the wider graduate market, and so they can leave these FD graduates at the mercy of the continued success of the occupational area in which they have specialised. The Quality Assurance Agency (2005) also reports a trend in student type which may indicate that groups are using these qualifications in ways that were not intended:

> Two distinctive student enrolment patterns emerge that appear to be particular to FDs. One group of students study full-time; they are primarily male, under 25 years of age, with traditional entry qualifications at level 3 on the National Qualifications Framework. The other group studies part-time; is predominantly female, mature, employed and holds a greater diversity of entry qualifications.

The former group was not that envisaged as the core target group in the design of foundation degrees. Foundation degrees were designed to attract people from a 'broader range of backgrounds', and provide alternative routes for people who are not the 'traditional A-level school leaver', in particular facilitating the development of skills of those already in the workplace (Department for Education and Employment, 2000). Therefore, there are questions around the assumptions inherent in many FDs that students have already worked and developed particular skills.

Work-Related Learning

Graduates need to be ready to add value in the workplace from their first day, according to evidence gathered for the Dearing Report (National Committee of Inquiry into Higher Education, 1997). Dearing found that most employers and graduates viewed work experience as a strong differentiating factor in graduates' potential employability. The QAA Code of Practice makes reference to the value of work-related learning: 'Institutions should consider: maximising and promoting the value of work experience and work-related learning to both students and employers' (Quality Assurance Agency, 2001a: Precept 11).

Foundation degrees are among the fastest-growing qualifications, with over 60,000 students in 2006–7, a figure projected to grow to 80,000–100,000 by 2010 (Higher Education Funding Council for England, 2007). The proportion of small and medium-sized businesses is also increasing, and consequently it is becoming increasingly difficult for students to access good-quality work experience; therefore, curriculum designers should become more creative in ensuring students have access to this learning. Work-related learning can act as a bridge between the classroom and the workplace, allowing skills to be built, but is not what was originally envisaged for FDs.

Case Study 2:
Building in Work Experience Through a Module

At Leeds Metropolitan University the BA (Hons) Media and Popular Culture produces graduates who are interested in entering the highly competitive media sector, though the course is non-vocational. Finding media-related work experience is difficult, and employers can be reluctant to provide opportunities until applicants have sufficient experience to be of use to them. Work experience can provide the 'foot in the door' necessary to build and use contacts and networks, and can act as the bridge necessary for students to operationalise and critique the theory they have learned, but it is hard to access. In the BA (Hons) Media and Popular Culture an employability programme was built into the whole course, incorporating many aspects of skills development, for example self-awareness activities and team building at level 1, and preparation for transition and communication skills at level 3. At level 2, students benefit from an innovative and successful work-related learning module.

The work experience module is compulsory and utilises the skills and knowledge of media professionals. It is built from three interrelated elements. The first is a work project that students must complete in small groups, with a media professional, employed for this purpose, acting as a mentor. This element focuses on developing negotiation,

continued

teamwork, communication skills and ability to compromise. The second element is a personal career strategy unit in which students choose an occupation of interest and research their entry into this role, including developing a five-year action plan and relevant CV. The third assessable element is a reflective log of the process, which draws together and synthesises the learning from the first two elements. As well as developing an insight into a particular role and an increased under-standing of employability skills, students gain valuable contacts with actual employers and develop the transferable skills that employers require.

This module has been in place since 2003 and it is possible to see an impact based on the number of graduates entering graduate-level work by the time of the Destinations of Leavers of Higher Education data collection. The module receives positive feedback from students, who comment on the impact it has had on their career intentions.

Laura Dean

Employability Skills Curriculum Modules and Courses

The inclusion of skills modules and courses is a popular and highly effective way to support the development of employability skills. These modules can target the development of many aspects of employability skills and can be tailored to reflect different discipline foci; however, the inclusion of such additional elements does not remove the need to refocus mainstream curriculum elements on the development of employability outcomes (see, for example, the Leeds Met curriculum review case study, p. 297). Indeed, the development of the full range of employability skills articulated in more complex conceptions of graduate attributes requires this refocusing of learning within the mainstream disciplinary curriculum as well as harnessing the full range of extra-curricular learning opportunities across and between disciplines (Barrie, 2007). Skills curriculum modules and courses play a vital role in an integrated strategy; however, such modules, no matter how excellent, cannot on their own achieve the full potential of employability. Indeed, the experience of some universities has been that the provision of excellent skills curriculum modules and courses can be seen by some in the institution as a tempting excuse to avoid mainstream curriculum renewal.

Case Study 3:
Integrating Academic and Transferable Skills at
Nottingham University

At Nottingham University Business School a variety of methods are used to integrate academic and transferable skills into the curriculum, combined with extra-curricular options to help students develop into capable and employable graduates. Within the curriculum there are modules that focus on developing key skills for undergraduate students; one such module is Entrepreneurship and Business, which is compulsory for all first-year Business School students. This module illustrates one of the ways companies can work with students as mentors. It is delivered and assessed using three interrelated methods: team work and poster presentation, coursework based around a reflective Integrative Learning Barometer and an Individual Innovation Report. The students are introduced to Creative Problem Solving (CPS), where as a group they are required to select a problem and design a solution and then they are mentored throughout the CPS process. The mentors are businesspeople who work outside the university. They come from a variety of occupations ranging from bankers and business advisers to entrepreneurs running their own enterprises.

Another example is the optional module on Career Management and Development, which provides students with an understanding of the key issues and challenges facing graduates as they enter the workplace. It does so by critically examining developments in career theory in the areas of both practice and management, as well as by examining how broader social forces have important implications for career possibilities.

Running alongside these modules is the Business School's Employer Programme, which includes some of the more traditional external employer presentations and skills workshops. The employer presentations focus on skills such as commercial awareness, leadership, communication skills and a variety of business games, combined with workshops on CV development and application skills, and develop students' expectations of company assessment days. They complement many sessions run by the Centre for Career Development but are more focused and subject-specific. There is a certificate attached to the Employer Programme to encourage attendance. Students have to attend a minimum of eight skills sessions, and produce a CV and a personal evidence statement that encourages them to reflect on the skills they have developed. They are then required to have a discussion with their personal tutor. There is no time limit on the programme, which enables

continued

participants to work at their own pace and fit it around their other commitments. Linked with this are some new and innovative projects that aim to utilise the corporate social responsibility agenda within companies. Corporate social responsibility (CSR) is a key strategy for the government, and one that it wishes to see implemented within all businesses; it is defined as 'the voluntary actions that business can take, over and above compliance with minimum legal requirements, to address both its own competitive interests and the interests of wider society' (csr.gov.uk, 2004), which, in very simplistic terms, translates into companies encouraging their staff to take part in voluntary schemes and providing them with time and support to undertake these activities. Some of the new projects therefore are aimed at linking this CSR by encouraging staff to work as mentors with students on voluntary projects within the local community; for example, a number of students are currently working with a local community centre in the heart of the student housing area to develop promotion and business strategies so as to raise awareness of the benefits of the centre among students and the local community. In another project, some of our international students put together and run Chinese cultural sessions in local primary schools. The voluntary projects enable students to put into practice, with a tangible result, some of the knowledge and skills they have acquired over the course of their degree.

Companies taking part in the Employer Programme often also contribute to the core curriculum by giving guest lectures or providing research material and case study information. A number of companies have employees who wish to speak at guest lectures for their own personal development, and this can demonstrate to students, who have opportunities to talk with them afterwards, the concept of lifelong learning: many of those taking part in the Employer Programme are alumni of the university. Many recruiters now recognise the value of using alumni, and from a university's perspective this can often be an effective way into a new company.

Jacqueline Andrews

The Particular Problem with 'Measuring' Employability

Assessment and measurement of graduate attributes and employability in general is a problem for universities. However, there are some particular problems that arise in relation to assessment strategies that perhaps unwittingly target some of the less complex notions of employability. These challenges are also seen in the sorts of assessments universities use to quality-assure the impact of their employability initiatives.

While the more complex understandings of the disciplinary nature of generic attributes for employability would render de-contextual standardised testing of such skills meaningless, and while the validation of existing 'standard' tests consistently finds that the variation in scores is a result of pre-existing variables rather than any value added by the university, there is a long history of the development of supplementary skills assessments for such purposes. Despite the apparent limitations, such assessments can be enticing for governments, employers and universities. They are often presented as an objective, standardised measure of employable skills (which is understandably attractive to employers and governments) and, as such, they appear to remove the need for universities to do anything about changing their existing assessment practices (possibly an attractive option to universities). However, the relationship between such skills tests and the sorts of high-level attributes that we have suggested as the focus of employability remains doubtful.

Case Study 4:
Curriculum Review at Leeds Metropolitan University

Leeds Met sees internationalisation as a process that is relevant to all its students, aiming to provide an education and a broader university experience that will prepare them to live and work as responsible citizens in the complexity and uncertainty of a globalising world. In this context, employability is not to be seen simply as a matter of building a relevant skills base, important though that is; rather, it should also incorporate attitudes and values that enable graduates to operate across cultural boundaries in multicultural and international contexts, and to do so with an understanding of the interconnected nature of the planet in relation to the personal and professional choices they face. Such a perspective on employability has much in common with the perspective on the graduate attribute of 'global citizenship' discussed earlier in this chapter.

The first objective in Leeds Met's Internationalisation Strategy refers to internationalising learning, teaching and research. In 2003, to begin the long-term process of change implicit in the first two strands of this objective the university embarked upon a five-year process of curriculum review against a set of guidelines (revised in 2006) based on the allied concepts of cross-cultural capability and global perspectives (Killick, 2006). All existing courses are undergoing reviews, and there

continued

is an ongoing requirement within the Assessment, Learning and Teaching Strategy that all new provision and all provision undergoing periodic review should include considerations of the guidelines in the review and approval process.

The guidelines for review advise courses teams that the curriculum review process should critically examine how the student, through participation on the course and as a member of the university community, is enabled:

- to develop the awareness, knowledge and skills to operate in multicultural contexts and across cultural boundaries;
- to develop the awareness, knowledge and skills to operate in a global context;
- to develop values commensurate with those of responsible global citizenship.

To facilitate the review process, staff development sessions have been offered through the annual Staff Development Festival, through year-round workshops and learning lunches, and by working with course and scheme teams. At least as significant to the process, though, have been activities across various areas of the university which demonstrate a commitment to these principles within the institution's own practice. In addition to high-profile international events, celebrations and partnerships, a daily 200-word International Reflection appears on the university website; the university operates a Fair Trade policy, and has won awards for its sustainability and 'green' practices; students and staff are supported if they wish to undertake international exchange and volunteering experiences; and Leeds Met Africa sets out an ethical basis for mutual partnerships across the continent. For many staff members, it is these varied and visible activities that evidence and encourage the change in culture which must inform and form the more concrete change in practice that the curriculum review process requires.

A series of key questions are laid out in the guidelines with examples of how they might be addressed, and the outcome of each course/scheme review has been collated annually to provide a bank of responses. The questions are organised around 'Knowledge' and 'Experience' gained on the course itself, or enabled through co-curricular activities encouraged or supported by the course. While the overall focus is to develop graduate attributes around the 'whole person' of a global citizen, sample questions serve to illustrate their relevance to employability:

- In what ways does the course seek to link issues of cross-cultural capability, diversity and global responsibility to employability?
- How does the course make students aware of the global impacts of professions related to the subject area?
- How is a student from this course prepared to interact with, benefit from and contribute to diversity in the world beyond the university?

The period for curriculum reviews is not yet fully complete, but it is clear that engagement with the process has been, predictably, variable across the institution. However, through a mandated process, tied in to two major university strategies, we believe that the dialogue generated provides the basis for academic staff to critically review their provision into the future, with an eye to enabling their students to make a successful transition into the complex and interconnected world(s) that await them.

A full description of this project, along with a complete copy of the guidelines, appears in Jones and Killick (2007).

David Killick

In addition to direct assessment of student learning and auditing of teaching and learning experiences (curriculum mapping and PDP records respectively), discussed earlier in the chapter, the simplest and most commonly used measures of employability are some variation of employment statistics: for instance, the percentage of graduates in work six months after graduation, or the percentage of graduates who are retained in employment over the next two years, or even the percentage of graduates who are satisfied with their employment. These measures do not of course take into account the other variables (e.g. gender, context, age) that affect employment, retention and job satisfaction. Moreover, the contested nature of what counts as 'work' is often ignored by such measures. For example, is it any work, or does it have to be graduate-level work? Must it be paid? And does self-employment count? Other measures used are employer surveys asking about satisfaction with graduate skills, and graduate surveys asking how well university equipped them for employment. These processes often default to the quick generation of skills lists from the survey respondents' personal perspectives.

There does not appear to be a fully adequate measure of employability at the point of graduation, and all that can be hoped for is indicators of its development through contextual integrated assessment of student learning and assessment of the extent of student engagement in activities likely to foster its development. Indeed, part of the challenge of fostering such complex outcomes might involve the realisation that nobody, apart possibly from the graduates themselves, and possibly not even then until the end of their careers, can truly judge the extent of development of 'employability'.

In presenting a variety of case studies in this chapter we have not attempted to describe the full range of employability strategies used by universities. Instead we have sought to illustrate some ideas that readers may wish to adapt and use in their own institutions rather than to suggest that any of the particular initiatives described here should be implemented. In deciding which ideas might work in a given university or degree course it is particularly important to consider the dynamics of the student population. For instance, PDP may be a suitable element for undergraduate students straight from school with little or no work experience, but for professional people taking an MBA it may be a less relevant activity of limited value. Strategies to foster graduate employability need to be cognisant of the unique institutional systems and contexts in which they are to be implemented. In particular, new strategies should be aligned with how the institutional understanding of 'employability' as an aspect of 'graduate-ness' is embodied in powerful institutional systems such as curriculum review, student assessment and quality assurance. Different universities have different dynamics and there is no one approach that fits all. In identifying a strategy, the aim is to be as adaptable, flexible and innovative as we would like our students to be.

Conclusions and Ways Forward

This chapter has outlined how employability can be approached by universities in different ways depending on what employability is thought to be. We have suggested that an integrated approach, where employability is seen as an integral facet of 'graduate-ness', is beneficial as it embeds the development of employability within the mainstream university curriculum and the broader university culture. Such an approach recognises that different members of the university community will have different contributions to make and that all these contributions are needed if the best outcomes are to be achieved. Central to this is the recognition that the university community encompasses more than staff and students; it includes members of the society in which the university is situated. Efforts are needed to further support the participation of some of the members of that community, employers in particular, in efforts to develop employability as a graduate quality.

Underpinning any effort by a university community to better encourage employability should be the development of a shared understanding as to what the term constitutes. As we noted in the opening sections of this chapter, different understandings of employability suggest different approaches. We have proposed that an effective and integrated approach requires all the various groups within the university community, including academics, careers advisers, administrators, managers and students, to be involved, and in order to be involved, the members of those groups need to share an understanding of employability as something with which it is relevant for them to be engaged. Clearly, if the understanding of employability is as something that can be addressed by work experience alone or solely by the provision of workshops by careers advisers, then academics will continue to teach in ways that are incompatible with its development. In a similar manner, if employer surveys and government reports of skills shortages portray employability simply as an additional set of low-level employment skills, then academics will continue to assert that the development of such skills is not their role. However, if students, teachers, careers staff and employers share a conception of employability that is not limited to low-level skills, but instead encompasses the sorts of holistic aptitudes which allow graduates to thrive, not only in work but in their lives, then they will all have something to contribute to fostering employability.

References

Barrie, S. C. (2004) 'A research-based approach to generic graduate attributes policy', *Higher Education Research and Development*, 23 (3): 261–75.

Barrie, S. C. (2006) 'Understanding what we mean by generic attributes of graduates', *Higher Education*, 51 (2): 215–41.

Barrie, S. C. (2007) 'A conceptual framework for the teaching and learning of graduate attributes', *Studies in Higher Education*, 32 (4): 439–58.

Bowden J., Hart, G., King, B., Trigwell, K. and Watts, O. (2000) *Generic Capabilities of ATN University Graduates*. Draft report, January. Online, available at www.clt.uts.edu.au/ATN. grad.cap.project.index.html (accessed April 2009).

Burniston, S., Rodger, J. and Brass, J. (2000) *Enterprise in Higher Education: Changing the Mindset*, London: Department for Education and Employment.

csr.gov.uk (2004) 'What is corporate responsibility (CR)?' Online, available at: www.csr.gov.uk/ whatiscsr.shtml (accessed 16 July 2008).

Department for Education and Employment (2000) 'Foundation degrees – consultation paper'. Online, available at: www.dfes.gov.uk/dfee/heqe/fdcd.pdf (accessed 20 March 2003).

Higher Education Funding Council for England (2007) *Foundation Degrees: Key Statistics 2001–02 to 2006–07*, London: HEFCE.

Institute for Employment Research (2007) 'Futuretrack project survey results'. Online, available at: www.futuretrack.ac.uk/public/2005entrants.php (accessed 15 January 2008).

Jones, E. and Killick, D. (2007) 'Internationalisation of the curriculum', in E. Jones and S. Brown (eds) *Internationalising Higher Education*, Abingdon: Routledge.

Kember, D., Leung, D. and Ma, R. (2007) 'Characterizing learning environments capable of nurturing generic capabilities in higher education', *Research in Higher Education*, 48(5): 609–32.

Killick, D. (2006) 'World-wide horizons: cross-cultural capability & global perspectives. Guidelines for curriculum review', Leeds: Leeds Metropolitan University.

National Committee of Inquiry into Higher Education (1997) *Higher Education in the Learning Society* (the Dearing Report), London: The Stationery Office.

Quality Assurance Agency (2001a) Code of Practice Section 8, 'Careers education, information and guidance', Gloucester: Quality Assurance Agency for Higher Education.

Quality Assurance Agency (2001b) 'Guidelines for HE progress files'. Online, available at: www.qaa.ac.uk/academicinfrastructure/progressFiles/default.asp (accessed 14 July 2008).

Quality Assurance Agency (2005) 'Learning from reviews of Foundation Degrees in England carried out in 2004–05'. Online, available at: www.qaa.ac.uk/reviews/foundationdegree/learningfrom05/default.asp#p3 (accessed 18 February 2007).

Training Agency (1990) *Enterprise for HE Initiative*, London: TA. Cited in MacLean, C., Semmens, M. and Silver, J. A. K. (2004) 'Enterprise learning: the process and the pedagogy', in 'Education in a Changing Environment', Conference Proceedings, 13–14 September 2004, University of Salford, downloaded from: www.edu.salford.ac.uk/her (accessed 17 July 2008).

CHAPTER 18

Conclusion

Leading the University Beyond Bureaucracy

SALLY BROWN with **STEVE DENTON**

Leeds Metropolitan University

Introduction

To review management of the university year without considering the role of senior managers would not be sensible. In this final chapter we explore one of the most complex, yet under-researched, areas of university management, that of university leadership. Both of the editors of this volume are pro-vice-chancellors working together in the university that provides many of the case studies within this volume, namely Leeds Met.

We wanted to investigate the nature of university leadership in an informal way, drawing upon some of the relevant literature but also on the advice provided by half a dozen or so vice-chancellors who kindly responded to our questions.

David Watson noted in his guest editorial for a special edition of *Higher Education Quarterly* on university leadership that systematic scholarly work on the topic was, with honourable exceptions, minimal until relatively late in the twentieth century. What did exist largely tended to comprise 'wry gentlemanly reflections by leaders towards or at the end of their careers on what seemed to have worked (at least for them)' (Watson, 2008).

Former Exeter Vice-Chancellor Sir Geoffrey Holland was quoted as calling for a major expansion of leadership training for universities: 'There are few sectors of our society so amateur, so apparently unconcerned, as higher education about the development of its leaders' (Midgley and MacLeod, 2003).

While a great deal has been written on leadership and leaders in general, there has until recently been less formal analysis of effective university leadership and the relationship of leaders with university administrators. In recent years, much more has been published, with particular stimulus in the United Kingdom from the work of the Leadership Foundation for Higher Education. We have drawn on this work, as well as contemporary journalistic articles, as a background against which to frame our responses from individuals.

From the Horse's Mouth

Without pretending this was a formal research project, we asked 17 current or previous vice-chancellors the following questions:

- As a Pro-Vice-Chancellor, I sometimes talk of myself as having no power but plenty of authority, which I derive from the trust and respect I have earned from my colleagues. I also influence people's behaviour by having funds to allocate to different areas in relation to assessment, learning and teaching. To what extent do you feel you as a Vice-Chancellor exercise power and authority and whence is this derived?
- In leading your university, how important to you is delegation? In what kinds of areas do you delegate fully to people you trust, and where do you feel you have to be most hands-on?
- To what extent have you shaped the mission/vision of your university and what means have you used to do so?
- If you were giving advice to a brand new Vice-Chancellor, what tips would you give him/her on setting off on the right note?

The responses, generously given by busy people, were extremely telling and aligned quite closely with some of the views proposed by the researchers in the field.

Balancing Power and Authority

Smith, writing about the roles of pro-vice-chancellors, summarises the outcomes of his follow-up research on a Leadership Foundation study as follows, coincidentally echoing the burden of our first question:

> The leadership roles of pro-vice-chancellors (PVCs) in the United Kingdom and elsewhere have evolved markedly over the last three decades while universities have been encouraged to shift towards

more executive styles of leadership and decision making. The change does not only reflect changing institutional needs, however, but an accommodation of deeper historical continuities around institutional autonomy and academic values. Most PVCs are drawn from the ranks of professors; typically have an Oxbridge, London or big-civic background; and are male. The role gains authority through influence rather than command, and depends on academic experience and credibility to be effective.

(2008: 340)

Most of the vice-chancellors who responded similarly linked the need for respect with the exercise of authority:

In my view, *mutatis mutandis*, the position of a PVC is quite similar to that of a VC, at least in a research-intensive university; that is, authority is exercised by virtue of consent. If that consent is withheld, then moving forward on a particular issue is difficult if not impossible. Of course, with a PVC there is the added need for explicit delegation, and the certainty that the VC will not, other than in truly extraordinary circumstances, overrule a decision made in his/her domain by the relevant PVC. This was certainly the case when I was PVC . . . when the then VC wholly delegated major areas of internal management to the Registrar and the PVCs, and would never himself allow anyone to approach him on the matters in question.

You may wonder about saying that a VC's position is essentially analogous. Let me qualify this. I have served on the Boards (Councils) of universities where the VC's word is law, provided only that the governing body retains confidence in their chief executive. Conversely, I have worked as VC only in universities where the consensus of academic opinion was decisive, and therefore authority derived from guiding that consensus in a desired direction. The 'governing body' in such institutions is essentially limited to hiring and firing the VC – an absolutely key role – and to helping to ensure the institution's ongoing financial stability. Of course, funding is important, but the more that funding is devolved and/or transparent, the less that particular power lies at the centre – except, of course, in a crisis (and every university has one of these from time to time).

(Male former Vice-Chancellor, pre-1992 university)

Another vice-chancellor similarly argued for a collegial approach:

> Whilst in a formal sense, it might be fair to say that there is a difference in this respect between a PVC and a VC role, I believe that in practice it is not possible to succeed in a senior management position by the exercise of power. Therefore, whilst some may seek or prefer to exercise chief executive power, I believe a successful leader will act on the basis of achieved trust, respect and credibility, allied with a clear vision which their colleagues can share and believe in. Any other approach will tend to achieve hollow and short-term results. The fact that absolute responsibility ultimately falls to the VC as chief academic and accounting officer is a key difference between the roles, but that is the 'burden' the VC chooses to shoulder in taking on the role and need not dictate a different approach to leadership.
>
> (Female VC, post-1992 university)

A third suggested:

> As a VC I do have power but only to the extent and for such time as I have authority. That authority is formally derived from the Governing Body but it retains confidence and therefore continues to extend its authority on the basis of what it perceives to be the confidence which a wide range of other individuals and organisations have in me, including my most senior colleagues, staff, students, the local and wider community, HEFCE, QAA, etc.
>
> (Male VC, post-1992 university)

And a fourth somewhat wryly commented:

> The Vice-Chancellor has much less 'power and authority' than staff sometimes realise and it is right that it should be like this.
>
> (Female VC, post-1992 university)

David Watson responded to our queries by providing the text of his valedictory presentation when stepping down as vice-chancellor of Brighton University. Having outlined what he considers to be the features of membership of the academic community of a university, he argues:

> Institutional *strategic choice* and decision-making should ideally come from all of these members of the university community, having of course consulted appropriately outside. But there is a

danger here. Universities can too easily become header-tank institutions, doing what is easy rather than what is right. That said, and to return to the question of autonomy, the evidence is that they make sounder choices when they decide what is right for themselves; when their first order commitments (who we are) guide their second order choices (what we do) rather than the other way around. I think that Brighton has been reasonably successful on this count.

(Watson, 2005)

Smith (2008) suggests there is a crumbling trust in academic leadership: 'Until comparatively recently it was taken as axiomatic that running a university was part of the "secret garden" of academic life'. As vice-chancellors have moved to recognising themselves as being more than just 'chief academic and administrative officers', he argues, they have been extending the influence and authority of the office beyond the ceremonial into what a number of researchers have described as a 'strengthened steering core', supported by a cadre of full-time professional administrators. The means by which the next tier down (PVCs, deputy vice-chancellors and deans, for example) is organised varies substantially from university to university, mirroring the power structures of the different organisations and the leadership styles of the vice-chancellors concerned.

Delegation

Delegation was an area about which our respondents expressed a degree of accordance, with all to a greater or lesser extent being in favour of delegating substantially.

Delegation is very important! It is at the heart of a successful institution. Much of my role is to appoint able people and allow them space to perform their role to the best of their abilities.

(Female VC, post-1992 university)

I delegate many areas of work completely. I am hands-on (a) in making sure that the delegated pieces of work follow complementary lines of action; (b) in high-level external relationships and with the Governing Body; and (c) in this University's particular circumstances, engaging with our Christian purposes.

(Male VC, post-1992 university)

A third VC made a useful distinction between delegation and abdicating responsibility, with a clear indication that full delegation is likely to be conditional on performance:

> It is crucial to be able to delegate to a senior team, both to ensure coverage of what is a very broad range of demands, challenges and ambitions, and to ensure they have the development opportunities they deserve and will need to progress in their own careers. Delegation for me does not mean abdicating knowledge of quite a lot of the detail, in all areas, but it does mean monitoring rather than interfering. I am happy to delegate in all areas, but monitor progress carefully and withdraw or switch delegation immediately it is apparent that progress is not being made.
>
> (Female VC, post-1992 university)

Bolden *et al.* (2008) argue for 'distributed leadership' as opposed to a somewhat individualistic and managerialist approach, which, they suggest, citing Fergussen, can exacerbate tensions, including individual versus collective performance, centralised versus decentralised control and economic versus social objectives.

A UK deputy vice-chancellor in a post-1992 university quoted in the Leadership Foundation study of PVCs (Smith, 2008) observed:

> [A] university is not like a command economy, it is not like an army. ... Leadership has to be within a collegiate, facilitative culture, where many people ... down to the level of principal lecturers, have to lead and inspire others.

This collegial approach came across strongly both in the literature and from our respondents as being a positive way to build loyalty to leaders within a university.

Shaping the Mission and Vision of the University

Professor David VandeLinde, the then vice-chancellor at Warwick University, was quoted (Midgley and MacLeod, 2003) as saying that a university's vision has to be shaped in partnership by Senate, university Council and the wider university community. While all our respondents recognised the need for a vice-chancellor to have a clear view of the direction in which their university needs to be heading, all acknowledged the value of participation of the university staff as a 'community of practice' (Wenger, 1998) helping to guide the vision to a greater or lesser extent:

I hope that I have had a significant role here. The mission outlives several Vice-Chancellors, but the vision can be developed by the Vice-Chancellor working with colleagues throughout the university.

(Female VC, post-1992 university)

After 11+ years, I guess to a significant extent. How has it been done? By working with all those from whom my authority is derived.

(Male VC, post-1992 university)

A third VC emphasised the importance of persuasion in bringing a university vision to life:

Setting priorities seems to me to be the key area of responsibility for a VC, preferably in some overall context ('the vision'), and then persuading the senior academics (the 'old' model) and/or the governing body (the 'new' model) that this is the way to move.

(Male VC, pre-1992 university)

David Watson emphasises the characteristics of an academic community that can work well in conjunction with an effective vice-chancellor for the benefit of the whole university community:

At the heart of academic citizenship is the concept of membership. When you sign up (most obviously as a student, but equally significantly as a staff member), what is the deal? What are the responsibilities that go along with all of your rights within the community; and, if you are a student, with your entitlements and expectations as a consumer? I think that such responsibilities include:

- A special type of academic honesty, structured most clearly around scientific procedure.
- Reciprocity and honesty in expression (for example by accurately and responsibly referring to other people's work within your own – avoiding plagiarism).
- Academic manners (as in listening to and taking account of other people's views).
- Striving towards self-motivation and the capacity for independent learning, along with 'learning how to learn'.
- Submission to discipline (most clearly in the case of assessment – for both assessors and the assessed).

- Respect for the environment in which members of the college or university work.
- Adherence to a set of collectively arrived at commitments and policies (on equalities, grievances, harassment, etc.).

(Watson, 2005)

These tenets are likely to be valuable to professional university administrators, echoing as they do many of the elements of the Association of University Administrators' *Code of Professional Standards* (AUA, 2000), as outlined in Chapter 1 of this volume.

Advice to New Vice-Chancellors

Advice proffered ranged from the highly practical to the fiercely idealistic and to many points in between.

David Watson's 'third envelope' lecture (Watson, 2005) included ten invaluable tips for VCs that he termed 'the laws of academic life':

1 Issues generate heat in inverse proportion to their importance (think of car-parking).
2 Academics grow in confidence the further away they are from their true fields of expertise (what you really know about is provisional and ambiguous, what other people do is clear-cut and usually wrong).
3 You should never go to a School or Department for anything which is in its title (which university consults its architecture department on the estate, or – heaven forbid – its Business School on the budget?).
4 The first thing a committee member says is the exact opposite of what he or she means ('I'd like to agree with everything the Vice-Chancellor has just said, but . . .'; or 'with respect . . .'; or even 'briefly').
5 Courtesy is a one-way street (social-academic language is full of hyperbole, and one result is the confusion of rudeness – or even cruelty – with forthrightness; however, if a manager responds in kind, it's a federal case).
6 On email nobody ever has the last word.
7 Somebody always does it better elsewhere (because they are better supported).
8 Feedback only counts if I agree with it.
9 The temptation to say 'I told you so' is irresistible.
10 There is never enough money, but there used to be.

Pragmatic advice from the VCs questioned included:

- Be visible both internally and externally.
- Avoid making non-urgent significant decisions within the first four months.
- Do not restructure for at least six months.
- Make sure that you are confident in your personal office team.
- Do not redecorate your office and similar things for at least a year.
- Do not refer in positive terms to how things worked at your previous university.
- When you don't know how to take the big steps, take the most sensible little step.
- Everyone deserves a second chance (including yourself).
- Trust your instincts, but be prepared to revise them in the light of experience.
- There is no difficult letter which cannot be improved by eight hours' sleep.
- Look at all of your post.
- Draft your emails.
- Try to learn people's names.
- Don't pretend to know when you don't (you will always be found out).
- Say thank you, even (especially?) when you don't mean it.
- Your most important (perhaps your only) tool for change is creative temporary cross-subsidy.

Watson (2005), who provided the last ten of these, argues that the last bullet is the most important. He suggests that this is a radically non-heroic proposition but it works. To make it work, he suggests you need to have (or to create) a sense of corporate commitment that taps into both altruism and self-interest. You also need financial discipline, in order to create the necessary margins, he concludes.

Further considered advice suggested:

- Be immediately highly visible, energetic and communicative, clearly committed to the values of the institution and proud of its existing achievements, but equally clear of the need to build on these and with a positive, engaging and inspiring vision of the future which colleagues can believe in and commit to.
- Take time to form your opinion of people and structures.
- Devote much time, at the start, to the university, rather than having too much focus on external roles.

- Personal chemistry and professional interactions are not the same thing. We all like some colleagues more than others, but we have to work with people, internally or externally, as required. Do not let your personal feelings show: you are much more likely to achieve what you are seeking to achieve.
- Identify quickly the key opinion formers within the institution (not always those with the formal titles) and make sure they fully understand the institution's policy goals and the principal means envisaged to achieve these.
- Go to talk face-to-face with major stakeholders, inside and outside the institution, to get key messages across.

David Watson's valedictory presentation explained the concept of the 'third envelope':

> There is a hoary old joke, much beloved of retiring principals and head teachers. On taking office, the new incumbent is handed three numbered envelopes by his or her predecessor and told to open them in sequence in response to crises. The first crisis reveals a note reading 'blame the previous administration'. The second advises 'say it's too early to judge'. The third [message] is brutal: 'prepare three envelopes'.
>
> (Watson, 2005)

Conclusions

Leadership styles of vice-chancellors vary substantially: the culture of the university is heavily dependent on the approach taken by the institution's leader, who can establish a positive collaborative working environment or who can set out to strengthen his (or, more rarely, her) own position by concentrating power in the higher echelons.

An Australian deputy vice-chancellor, one of the respondents to the Leadership Foundation study analysed by Smith (2008), describes a dysfunctional university as being 'a bit like Italy, before Garibaldi . . . and a series of warring chieftains who come together occasionally to fight the common enemy'. The role of the vice-chancellor is crucial in preventing this kind of internecine warfare breaking out in a university; the support of university administrators who work collegially across the institution is similarly of high importance in ensuring that the vision of the leaders is translated into effective practice.

References

Association of University Administrators (2000) *Code of Professional Standards*. Online, available at: www.aua.ac.uk/about/code/ (accessed December 2008).

Bolden, R., Petrov, G. and Gosling, J. (2008) 'Tensions in higher education leadership: towards a multi-level model of leadership practice', *Higher Education Quarterly*, 62 (4): 358–76.

Leadership Foundation for Higher Education. Online, available at: www.lfhe.ac.uk (accessed December 2008).

Midgley, S. and MacLeod, D. (2003) 'Vice squad: what sort of people make successful vice-chancellors and what exactly is their business?', *Guardian* (London), 1 April.

Smith, D. (2008) 'Academics or executives? Continuity and change in the roles of pro-vice-chancellors', *Higher Education Quarterly*, 62 (4): 350–7.

Watson, D. (2005) 'The third envelope: a farewell to Brighton University', Brighton: University of Brighton Educational Research Centre Occasional Paper.

Watson, D. (2008) Editorial, *Higher Education Quarterly*, 62 (4): 319–21.

Wenger, E. (1998) *Communities of Practice: Learning, Meaning, and Identity*, Cambridge: Cambridge University Press.

Contributors

Jill Adam is Associate Dean in the Carnegie Faculty of Sport and Education. She has responsibility for a number of Leeds Metropolitan partnerships, including the Hollybank Trust, schools and Harrogate International Festivals. Jill's doctoral research focused upon conceptions of expertise in teaching; her other professional interests and responsibilities include continuing professional development for those working in educational contexts and schools specifically.

Katie Akerman is Head of Quality Management at Bath Spa University. Katie has worked in higher education for around ten years in both English and Australian institutions, and for two national bodies, the Quality Assurance Agency for Higher Education and the Higher Education Academy.

Jacqueline Andrews is the Undergraduate Learning Officer of the Nottingham University Business School, where she developed and manages the Employer Programme, Study Skills Programme and Volunteering Programmes aimed at developing and enhancing the transferable skills and employability of Business School undergraduate students.

James Arthur works at the University of Bath as Assistant Registrar (Management Information and Ceremonies). He has worked in higher education for approximately six years, joining the Academic Registry at the University of Bath in 2005. His previous experience has focused on management information, so taking on responsibility for the student aspect of award ceremonies at Bath has proved to be both challenging and rewarding.

Kathy Ashton is People Development Manager at Leeds Metropolitan University with particular responsibility for management and leadership development. She is an experienced organisational development professional with accredited qualifications in business coaching and five years' experience of introducing coaching to the Leeds Partnerships Foundation Trust.

Chris Bailey is Professor of Cultural History and Dean of the Faculty of Arts and Society at Leeds Metropolitan University. His research covers the fields of design history, the impact of new technology on arts disciplines and the relationship of culture to social and economic regeneration. He shares responsibility for managing and developing cultural partnerships at Leeds Metropolitan University.

Simon Barrie is Associate Director, Institute of Teaching and Learning at the University of Sydney. Simon's recent research has focused on issues surrounding the development of generic graduate attributes and the assurance of the quality of university teaching and learning. His academic development work focuses on supporting organisational change in teaching and learning using systemic and structural approaches.

Christine Bexton is Postgraduate Registry Manager at the University of Nottingham. Her team maintains the records for the majority of the university's postgraduate students for both taught courses and research degrees, and handles recommendations for the award of degrees.

Maz Brook works at the University of Essex as Estate Management Administration Officer. After graduating from the University of Leeds, Maz spent nine years in a number of administrative roles in both the public and the private sector before joining the University of Essex Estate Management Section in 1999, where the wide variety and breadth of scale of the post ensures that life is never too boring!

Sally Brown is Pro-Vice-Chancellor for Assessment, Learning and Teaching at Leeds Metropolitan University. She has published widely on innovations in teaching, learning and, particularly, assessment.

Liz Buckton works as head of the Service Quality Unit at the University of Sheffield. She has responsibility for the area of student rights and responsibilities. This includes the management of discipline, complaints and appeals procedures for both taught and research students. Liz has worked at

Sheffield University since 1993, mostly in faculty support (including one year on secondment at the University of Sydney, Australia).

Phil Cardew is Pro-Vice-Chancellor (Students and Quality) at London South Bank University. He has been employed in various capacities within higher education for 18 years, also spending some of that period with the Quality Assurance Agency, for which he remains an institutional auditor. He has also been extensively involved in the development of quality assurance systems around the world, particularly the Gulf States (chiefly Kuwait, Qatar, the United Arab Emirates and Oman) but also in South Africa, Azerbaijan, the Netherlands and Pakistan.

Christine Child is the Head of the Student Services Centre at the London School of Economics. She has worked for higher education institutions and trade unions, and has considerable experience of academic administration and management and particular interests in staffing issues and managing change.

Lis Child has worked in higher education administration for over 20 years at the University of Durham, the University of Sunderland and Nottingham Trent University. She has extensive experience in student-related policies, procedures and systems, having held the post of Deputy Registrar for many years and latterly Student Liaison Manager in Student Support Services.

Tina Conkar is a Business Development Manager at Leeds Metropolitan University. She has held various business management posts at the university and is currently working with the Sporting Partnership Team. Following on from her DPhil from the University of York (2000), she continues to write about the social and collaborative impact of information and its strategic use.

Roseanna Cross is currently Head of Undergraduate Admissions at the University of Bristol. She previously worked as Admissions Projects Officer at the same institution.

Laura Dean is an occupational psychologist and employability specialist with a particular interest in equality of access to graduate opportunities for widening participation students. She is Head of Employability at Leeds Metropolitan University.

Steve Denton is Pro-Vice-Chancellor and Registrar and Secretary at Leeds Metropolitan University, where his role involves bringing together a range of university-wide student administrative and support services, including governance and legal matters, the academic registry, planning, student services, communication and marketing, and widening access and participation. Steve is also Chair of UNIPOL Student Homes, Honorary

Treasurer of AHUA and a member of the national executive of the Association of University Administrators (AUA).

John Dishman has worked in further and higher education for over 20 years and is currently a Dean at Leeds Metropolitan University. In addition to having served as principal of a further education college, he has worked extensively in curriculum and quality development, publishing and presenting nationally and internationally in these fields.

Max Farrar is Professor for Community Engagement at Leeds Metropolitan University. His sociological research and publications over the past 15 years have been on the struggles by the multi-ethnic populations of the British inner cities to achieve their longing for community. For the past 35 years he has actively engaged in community development work in the inner city area of Leeds.

Pam Fearnley works at Leeds Metropolitan University as Senior Officer, Awards, Examinations and Graduations Office. Pam worked for the Civil Service for eight years and moved into the private sector briefly before joining Leeds Metropolitan University where she has spent the last 18 years working in a variety of roles. Using her knowledge of the University and previous experience, she is now Project Manager of the graduation ceremonies on campus and in Hong Kong. Pam was runner up in 2007 for the AUA Awards for Excellence in Higher Education Administration and Management.

Jackie Flowers works at Birmingham City University, where she has held a range of posts in university and faculty administration. For the past eight years she has had responsibility for managing student casework for appeals, complaints, disciplinary procedures and fitness to practise.

James Forshaw has worked at Liverpool John Moores University for ten years and has witnessed at first hand student funding systems morphing several times in this period. Part of his professional experience comprises providing information regarding funding and the associated processes involved to both new and prospective higher education students. Since 2002 he has been administering scholarships funded by private donors for students at Liverpool John Moores University. His role has subsequently evolved with the introduction of variable tuition fees so that he now administers all non-course-specific scholarships at Liverpool John Moores University.

Rachel Frost works at the University of Essex as Administrative Officer (Registration and Graduation). She worked for almost 20 years in the private sector before joining the University of Essex in 2003, where she has carried out roles in the Research and Enterprise Office and central Academic Administration. She moved into higher education administration and management following her experience as a full-time mature international student completing her Master's degree in Australia.

Peter Funnell is Director of Enterprise and Executive Dean of the Faculty of Arts, Business and Social Sciences at University Campus Suffolk. He was previously Assistant Principal at Suffolk College and Executive Director of the Project for a University for Suffolk. He has published extensively in the fields of quality in vocational education and e-learning, and is currently a Director of the Suffolk Chamber of Commerce and a member of the JISC Joint Organisational Support Committee.

Michael Gray is Director of the Headingley Carnegie Partnership involving Leeds Rhinos, Leeds Carnegie and Yorkshire County Cricket Club, based at the Headingley Carnegie Stadium. This pioneering partnership was the first in the United Kingdom between a higher education institution and professional sport. Michael started his career in teaching and community education before moving into lecturing in higher education at Leeds Metropolitan University.

Sarah Gray is Associate Director of Human Resources at Leeds Metropolitan University, where she has worked since 2002. A human resources professional with over 15 years' experience, she has worked across the public and private sectors, including at the Universities of Sheffield and Oxford, the Royal Bank of Scotland and the Guide Dogs for the Blind Association. Her current focus is on the development and implementation of organisational development initiatives around performance, development, engagement, reward and talent management.

Mark Grayling has been General Manager at Nottingham Trent Students Union since 2003, previously having occupied a similar position at the University of Bradford Union after 12 years at NUS(UK) as a Regional Officer and then Director of Research and Policy. He was Chair of the Association for Managers in Students' Unions (AMSU) from 2004 to 2008.

Jean Grier has worked in a wide range of administrative posts at the University of Edinburgh, including a number of years in postgraduate student administration. She runs professional development courses through the Association of University Administrators (AUA), and is the author of several AUA good practice guides.

Ian Hamley has worked in the higher education sector since graduating from Warwick University in 1995. His early career was spent in administration roles at the University of Central England (now Birmingham City

University) and Coventry University. In 2001 he moved to the Registrar's Department at the University of Nottingham and since 2004 he has been the Undergraduate Registry Manager based in the Academic Services Division of the Registrar's Department.

Stewart Harper is Chief Operating Officer for the International Faculty at Leeds Metropolitan University, previously having worked at Leeds Trinity and All Saints, and Keele University, having joined the sector in 2001. He is a graduate of the University of Leicester, and is a member of the Board of Trustees of the Association of University Administrators.

Inta Heimanis has a strong background in tertiary education management, with a focus on the provision of careers services and employability issues spanning the last decade. She is an active member of the National Association of Graduate Careers Advisory Services (NAGCAS), the Australian voice for career development in higher education.

Inder Hunjan studied for a BA (Hons) in Youth and Community at the then Leeds Polytechnic, during which time she was also offered a post as a development worker for Asian girls and women. Inder has since held several roles within Leeds Metropolitan University. Currently Inder leads the Get Ahead team – the university's central widening participation team within the Registrar and Secretaries' Office – working across Yorkshire and Humberside raising the aspirations and attainment of the region's young people.

Dennis Kelly is the Director of Marketing and Student Recruitment at the University of Teesside, where he is responsible for managing the reputation of the university, for marketing and for the recruitment of students. Dennis is an experienced marketing and communications professional and a Fellow of the Chartered Institute of Public Relations. As a communications consultant he has worked in both public- and private-sector organisations, and has participated in research into the management structures of successful communications and marketing functions and into the behaviours of senior communications professionals.

Paul Kelly is Director of Academic Registry at Northumbria University. Previously an Associate Dean in the School of Computing, he manages the university's student and programme data systems and their supporting policies and procedures. He is also responsible for timetabling and the approval, review and enhancement of learning and teaching.

Sue King moved from a management career in the private sector to become a Senior Lecturer in Human Resource Management and Industrial Relations at Glyndŵr University Business School (formerly the North East Wales Institute) in 1990. She is a programme leader, lectures on undergraduate, postgraduate and professional courses and is a University and College Union trade union activist.

Rachel Lander is a Senior Lecturer in the Department of Business Information Management and Operations at the University of Westminster. She has worked in higher education for 15 years and currently specialises in business process management.

Brigid McClure, otherwise known as Chip, was educated at St John's College, Cambridge, and moved to Leeds Metropolitan University in 2005. In January 2007, Chip was appointed to manage the ground-breaking partnership with the Rugby Football League, including the sponsorship of the Carnegie Challenge Cup and Carnegie Champion Schools tournament. As Director of Rugby League Partnerships, Chip also negotiated the partnership agreement with Rugby League Ireland.

Anne Maruma is Quality and Standards Officer, Information Services at the University of Kent. Her role includes recording and responding to feedback received by Information Services. She is also Investigating Officer for computing and library complaints and breaches in computing and library regulations. She is responsible for IS surveys, a critical function that maps and reports upon stakeholder expectations and experience of the university's library and IT services.

Sandra Mienczakowski is Head of Assessment at the University of Nottingham. She manages the delivery and development of the university's assessment systems, policies and procedures, and has wide-ranging experience of administration and management, having previously worked with academic staff and students in the university's School of Law and the University of Nottingham Business School.

Michelle Morgan is presently a Teaching and Learning Co-ordinator and Student Experience Manager at Kingston University. She has been specifically involved in the field of the student experience for eight years and was 'Highly Commended' in the Association of University Administrators Inaugural National Excellence Awards in recognition of outstanding achievements in higher education, management and administration 2004.

Sue North is Equality and Diversity Manager in the Widening Participation section of the Registrar and Secretary's Office at Leeds Metropolitan University. With a background in human resources, she has a strong commitment to equality issues and an abiding interest in mentoring in higher education.

Oluwatoyin Gladstone Oshun commenced his career in university administration at the Federal University of Lagos, Akoka, Nigeria in

September 1978. He is currently Registrar and Secretary at Lagos State University, Nigeria.

Tony Rich has been Registrar at the University of Essex since 1999, having previously worked at the Universities of Warwick, Sheffield and East Anglia. He has a PhD in African politics from the University of Manchester. Tony is currently a member of the board of University Campus Suffolk Ltd, Chair of SUMS Consulting, a member of the Colchester Local Strategic Partnership and a member of Renaissance Southend Ltd, the town's urban regeneration company.

Pete Rodgers is the Dean of Sporting Partnerships at Leeds Metropolitan University. Following a Unilever scholarship to Reading University, he worked with the company in marketing, commercial and human resource roles before starting as a part-time lecturer in FE in 1972 alongside a career in small business and the completion of an MBA at Bradford University. He joined Leeds Polytechnic (now Leeds Metropolitan University) in 1986 and has held a variety of posts there. Following senior management roles in the Office for Leeds and Yorkshire, Yorkshire First and the Business faculty, he jointly developed the university's commercial strategy and sporting partnerships.

John Ryan is Registrar and Secretary at the University of Worcester, where he is responsible for a range of central services, including Registry and Student Services. He has extensive experience of higher education management and administration at four different universities. John is a previous Chair of the Association of University Administrators and is currently a member of the Universities and Colleges Admissions Service (UCAS) board and chairs the UCAS Audit Committee.

Rosemary Stamp is Director and Principal Consultant of Stamp Consulting. She works with education, public-sector and commercial organisations providing strategic management, business and marketing direction through specialist consultancy, with a portfolio that includes international marketing strategies; competitive brand development; location brand strategy; business, foresight and policy response planning; competitor analysis; plus digital and online strategies.

Gail Stephens of Sheffield Hallam University Union of Students joined the students' union movement relatively recently, but brings with her many years of experience of senior management in the commercial and public sectors.

Richard Taylor is Professor and Director of Continuing Education and Lifelong Learning at the University of Cambridge and a Professorial Fellow of Wolfson College. He was previously Professor of Continuing Education at the University of Leeds, where he had been Head of Department and, subsequently, Dean of the Faculty of Business, Law, Education and Social Studies. He was Secretary of the Universities' Association for Continuing Education (UACE) from 1994 to 1998 and has been Chair of the National Institute of Adult Continuing Education (NIACE) from 2001 to 2006. In 2006 he became the Chair of the Board of Trustees of the Workers' Educational Association (WEA).

David Ward was a Principal Lecturer in Events Management at Leeds Metropolitan University when in August 2003 he was seconded to Bradford City Football Club, which at the time was in administration. David's remit was to support the club in its efforts to broaden its grassroots support, especially with the local Pakistani and Bangladeshi community, through community development activities and partnerships. In November 2006 the university received the *Times Higher Education Supplement*'s 'Outstanding Contribution to the Local Community' award for its work at the football club.

Index

All universities and colleges are arranged under the heading 'universities'